Failure to PROTECT

Failure to PROTECT

Moving Beyond Gendered Responses

Edited by
Susan Strega, Julia Krane, Simon Lapierre,
Cathy Richardson, and Rosemary Carlton

Fernwood Publishing • Halifax & Winnipeg

Editing: Eileen Young
Cover design: Ellissa Glad
Printed and bound in Canada by Hignell Book Printing

Published in Canada by Fernwood Publishing
32 Oceanvista Lane, Black Point, Nova Scotia, B0J 1B0
and 748 Broadway Avenue, Winnipeg, Manitoba, R3G 0X3
www.fernwoodpublishing.ca

Fernwood Publishing Company Limited gratefully acknowledges the financial support
of the Government of Canada through the Canada Book Fund and the Canada Council
for the Arts, the Nova Scotia Department of Communities, Culture and Heritage,
the Manitoba Department of Culture, Heritage and Tourism under the
Manitoba Book Publishers Marketing Assistance Program and the Province of Manitoba,
through the Book Publishing Tax Credit, for our publishing program.

Library and Archives Canada Cataloguing in Publication

Failure to protect : moving beyond gendered responses / Susan
Strega ... [et al.], editors.

Includes bibliographical references.
ISBN 978-1-55266-556-5

1. Child welfare. 2. Child abuse--Prevention. I. Strega, Susan

HV713.F35 2013   362.76   C2012-908134-5

Contents

About the Authors

Ramona Alaggia is the Factor-Inwentash Chair in Children's Mental Health at the University of Toronto. She uses her considerable practice experience in the areas of child sexual abuse, intimate partner violence, and children's exposure to inform her teaching and research.

Claudia Bernard is a senior lecturer in the Department of Social, Therapeutic and Community Studies at Goldsmiths, University of London. Her research, teaching and writing focus on the intersection of race, gender, social class, and child and family welfare. She has undertaken research into mothers' emotional and behavioural responses in the aftermath of the sexual abuse of their children, and has investigated how teenage mothers create narratives of their childhood histories of maltreatment to develop insights into its impact on their parenting.

Rebecca Bolen is an associate professor at the University of Tennessee College of Social Work where she teaches courses in human behaviour, neuroscience, and child maltreatment and trauma. Her area of expertise is child sexual abuse, with a primary focus on the non-offending mothers of the child victims and the support these mothers provide to the children.

Rosemary Carlton is a PhD candidate who teaches at the School of Social Work, McGill University. She has substantial front-line experience in the areas of child protection and child sexual abuse. Her doctoral research explores how contemporary notions of risk and autonomy shape teenage girls' experiences of child protection involvement arising in the aftermath of sexual abuse.

Kyllie Cripps is a Pallawah woman whose research interests include issues relating to Indigenous family violence, sexual assault and child abuse, including policy development and program delivery; Indigenous research processes and practices; and Indigenous health and Indigenous education. She is a senior lecturer in the Faculty of Law, University of New South Wales. As one of only a handful of researchers in Australia working in the area of Indigenous family violence, she is very involved in work on knowledge transfer; she also regularly provides advice to state and federal governments and professional and community groups to improve services and programs for Indigenous people.

Caitlin Janzen is a researcher and writer in the School of Social Work at the University of Victoria. Caitlin is currently a research coordinator in the Centre for Addictions Research of British Columbia.

Julia Krane is an associate professor in the School of Social Work at McGill University and Clinical Consultant for a number of local shelters. Her teaching and SSHRC-funded research endeavours centre on child protection, child sexual abuse, and violence against women, from feminist, critical, and intersectionality perspectives with particular attention to the disrupting attributions of mother-blame in front-line social work practice with vulnerable women. At present, Krane is working on a funded project with cultural and linguistic interpreters that aims to determine the needs of ethno-racial minority women following temporary residency at a shelter: the goal of the project is to develop a model for assisting them to establish their independence, following experiences of intimate partner abuse.

Simon Lapierre is an assistant professor at the School of Social Work, University of Ottawa. He teaches courses on feminist practices, as well as on the theoretical foundations of social work intervention. His work is focused on both women's and children's experiences in the context of domestic violence, and proposes a feminist-critical perspective on policies and practices in the area of child and family social work.

Sarah Maiter is an associate professor in the School of Social Work at York University's Faculty of Liberal Arts and Professional Studies. She brings more than twenty years of practice experience in child welfare and children's mental health services to her teaching, and to research that explores services from a critical race framework for ethnically and racially diverse individuals, families and groups.

Baldev Mutta is the founder and the chief executive officer of Punjabi Community Health Services. Beginning in the 1980s, the agency has provided health, settlement and social services to the community in an integrated, holistic, and family-centred framework in Brampton, Ontario. His work spans more than four decades in Ontario, during which time he has developed innovative addiction, mental health and family violence programs from a culturally appropriate framework.

Kendra Nixon teaches in the Faculty of Social Work at the University of Manitoba. Kendra's research interests include violence against women, mothering in the context of intimate partner violence, child exposure to intimate partner violence, and family and social policy. Kendra has worked as a child protection social worker and as a counsellor/advocate for abused women.

Cathy Richardson is a Métis mother, researcher, scholar, writer, counsellor and activist living on southern Vancouver Island. Cathy's areas of research and activism include Indigenous family well-being, anti-colonial child welfare, and response-based practice. Cathy teaches in the School of Social Work at the University of Victoria and is currently involved in various projects that assist in the recovery from violence, as well as promoting social justice.

Susan Strega teaches in the School of Social Work, University of Victoria, where she is responsible for the Child Welfare Specialization. She has conducted research with young mothers in care, fathers whose children are involved with child welfare, and sex workers and their families. Susan is the co-editor, with Sohki Aski Esquao (Jeannine Carrière), of *Walking this Path Together: Anti-Racist and Anti-Oppressive Child Welfare Practice* (Fernwood 2009).

Allan Wade works on Vancouver Island as a therapist, consultant and researcher.

About the Cover Art

Born in Victoria in 1986, Qwul'thilum (Dylan Thomas) is a Coast Salish artist from the Lyackson First Nation, who are originally from Valdes Island. Dylan was exposed to Coast Salish art at a young age because his family continues to participate in their culture and tradition. He has done training in jewellery with the late Seletze (Delmar Johnnie) and has apprenticed under Rande Cook in all mediums of the art. Rande has been a major influence on Dylan's art as have the late Art Thompson, Susan Point and Robert Davidson.

Birds of Change: In Salish culture the sighting of a white raven means that great change is coming. I was inspired to do this print by the recent sightings of white ravens on Vancouver Island. I believe that if we do not change the way we have been treating the earth, the change that is coming could be irreversible. So in this print I have depicted a giant flock of white ravens rushing towards the moon, who is known as the protector of the earth. Although the moon is not in view on the print, its glow can be seen radiating from the top right corner. —Qwul'thilum

Acknowledgments

This book grew out of a research workshop held at the University of Victoria in April 2010. Funding for the original workshop and for some of the work involved in developing this book was provided by SSHRC (Social Sciences and Humanities Research Council) Canada through its "Aid to Workshops and Conferences" program. Although we are unable to include the work of all of the workshop participants in this volume, we extend our appreciation to them: Elizabeth Comack (University of Manitoba), Shelly Johnson (Thompson Rivers University), Mehmoona Moosa-Mitha (University of Victoria), Gary Dumbrill (McMaster University), Michael Hart (University of Manitoba) and Carl Lacharité (Université du Québec à Trois-Rivières). Their involvement in presentations and discussions at the original workshop, while not overtly visible here, made material contributions to the writers whose work appears here. A special word of thanks to Cathy Humphreys (RMIT, Melbourne), whose years of research, scholarship and activism against violence against women inspired participants and contributors to this volume. We acknowledge the work of Caitlin Janzen in organizing and managing the original workshop and the contributions of the School of Social Work and the University of Victoria in making it a success.

We also extend our appreciation to Wayne Antony and all the team at Fernwood Publishing: Beverley Rach for producion coordination, Eileen Young for copyediting, Debbie Mathers for pre-production, and Ellissa Glad for cover design. Wayne has believed in this book since its inception and has encouraged us through the challenges of bringing the project to a successful conclusion. In these neoliberal times, we appreciate and celebrate the continued existence of a publisher committed to social justice.

1. G-d Couldn't Be Everywhere so He Created Mothers

The Impossible Mandate of Maternal Protection in Child Welfare

Susan Strega, Julia Krane, and Rosemary Carlton

A local women's crisis centre contacted Child Protection Services with concerns about the safety of Andrea Hernandez and her three children, Reuben, Sonia and Rosa, ages fifteen, ten, and five. Mrs. Hernandez approached the centre, expressing fear of her husband, Antonio, after he hit her in the face and threw her out of the house when she refused to cook for him the previous evening. She told the crisis worker that her children awoke during the fight and were afraid of their father's drunken rage. When the children begged their father to allow their mother back in the house, he demanded that they throw her personal belongings outside. Reuben refused. Mr. Hernandez grabbed his arms, shook him, and pulled him close to his face, threatening to throw him out of the house along with Andrea. He screamed at the children, demanded that they stop their crying and insisted that Sonia cook his meal. Two hours later, Mr. Hernandez fell asleep and the children let their mother back in the house. Though she had sustained broken bones and multiple bruises during the past ten years of abuse, she viewed this latest violent episode as the worst ever.[1]

Tammy, age fifteen, has been cutting herself again. Though she tried to keep it secret from those around her, her best friend accidentally witnessed the act and reported it to the school guidance counsellor who then made contact with Child Protection Services. Her assigned worker arranged for a psychiatric consultation through the Emergency Department at the Children's Hospital, revealing allegations of sexual abuse by her mother's partner. Upon hearing the allegations, Tammy's mother, Tabatha, vowed to cut ties with this man in order to protect her daughter. As the weeks progressed post-disclosure, Child Protection Services received calls from neighbors with reports that the partner was seen at Tabatha's home, sparking off a second round of investigation.[2]

These scenarios capture the essence of typical practice challenges in today's Child Protection Services (CPS) systems that rely largely on the protection of children by their non-offending mothers in situations of intimate partner abuse and child sexual abuse. Considered to be in the best interests of children to maintain them under the care of their non-offending mothers, the expectation of maternal protection is now well ensconced in legislation across Anglo-American CPS systems through the concept of "failure to protect." Whereas child maltreatment in its various forms was once defined by CPS as the actions or inactions of an abusive or neglectful parent or caregiver, the definition is now extended to encompass the actions or inactions of the non-offending parent or caregiver through the concept of "failure to protect." When a child is sexually abused or a mother is assaulted, child protection authorities now commonly devote more attention to how the non-offending caregiver has behaved than they do to the behaviour of the offending parent. Thus, if Mrs. Hernandez or Tabatha cannot keep their children safe from the offending men in their lives, they can then be defined by CPS policy as having failed to protect their children: as a result of that decision, they risk losing their children for a period of time.

Of particular concern in this book are CPS systems that are based on a threshold approach. We refer to these systems as "Anglo-American" to reflect that this approach is common to Canada, the United States, the United Kingdom, Australia, and New Zealand. Although there are variations amongst threshold systems, they share some defining characteristics that influence failure-to-protect labelling and generate similar legislation, policy, and interventions across geographical boundaries. These systems all evolved from a child-saving mission in which children were "rescued" from immoral, dangerous, or deviant parents. Anglo-American systems are threshold systems in that they define minimal standards of acceptable care, parental behaviour, and child development trajectories (Cameron et al. 2007). Definitions of acceptable care and parental behaviour are, of course, subject to ideological influences and have varied over time.

The two foundational pillars of threshold systems are the notions that individual parents are responsible for the care, nurturance, and protection of their children and that child protection authorities should be legally sanctioned to intervene with children and their families only when parental care is deemed to have fallen below a prescribed minimum standard (Cameron, Coady and Adams 2007; Cameron et al. 2007). Though many parents might struggle to care for their children, threshold systems expect that parents can overcome those struggles with minimal or no assistance from the state. It is only situations considered to pose serious risk to a child's well-being, safety or security that warrant intervention in the assumed private sphere of the family. Under the influence of neoliberal approaches to social policy, the supportive functions of Anglo-American states have diminished or disappeared (Daly 2010; Naiman 2012). Rather than providing support to families, CPS interventions are primarily devoted to investigating allegations of abuse or neglect, protecting children if allegations are substantiated, providing alternate care or supervision of children as needed, and overseeing adoption. The threshold approach in Anglo-American CPS systems is distinct from both the community-caring systems preferred by Indigenous peoples, wherein child welfare is a collaborative community concern that involves the extended family, and the European family services orientation seen in the Nordic countries and countries like Belgium, Sweden, and Germany, wherein child protection is part of a universal and preventative approach to social problems.

Failure to Protect in Anglo-American CPS Legislation

Anglo-American CPS systems, despite variations, are guided by a set of principles reflecting deeply held beliefs about parental responsibilities for the care and welfare of their children and the conditions under which parental care can be challenged, interrupted, or even terminated.

For example, in Canada, the paramount purpose of child protection intervention is to protect children's best interests, safety and well-being. While provincial statutes assert the right of parents to raise, care, discipline, and provide for their children as they see fit, such rights are considered secondary to children's safety when their welfare is in question. The key principles guiding child protection practice in the U.S. are primarily delineated in federal statutes, specifically the *Child Abuse Prevention and Treatment Act (CAPTA)* and the *Adoption of Safe Families Act (ASFA)*. Alongside explicit recognition that parents have the right to raise their children as they choose and the presumption that parents will act in accordance with their children's best interests, these statutes attest that "the child's health and safety shall be the paramount concern" guiding child protection efforts (*ASFA*, section 101.A (15.a)). In the U.K., the *Children Act* explicitly acknowledges "parental responsibility" — within the definition of "all the rights, duties, powers, responsibilities and authority which by law a parent of a child has in relation to the child and his [sic] property" (section 3.1) — in all interventions with families. It privileges the commitment to children by legislating that the child's welfare must be the "paramount consideration" (section 1.1), notwithstanding parental responsibility, when risk to a child is determined with respect to her/his "upbringing." Thus, one can see a thematic philosophy echoed in legislation in threshold systems such as Canada, the U.S., and the U.K.

Other guiding principles common to Anglo-American legislation include support for the autonomy and integrity of families; priority given to intervening on the basis of mutual consent; commitment to pursuing the least disruptive course of action; recognition of the importance of providing services that respect a child's need for continuity of care and stable family relationships; promotion of early assessment, planning, and decision making to achieve permanent plans that include participation by children, parents, and relatives; and provision of services that respect cultural, religious, and regional differences (Bala 2004; Goldman, Salus, Wolcott, and Kennedy 2003; U.K. Department of Children, Schools and Families 2010). As is evident here, threshold CPS systems regard parents as first and foremost responsible for the care of their children and view families as autonomous in making decisions around their children's welfare. When there is a need for CPS to intervene in families, that intervention would aim to be the least intrusive or disruptive to children and their parents.

All child protection legislation defines the circumstances under which a child may be deemed "in need of protection" by CPS through establishing child maltreatment categories. As will be shown, the concept of failure to protect is embedded in all Anglo-American child protection legislation. In Canada, for example, there is no federal child protection legislation. Instead, provincial and territorial statutes refer to, and offer brief definitions of, specific categories of child maltreatment, thereby delineating the circumstances under which a child may be considered to be at risk and in need of protection. Commonly, these categories include abandonment, neglect, physical, sexual or emotional abuse, and deprivation of necessary health care. In addition to suspected or actual neglect or abuse, provincial statutes now include clauses stating that a child may be deemed to be in need of protection when risk factors are taken into account. For example, in Alberta, a child is considered to be in need of protective intervention when "the child has been or there is substantial risk that the child will be physically injured or sexually abused by the guardian of the child" (*Child, Youth and Family Enhancement Act* 2000: article 2(d)). Similarly, in New Brunswick, "the security or development of a child may be in danger when ... the child is physically or sexually abused, physically or emotionally neglected, sexually exploited, including sexual exploitation through child pornography or in danger of such treatment" (*Family Services Act* 1983: article 31.1(e)).

Turning to the U.S., *CAPTA* provides the minimum standards for defining physical abuse, child neglect, and sexual abuse, which each state must incorporate into its respective statutory definitions. *CAPTA* contains clear and explicit references to the "failure to act," a cognate for "failure to protect." According to *CAPTA*, "the term 'child abuse and neglect' means, at a minimum, any recent act *or failure to act* on the part of a parent or caretaker, which results in death, serious physical or emotional harm, sexual abuse or exploitation, or an act *or failure to act* which presents an imminent risk of serious harm" (section 111.2, our emphasis). Similarly, in the U.K., the *Children Act* states that local CPS authorities have a "duty to investigate" when there is "reasonable cause to suspect that a child who lives, or is found, in their area is suffering, or is likely to suffer, *significant harm*" (section 47.1.b., our emphasis). Determining significant harm — without legislated criteria that set out the threshold justifying child protection intervention — thus relies on professional judgement that is specific to individual situations. Definitions of categories of significant harm, including physical abuse, sexual abuse, emotional abuse, and neglect, are offered in the *Working Together to Safeguard Children* (2010) document in the U.K., which states that "somebody may abuse or neglect a child by inflicting harm, or by failing to act to prevent harm" (paragraph 1.32). The *Children Act* adds further weight to the understanding of parental failure to protect as a determining factor in interventions, stating that a child protection order can be enacted on the basis "that the child concerned is suffering, or is likely to suffer, significant harm; and that the harm, or likelihood of harm, is attributable to the care given to the child, or likely to be given to him [sic] if the order were not made, not being what it would be reasonable to expect a parent to give to him [sic]" (section 31.2).

As can be seen, the concept of failure to protect is embedded in the legislative frameworks of the U.S. and the U.K.; it also weaves its way into Canadian child protection legislation. For example, in Nova Scotia, a child may be deemed to be in need of protection due to the "failure of a parent or guardian to supervise and protect the child adequately" (*Children and Family Services Act* 2002: article 22.2). In Manitoba and Saskatchewan, a child may be considered to be endangered as a result of a parent's "action or omission" (*Child and Family Services Act* 1985: article 17.2; *Child and Family Services Act*, 1989–1990, article 11 (a)). In Newfoundland, failure to protect is addressed as the "action or lack of appropriate action by the child's parent" (*Children and Youth Care and Protection Act* 2010: article 10.1). In Quebec, a child's security or development may be compromised should her/his parent "fail to take the necessary steps to put an end to the situation [of risk]" (*Youth Protection Act* 2007: article 38), while in Alberta, British Columbia, Manitoba, New Brunswick, and Nunavut, a child is in need of protection when her/his parent is "unable or unwilling" to protect the child from harm or to provide him/her with adequate care or supervision. In Ontario, *The Child and Family Services Act* (1990) states that protective intervention is required when a child has suffered harm or is at risk of suffering harm as a result of her/his parent's "failure to adequately care for, provide for, supervise or protect the child" (article 37.2).

These statutes make explicit the expectation that even the parent who is not the perpetrator of abuse should predict and recognize the risks to the child and prevent and react accordingly, either to bring to an end actual abuse or neglect, or the potential for abuse or neglect. Otherwise, that non-offending parent is seen as having failed to protect. Though not explicitly stated in any piece of official legislation, the non-offending parent in such situations is almost always the child's mother. According to the most recent *Canadian Incidence Study of Reported Child Abuse and Neglect — 2008* (Trocmé et al. 2010),[3] women comprise 91 percent of all primary caregivers with mothers comprising 86 percent of primary caregivers; in other words, 5 percent of women caregivers are not mothers; they may be aunts, grandmothers, etc. The responsibility for determining whether a parent's responses are appropriate or adequate to alleviate the specific circumstances associated with risk to the child rests with individual child protection workers.

Gender disproportionality is particularly acute in situations of intimate partner violence and child sexual abuse. Notably, failure to protect in the context of child sexual abuse falls on the shoulders of non-offending mothers. In one of the *Canadian Incidence Studies*, only 5 percent of perpetrators of child sexual abuse were found to be the biological mother or stepmother (Trocmé et al. 2005). Demonstrating gender disproportionality related to intimate partner violence is somewhat trickier since data collection dealt with exposure to,[4] not perpetrators of, such abuse. In the study, 88 percent of biological fathers/stepfathers were considered to be responsible for having exposed their children to intimate partner violence; yet 28 percent of biological mothers/stepmothers were considered to have failed to protect their children from exposure to domestic violence (Trocmé et al. 2005). Presumably, the remaining biological mothers/stepmothers victimized by intimate partner violence were not exempt from the responsibility to protect their children from exposure. With mothers/stepmothers held to account, as scholars have noted, perpetrators' accountability is diminished or ignored (Alaggia et al. 2007; Nixon et al. 2007). These practices accord with everyday work processes in child protection, which are historically, and currently, mother-blaming and father-absenting (Risley-Curtiss and Heffernan 2003; Scourfield 2003; Strega et al. 2008; Swift 1995). Widespread societal interest in the role of fathers in child development (Tamis-LeMonda 2004) has had little impact in child protection systems, whereas gender-inequitable practice remains routine (Scourfield 2003).

Theoretically, the requirement to protect and the corollary allegation of failing to protect could be applied equally to mothers and fathers/father-figures. Indeed, the gender-neutral language employed in most child protection legislation and policy would seem to support equal treatment. In practice, however, men are rarely, if ever, assessed for failure to protect. Even when children have two parents, neglect investigations focus primarily on mothers (Coohey and Zhang 2006). Child protection workers routinely engage with mothers and ignore fathers and father-figures, even when fathers are the identified source of a family's difficulties (Scourfield 2003; Strega et al. 2008). While mothers are particularly likely to be held responsible when men assault them (Coohey 2007; Landsman and Hartley 2007), when men physically or sexually abuse children, mothers are routinely held to be at fault even when the assailant is the father or father-figure (Krane 2003; Radhakrishna et al. 2001). Further, in order to be seen as acting in a protective manner, women are routinely expected to monitor and manage the behaviour of violent men and ameliorate the consequences of their violence (Hughes, Chau, and Poff 2010; Scourfield 2003).

Shifting Terrains: CPS Practice Context

Failure to protect as a marker of risk to children speaks to a deepened preoccupation with child safety, in tandem with a commitment to family preservation and autonomy. Historically, in Canada, policy and practices had long been centred only on the most obvious cases of abuse and neglect, and child protection services intervention consisted primarily of the removal of children from unsafe care or circumstances (Bala 2004). However, family preservation practices became paramount when it was recognized that, as noted by Bala (2004), decisions to remove children from parental care reflected class and race biases.

Various authors in this book note that, in addition to bringing greater cultural sensitivity to CPS work with families, it is important to attend to children's attachments to their primary caregivers and the fear of causing harm to children through placing them in out-of-home care. As we have argued elsewhere, "by the mid-1980s, a swell of concern for the emotional damage caused by separating children from their primary caregivers with whom they may have formed attachments gave rise to practices that now made every effort to maintain children in their families" (Krane et al. 2010: 157). Only a decade later, public outcry over the death of children entrusted to state care would lead to the scrutiny of the family preservation approach, and a shift towards protecting and preserving the safety of the child was once again in evidence (Dumbrill 2005). Intense media scrutiny of child deaths associated with child protection authorities led many Anglo-American jurisdictions to "[swing] back in favour of protecting children, hopefully before harm occurred. Thus substantial risk became risk in law" (Swift and Callahan 2009: 119). At that time, "swift reactions to potential child risk were promoted and realized through interventions that prioritized stability, consistency, and the opportunity for children to form secure attachments for their healthy development" (Krane et al. 2010: 157). In practice, this has translated into the expectations that parents, predominantly mothers, must immediately take a protective stance in the face of their children's exposure to intimate partner violence or sexual abuse. Failure to do so has dire consequences.

A renewed focus on children's safety and protection has been accompanied by the widespread adoption of standardized tools for risk assessment.

These tools for assessing risk were meant to enhance the effectiveness and accuracy of child protective service investigations and procedures related to service provision "as well as filter out high risk cases from the rest" (Krane and Davies 2000: 36). Simply put, risk assessment tools were intended to guide workers to assess risk of further abuse or neglect as well as the capacity of non-offending parents to protect their children from further harm. By using standardized risk assessment tools, the hope was to improve CPS practice by "[reducing] worker professional and personal bias, [streamlining] worker decision making, [reducing individual workers'] discretion, and generally [sharpening] professional thinking about the broad range of factors related to assessing risk" (Krane and Davies 2000: 37). Critics of risk assessment tools saw these standardized measures as potentially promoting "the rapid scrutiny and classification of parents, largely mothers, through a filter of cultural, class, and gender assumptions"; they feared that "the ideological and material contexts in which the mothering of children takes place are concealed while deviations from the Eurocentric, middle-class standard of good mothering are suspect" (Krane and Davies 2000: 42). In other words, the daily struggles that women face to keep themselves and their children safe can go unrecognized when there are worries for their children's safety or protection or worse, these struggles can be interpreted as putting their children at greater risk. For example, when women seeking to protect themselves and their children from a perpetrator frequently change housing, CPS might interpret these actions as creating instability for children.

In contemporary practice, failure to meet minimal parenting standards is generally ascribed to individual dysfunction, inadequacy or pathology. An underlying assumption is that adequate or functional parents will not normally need external assistance with child-rearing, and thus CPS places little emphasis on providing social or systemic supports. Although Anglo-American child protection legislation usually mentions both care (providing supports and assistance to enhance child, parent, and family functioning) and control (investigating and monitoring parents), it is control functions that are legislatively mandated while supports and resources are usually discretionary. Indeed, the bulk of child protection practice is occupied with responding to reports of maltreatment and engaging in the activities related to protection: identifying abuse, investigating and assessing risk, policing families, and providing involuntary/coercive protection services (Krane 2003). As Rogowski (2012) notes, with reference to practice in England, once assessment forms are completed, CPS offers little in the way of help and support unless there are serious child protection concerns.

The past two decades or so has seen a troubling shift from a concern for the general welfare of children and families to a preoccupation with having the legislated means to intervene in what are often considered "failed" families (Krane 2003). This preoccupation with risk (evaluating, monitoring and avoiding), coupled with neoliberal reforms that put greater emphasis on individual responsibility and reduce the availability of supports to help care for their children, further skewed the focus of child protection services towards surveillance and control (Swift and Callahan 2009). As Chen (2005: 143) pointed out, risk assessment "embodies the paradigm shift from considering certain aspects of reality to be social problems to considering them to be risk factors." Not surprisingly, CPS workers are consumed by documentation of risk and ensuring parental compliance (Cameron, Coady, and Adams 2007). They are "granted less discretionary power and less time for direct engagement with mothers and fathers. As well, they experience less clinical supervision in their work and yet remain responsible for life-altering decisions and liable for managing risk" (Krane et al. 2010: 159). Research with CPS workers provides some insights into the difficulties inherent in being charged with managing challenging, complex, and emotional situations within strict time limits, with few resources, and while ensuring the timely completion of mandated paperwork (Kemp et al. 2009). While some child protection teams and offices manage to create a supportive environment, most CPS workplaces have a pervasive preoccupation with "risks of fear and fears of risk" (Littlechild 2009: 113).

Research with parents has helped to elucidate key components of positive engagement between families and CPS workers who adopt respectful and anti-oppressive approaches. Worker characteristics that promote positive engagement include: attending to stigma and structural inequities; validating parents' negative perceptions of child welfare; normalizing angry and anxious responses to CPS involvement; communicating clearly and directly about the reasons for CPS involvement and showing willingness to listen to parents' perceptions; ensuring parents have accurate information; providing concrete resources and supports; remaining respectful and empathic; and following through on commitments and tasks (de Boer and Coady 2007; Dumbrill 2006; Palmer, Maiter and Manji 2006; Spratt and Callan 2004).

Further complicating this challenging area of practice, in which workers face overwhelming demands, is an understanding that resources are limited and accessible only by those families and children with the most severe problems. In legislation, policy, and practice, "the best interests of the child" have been severed from commitments to support and provide resources to families (Swift and Callahan 2006). At the same time, in most Anglo-American countries, income inequality and income poverty has increased significantly over the last few decades (OECD 2008), leaving poor families with few resources. The poorest of the poor are women, especially single mothers (Statistics Canada 2011). It is these families, who are living the effects of inequality, marginalization, and poverty, that CPS authorities most often encounter.

Class, Gender, Race, and Indigeneity: CPS Client Context

In theory, any family has the potential to come into contact with child protection systems, but in practice, the primary determinants of whether or not a family comes to the attention of CPS authorities are poverty and race, as a multitude of writers have observed (see, for example, Blackstock 2008; Lindsey 2003; Roberts 2002; Swift 1995). Moreover, in Canada and Australia, Indigenous children and families are vastly over-represented in child welfare caseloads. In all Anglo-American jurisdictions, CPS disproportionately engages with racialized minorities, poor single mothers, and the otherwise disadvantaged, including poor immigrants and refugees, and people with disabilities (Cameron et al. 2007; Lindsey 2003; Roberts 2002; Swift 1995).

Families involved with CPS typically live in very precarious circumstances. Their housing conditions are often unsafe (Chau et al. 2009), and they are significantly more likely than the general population to be living on social assistance. Single poor mothers are especially likely to be targeted (Dworsky et al. 2007; Cross 2008; Trocmé et al. 2010). The *Canadian Incidence Study on Reported Child Abuse and Neglect — 2008* found that 33 percent of all families substantiated for child abuse and neglect were financially supported by social assistance, EI or other sources of benefits: "Ten percent relied on part-time work, multiple jobs or seasonal employment. In 5% of substantiated investigations, the source of income was unknown by the workers, and in 2%, no reliable source of income was reported" (Trocmé et al. 2010: 41). While CPS workers reported that half of the families with whom they were engaged listed full-time employment as their primary source of income, the *CIS* does not identify annual earnings. We can only surmise that at least 50 percent of families substantiated for maltreatment had poverty-level incomes. According to the U.S. *National Incidence Study of Child Abuse and Neglect (NIS-4)* (Sedlak et al. 2010), children living in families of low socio-economic status are at significantly higher risk of maltreatment. Sedlak et al. (2010) report that an estimated 55.1 children per 1,000 children in families of low socio-economic status experienced at least one form of maltreatment, a rate which is more than five times that for children from families with higher income levels (found to be 9.5 children per 1,000 children).

Research conducted for the *Canadian Incidence Study on Reported Child Abuse and Neglect — 2003* (Trocmé et al. 2005) documented the experiences of female caregivers who become involved with child protection, and found in their histories, in order of frequency: intimate partner violence, few social supports, mental health problems, maltreatment as a child, and drug and alcohol use. The most recent *CIS* notes that child protection workers either suspected or confirmed that the primary caregiver had experienced intimate partner violence in 46 percent of all substantiated cases of abuse or neglect (Trocmé et al. 2010). This finding suggests heightened child protection attention to intimate partner violence as a risk factor in situations of abuse or neglect. Despite the demonstrated fact that, almost exclusively, it is men who perpetrate intimate partner violence, the protection mandate falls squarely on the shoulders of women. It is mothers whose parenting is scrutinized and mothers who are held accountable for any failure to ensure their children's safety.

There is extensive documentation of racial disproportionality in Anglo-American child protection systems. In Canada, Indigenous children comprised approximately 18 percent of children reported to child protection authorities in 2003, yet they represent only 5 percent of the child population (Lavergne et al. 2008). Black children account for 65 percent of the children in care in Toronto, the largest urban centre in Canada, whereas only 8 percent of the city's population is Black (Child Welfare Anti-Oppression Roundtable 2009: 8). In Australia, Aboriginal and Torres Strait Islander children comprised 28 percent of children in care in 2006, but account for only 5 percent of the child population (Tilbury 2009). In New Zealand, Maori and other Indigenous children comprised 47 percent of children in care, but only 24 percent of the child population (Tilbury 2009). In England, in 2002, 5.2 percent of children in care were of African or African-Caribbean descent, though this group represents only 2.6 percent of the total child population; in addition, Black and other ethnic minority children were also vastly over-represented on child protection registers (Owen and Statham 2009).

Similarly, research by Hill (2005, 2008) and Blackstock (2008) has documented racial and ethnic disproportionality at national, state, and county levels in the United States. It has also been demonstrated that African-American children and families often receive unequal treatment, such as reduced access to services and fewer visits from caseworkers when compared to other racial groups, particularly Whites (McRoy 2004). U.S. researchers note that racialized children are more likely to be apprehended, spend more time in out-of-home care, and experience a greater number of placements than White children (Hines et al. 2004; Lu et al. 2004).

The *NIS-4* indicates that abuse is more likely to be substantiated with African-American children (Sedlak, McPhearson, and Das 2010). However, it is essential to note that research does not affirm disproportionality in the maltreatment of children. Two studies conducted ten years apart indicated no significant differences in the incidence of child maltreatment amongst different U.S. racial groups (Sedlak and Broadhurst 1996; Sedlak and Schultz 2005). Indeed, after controlling for factors like income and family structure, the *NIS-3* found significantly higher rates of maltreatment in White families than in non-White families (Sedlak and Schultz 2005). While the most recent *NIS-4* revealed that African-American children experienced significantly higher rates than White children of physical abuse, overall abuse, emotional neglect, overall neglect and overall maltreatment, race differences in rates of sexual abuse and overall neglect were found to be statistically insignificant (Sedlak et al. 2010).

In addition to the over-representation of visible minority children and their families, researchers in different jurisdictions have also highlighted racial discrimination in reporting to CPS and in decisions to substantiate alleged maltreatment (see, for example, in Canada, Lavergne et al. (2008); in the U.K., Chand and Thoburn (2006) and Thoburn et al. (2005); in the U.S., Ards et al. (2003), and in Australia, Bamblett and Lewis (2007) and Delfabbro et al. (2010)). While Indigeneity, race, and poverty do not cause child protection involvement, they are implicated in the pathways through which families come to the attention of CPS authorities (Dworsky et al. 2007; Cross 2008). Most families come into contact with CPS as a result of third-party reports. Biases related to poverty and social class have been found to be even more significant than those related to race in studies of factors influencing whether or not allied professionals (police, teachers, doctors, and nurses) report suspected maltreatment to CPS. In their analyses of factors influencing decisions to report maltreatment, Dettlaff and Rycraft (2010) and Hines et al. (2004) demonstrated that decisions by mandated reporters about whether or not to report to CPS were significantly influenced by parental race and social class. In a later analysis that controlled for race, Dettlaff et al. (2011) found social class to be the most influential determinant in substantiating maltreatment, a finding that accords with Berger's (2005) report that income level was the most significant variable in whether families were reported and/or investigated for child physical abuse. Taken together, this research leads to the reasonable presumption that failure-to-protect interventions are disproportionately enacted on Indigenous, racialized, poor, and otherwise marginalized women.

Reframing Failure to Protect

Failure-to-protect policies and practices that permeate Anglo-American child protection systems are disproportionately enacted on Indigenous, racialized, poor, and otherwise vulnerable and marginalized women. This problem has been particularly evident in situations of child sexual abuse for a number of decades, and, more recently, it emerged in response to children witnessing or being exposed to intimate partner violence. As such, it is these areas of CPS policy and practice that comprise the focus of this book. As documented in Chapters 2 and 3, it is most often men who perpetrate both forms of child maltreatment and yet it is women who are overwhelmingly charged with having to protect their children and/or themselves from such abuses and who fall prey to CPS interventions based in the concept of failure to protect. Although the particular legislative, historical, and ideological underpinning of failure-to-protect practices and policies vary somewhat according to location, contributors to this book argue that a pervasive child protection concept holds women primarily or solely responsible for protection, exculpates perpetrators of their violence, and thus fails to protect both children and women from violence and abuse. Contributors demonstrate that the proliferation of failure-to-protect policies and practices is not indicative of progress in child protection. Rather, these policies and practices reflect longstanding and deeply embedded mother-blaming and father-absenting ideologies that shape Anglo-American child protection systems. We believe that current manifestations of the concept of failure to protect not only increase danger for children and the women who care for them, but may also frequently deprive all parties of essential resources and support.

How might a critical analysis of failure to protect shape practice? This book describes the ideological scaffolding upon which failure to protect has been built; most importantly, it explains how dismantling the ideological scaffolding upon which failure to protect has been built might allow a space for rethinking alternative policies and practices to better protect children at risk. These are the challenges undertaken here with the aim of providing a route out of the difficulties and dilemmas that failure-to-protect statutes currently create for families and for CPS systems and workers.

The starting point is a recognition that there are, in fact, many aspects of CPS policies and practices that lend themselves particularly well to reframing situations in which mothers like Mrs. Hernandez and Tabatha might be blamed and held to account for the protection of their children in situations of child sexual abuse and intimate partner violence perpetrated by the men in their lives. Contributors to this book demonstrate the contradiction between the recent proliferation of gender-neutral language and the extent to which gendered and hierarchical relations remain deeply embedded in child protection statutes, discourses, and practices. Several contributors explore how CPS interventions based on notions of failure to protect are differentially interpreted and applied along lines of gender, race, and class. Together, the contributors in this book imagine alternatives to failure to protect and describe concrete ways to move forward that engage men, affirm women and protect children.

In Chapter 2, Rosemary Carlton and Julia Krane show how failure to protect in situations of child sexual abuse appears, often implicitly, in CPS legislation. They explore the complicated terrain on which non-offending mothers exist and tie present-day approaches to a history of blaming mothers when their children are sexually abused. Carlton and Krane explain how dominant ideologies of motherhood complicate both the responses of mothers and how CPS workers engage with them, providing a starting point from which other authors deconstruct the application of failure to protect in child sexual abuse. Similarly, in Chapter 3, Susan Strega and Caitlin Janzen provide a foundational overview of failure to protect in situations of intimate partner violence. They demonstrate how current policies and practices are demonstrably ineffective at eliminating, and may even increase, danger to mothers and children, and explain how CPS systems can engage directly with domestically violent men.

In Chapter 4, Rebecca Bolen and Julia Krane draw extensively from their own and others' research to challenge existing assumptions about the roles and responses of non-offending mothers in cases of child sexual abuse. In Chapter 5, Rosemary Carlton and Julia Krane draw from these ideas, as well as those in Chapter 2, in their proposal for a new approach to CPS engagement with non-offending mothers. Because the responses of mothers are normatively mixed and change over time, Carlton and Krane explain how a worker's ability to tolerate some uncertainty around risk is likely to increase, rather than diminish, children's safety.

In this introductory chapter, we detailed significant racial disproportionality in child protection. Chapters 6 and 7 explore in more detail how race intersects with notions of failure to protect. In Chapter 6, Claudia Bernard draws on Black feminist thinking, especially the concept of intersectionality, to highlight the complexities faced by Black mothers when they contend with child sexual abuse. She provides a number of ideas to help practitioners build respectful helping relationships with Black mothers. In Chapter 7, Sarah Maiter, Ramona Alaggi, and Baldev Mutta bring their extensive practice and research experience to elucidating the challenges faced by ethno-racial families, especially mothers, in situations of intimate partner violence. They consider the potential that differential response approaches recently introduced in CPS, hold for more anti-oppressive ways of engaging both victimized mothers and domestically violent fathers.

In Chapter 8, Cathy Richardson and Allan Wade describe the philosophical basis and key practices of the "Islands of Safety" intervention model that they have used successfully with Indigenous families experiencing both paternal violence and CPS involvement. Their chapter details respectful practice strategies for supporting victimized mothers and engaging violent men. In Chapter 9, Kendra Nixon and Kyllie Cripps bring attention to policy. They demonstrate how existing failure-to-protect statutes and policies in Canadian and Australian CPS systems have created unintended negative impacts, particularly for Indigenous peoples. Their work questions the usefulness of these policies: they recommend changes to policy as well as to the processes by which policies are developed.

Notes

The title of this chapter is a Jewish proverb.

1. The Hernandez scenario is a modified version of a case written in Brown 2002.
2. This scenario is a modified version of a case appearing in Krane 2003.
3. In total, three *Canadian Incidence Studies of Reported Child Abuse and Neglect* have been produced (1998, 2003, 2008). Each *CIS* provides national estimates of child abuse and neglect reported to, and investigated by, child welfare services in Canada. In addition to documenting incidence rates of child maltreatment, data from the *CIS* offer insights into the characteristics of the children, youth, and families who were the subject of child welfare investigations for alleged child abuse and neglect.
4. "Exposure" to intimate partner violence refers to children who are, in some ways, affected by such violence that may or may not include directly observing acts of violence. According to the *CIS*-2008 (Trocmé et al. 2010: 88), exposure to intimate partner violence includes "direct witness to physical violence: The child is present during physical or verbal violence between intimate partners. The child can see and/or hear the violence…; indirect exposure to physical violence: The child is not present during the violence between intimate partners, but suffers the consequences, hears about it, or experiences changes in his or her life that are attributed to this violence (e.g., frequent moves)…; exposure to emotional violence: The child is exposed to or witnesses the consequences of emotional violence between intimate partners…; exposure to non-partner physical violence: The child is exposed to or witnesses the consequences of physical violence between a caregiver and another individual who is not the spouse/partner of the caregiver (e.g., between the caregiver and a neighbour, grandparent, uncle, or aunt)."

References

Alaggia, Ramona, Angelique Jenney, Josephine Mazucca, and Melissa Redmond. 2007. "In Whose Best Interest? A Canadian Case Study of the Impact of Child Welfare Policies in Cases Of Domestic Violence." *Journal of Brief Therapy and Crisis Intervention* 7, 4.

Alberta. 2000. *Child, Youth and Family Enhancement Act*, R.S.A. 2000, c. C-12.

Ards, Sheila, Samuel Myers, Allan Malkis, Ellen Sugrue and Li Zhou. 2003. "Racial Disproportionality in Reported and Substantiated Child Abuse and Neglect: An Examination of Systematic Bias." *Children and Youth Services Review* 25, 5/6.

Bala, Nicolas. 2004. "Child Welfare Law in Canada: An Introduction." In N. Bala, M.K. Zapf, R.J. Williams, R. Vogl and J.P. Hornick (eds.), *Canadian Child Welfare Law: Children Families and the State*. Second edition, Toronto: Thompson Education Publishing.

Bamblett, Muriel, and Peter Lewis. 2007. "Detoxifying the Child and Family Welfare System for Australian Indigenous Peoples: Self-Determination, Rights and Culture as the Critical Tools." *First Peoples Child and Family Review* 3, 3.

Berger, Lawrence. 2005. "Income, Family Characteristics, and Physical Violence Toward Children." *Child Abuse and Neglect* 29, 2.

Blackstock, Cindy. 2008. "Reconciliation Means Not Saying Sorry Twice: Lessons from Child Welfare in Canada." In Marlene Brant Castellano, Linda Archibald and Mike DeGagne (eds.), *From Truth to Reconciliation: Transforming the Legacy of Residential Schools.* Ottawa: Aboriginal Healing Foundation.

British Columbia. 1996. *Child, Family and Community Service Act,* BC Reg 533/95.

Brown, Venessa. 2002. *Child Welfare Case Studies.* Toronto: Allyn & Bacon.

Cameron, Gary, Nick Coady and Gerald Adams. 2007. *Moving Toward Positive Systems of Child and Family Welfare.* Waterloo: Wilfrid Laurier Press.

Cameron, Gary, Nancy Freymond, Denise Cornfield and Sally Palmer. 2007. "Positive Possibilities for Child and Family Welfare: Expanding the Anglo-American Child Protection Paradigm." In Gary Cameron, Nick Coady and Gerald Adams (eds.), *Moving Toward Positive Systems of Child and Family Welfare.* Waterloo: Wilfrid Laurier Press.

Chand, Ashok, and June Thoburn. 2006. "Child Protection Referrals and Minority Ethnic Children and Families." *Child and Family Social Work* 11, 4.

Chau, Shirley, Ann Fitzpatrick, David Hulchanski, Bruce Leslie, and Debbie Schatia. 2009. "One in Five: Housing as a Factor in the Admission of Children in Temporary Care." In David Hulchanski, Philippa Campsie, Shirley Chau, Stephen Hwang and Emily Paradis (eds.), *Finding Home: Policy Options for Addressing Homelessness in Canada.* Toronto: Cities Centre Press, University of Toronto.

Chen, Xiaobei. 2005. *Tending the Gardens of Citizenship: Child Saving in Toronto, 1880s–1920s.* Toronto: University of Toronto Press.

Child Welfare Anti-Oppression Roundtable. 2009. *Anti-Oppression in Child Welfare: Laying the Foundation for Change. A Discussion Paper.* Toronto: The Child Welfare Anti-Oppression Roundtable.

Coohey, Carol. 2007. "What Criteria Do Child Protective Services Investigators Use to Substantiate Exposure to Domestic Violence?" *Child Welfare* 86, 4.

Coohey, Carol, and Ying Zhang. 2006. "The Role of Men in Chronic Supervisory Neglect." *Child Maltreatment* 11, 1.

Cross, Terry. 2008. "Disproportionality in Child Welfare." *Child Welfare* 87, 2.

Daly, Mary. 2010. "Shifts in Family Policy in the U.K. under New Labour." *Journal of European Social Policy* 20, 5: 433–43.

de Boer, Catherine, and Nick Coady. 2007. "Good Helping Relationships in Child Welfare: Learning from Stories of Success." *Child and Family Social Work* 12, 1.

Delfabbro, Paul, Craig Hirte, Nancy Rogers and Ros Wilson. 2010. "The Over-Representation of Young Aboriginal or Torres Strait Islander People in the South Australian Child Welfare System: A Longitudinal Analysis." *Children and Youth Services Review* 32, 10.

Dettlaff, Alan, Stephanie Rivaux, Donald Baumann, John Fluke, Joan Rycraft and Joyce James. 2011. "Disentangling Substantiation: The Influence of Race, Income, and Risk on the Substantiation Decision in Child Welfare." *Children and Youth Services Review* 33, 9.

Dettlaff, Alan, and Joan Rycraft. 2010. "Factors Contributing to Disproportionality in the Child Welfare System: Views from the Legal Community." *Social Work* 55, 3.

Dumbrill, Gary. 2006. "Parental Experience of Child Welfare Intervention: A Qualitative Study." *Child Abuse and Neglect* 30, 1: 27–37.

Dworsky, Amy, Mark Courtney and Andrew Zinn. 2007. "Child, Parent, and Family

Predictors of Child Welfare Services Involvement among TANF Applicant Families." *Children and Youth Services Review* 29, 6.

Goldman, Jill, Marsha Salus, Deborah Wolcott and Kristie Kennedy. 2003. *A Coordinated Response to Child Abuse and Neglect: The Foundation for Practice.* Washington, DC: Office on Child Abuse and Neglect (HHS).

Hill, Robert. 2005. "The Role of Race in Parental Reunification." In D. Derezotes, J. Poertner and M. Testa (eds.), *Race Matters in Child Welfare: The Overrepresentation of African American Children in the System.* Washington: CWLA Press

_____. 2008. *An Analysis of Racial/Ethnic Disproportionality and Disparity at the National, State and County Levels.* Seattle, WA: Casey Family Programs.

Hines, Alice, Kathy Lemon, Paige Wyatt and Joan Merdinger. 2004. "Factors Related to the Disproportionate Involvement of Children of Color in the Child Welfare System: A Review and Emerging Themes." *Children and Youth Services Review* 26, 6.

Hughes, Judy, Shirley Chau and Deborah Poff. 2011. "They're Not My Favourite People: What Mothers Who Have Experienced Intimate Partner Violence Say about Involvement in the Child Protection System." *Children and Youth Services Review* 33, 7.

Kemp, Susan, Maureen Marcenko, Kimberly Hoagwood and William Vesneski. 2009. "Engaging Parents in Child Welfare Services: Bridging Family Needs and Child Welfare Mandates." *Child Welfare* 88, 1.

Krane, Julia. 2003. *What's Mother Got to Do with It? Protecting Children from Sexual Abuse.* Toronto: University of Toronto Press.

Krane, Julia, and Linda Davies. 2000. "Rethinking Risk Assessment in Mothering and Child Protection Practice." *Child and Family Social Work* 5, 1.

Krane, Julia, Linda Davies, Rosemary Carlton and Meghan Mulcahy. 2010. "The Clock Starts Now: Rethinking Attachment Theory in Child Protection Practice." In Brid Featherstone, Carol-Ann Hooper, Jonathan Scourfield and Julie Taylor (eds.), *Gender and Child Welfare in Society.* Chichester, UK: John Wiley and Sons.

Landsman, M.J., and Carolyn C. Hartley. 2007. "Attributing Responsibility for Child Maltreatment when Domestic Violence Is Present." *Child Abuse and Neglect* 31.

Lavergne, Chantal, Sarah Dufour, Nico Trocmé and Marie-Claude Larrivée. 2008. "Visible Minority, Aboriginal, Caucasian Children Investigated by Canadian Protective Services." *Child Welfare* 87, 2.

Lindsey, Duncan. 2003. *The Welfare of Children.* Second edition. New York: Oxford University Press.

Littlechild, Brian. 2009. "Child Protection Social Work: Risks of Fears and Fears of Risks." In David Denney (ed.), *Living in Dangerous Times: Fear, Insecurity, Risk and Social Policy.* Chichester, UK: John Wiley and Sons.

Lu, Yuhwa, John Landsverk, Elissa Ellis-MacLeod, Rae Newton, William Gangerand Ivory Johnson. 2004. "Race, Ethnicity, and Case Outcomes in Child Protective Services." *Children and Youth Services Review* 26, 5.

McBride, Stephen, and Heather Whiteside. 2011. "Austerity for Whom?" *Socialist Studies/Études socialistes* 7, 1/2.

McRoy, Ruth. 2004. "The Color of Child Welfare." In King Davis and Tricia Bent-Goodley (eds.), *The Color of Social Policy.* Alexandria, VA: Council on Social Work Education.

Manitoba. 1985. *The Child and Family Services Act*, C.C.S.M. c. C80.

Naiman, Joanne. 2012. "Neoliberalism and Globalization." In *How Societies Work: Class, Power and Change*. Fifth edition. Winnipeg: Fernwood.

New Brunswick. 1983. *Family Services Act*, S.N.B. 1980, c. F 2-2.

Newfoundland and Labrador. 2010. *Children and Youth Care and Protection Act*, S.N.L. 2010, c.C-12.2.

Nixon, Kendra, Leslie Tutty, Gillian Weaver-Dunlop and C. Walsh. 2007. "Do Good Intentions Beget Good Policy? A Review of Child Protection Policies to Address Intimate Partner Violence." *Children and Youth Services Review* 29, 12.

Northwest Territories. 1997. *Child and Family Services Act*, S.N.W.T. 1997, c 13.

Nova Scotia. 2002. *Children and Family Services Act*, S.N.S. 1990, c.5.

Nunavut. 1997. *Child and Family Services Act*, S.N.W.T. (Nu) 1997, c 13.

OECD (Organization for Economic Co-operation and Development). 2008. *Growing Unequal? Income Distribution and Poverty in OECD Countries*. <oecd-ilibrary.org/social-issues-migration-health/growing-unequal_9789264044197-en>.

Ontario. 1990. *Child and Family Service Act*, R.S.O. 1990, c. C.11.

Owen, Charlie, and June Statham. 2009. *Disproportionality in Child Welfare: The Prevalence of Black and Minority Ethnic Children within the "Looked After" and "Children in Need" Populations and on Child Protection Registers in England*. London, UK: Department for Children, Schools and Families.

Palmer, Sally, Sarah Maiter and Shehenaz Manji. 2006. "Effective Intervention in Child Protective Services: Learning from Parents." *Children and Youth Services Review* 28, 7.

Prince Edward Island. 2003. *Child Protection Act*, R.S.P.E.I. 1988, c. C-5.1.

Quebec. 2007. *Youth Protection Act*, R.S.Q., c P-34.1.

Radhakrishna, Aruna, Ingrid Bou-Saada, Wanda Hunter, Diane Catellier and Jonathan Kotch. 2001. "Are Father Surrogates a Risk Factor for Child Maltreatment?" *Child Maltreatment* 6, 4.

Risley-Curtiss, Christina and Kristin Heffernan. 2003. "Gender Biases in Child Welfare." *Affilia* 18, 4.

Roberts, Dorothy 2002. *Shattered Bonds: The Color of Child Welfare*. New York: Basic Books.

Rogowski, Steve. 2012. "Social Work with Children and Families: Challenges and Possibilities in The Neo-Liberal World." *British Journal of Social Work* 42, 5.

Saskatchewan. 1989–1990. *Child and Family Services Act*, S.S. 1989-1990, c. C-7.2.

Scourfield, Jonathan. 2003. *Gender and Child Protection*. Basingstoke, UK: Palgrave Macmillan.

Sedlak, Andrea, and Diane Broadhurst. 1996. *Third National Incidence Study of Child Abuse and Neglect — Final Report*. Washington, DC: U.S. Department of Health and Human Services, National Clearinghouse on Child Abuse and Neglect Information.

Sedlak, Andrea, and Dana Schultz. 2005. "Racial Differences in Child Protective Services Investigation of Abused and Neglected Children." In Dennette Derezotes, Mark Testa and John Poertner (eds.), *Race Matters in Child Welfare: The Overrepresentation of African American Children in the System*. Washington, DC: CWLA Press.

Sedlak, Andrea, Karla McPherson and Barnali Das. 2010. *Supplementary Analyses of Race Differences in Child Maltreatment Rates in the NIS-4*. Washington, DC: U.S. Department of Health and Human Services, Administration on Children, Youth and Families.

Spratt, Trevor, and Jackie Callan. 2004. "Parents' Views on Social Work Interventions in Child Welfare Cases." *British Journal of Social Work* 34.

Statistics Canada. 2011. *Income of Canadians.* <statcan.gc.ca/daily-quotidien/110615/dq110615b-eng.htm>.

Strega, Susan, Clair Fleet, Leslie Brown, Lena Dominelli, Marilyn Callahan and Christopher Walmsley. 2008. "Connecting Father Absence and Mother Blame in Child Welfare Policies and Practice." *Children and Youth Services Review* 30, 7.

Swift, Karen. 1995. *Manufacturing "Bad Mothers:" A Critical Perspective on Child Neglect.* Toronto: University of Toronto Press.

Swift, Karen, and Marilyn Callahan. 2006. "Problems and Potential in Canadian Child Welfare." In Nancy Freymond and Gary Cameron (eds.). *Towards Positive Systems of Child and Family Welfare: International Comparison of Child Protection, Family Service, and Community Caring Systems.* Toronto, ON: University of Toronto Press.

____. 2009. *At risk: Social Justice in Child Welfare and Other Human Services.* Toronto: University of Toronto Press.

Tamis-LeMonda, Catherine. 2004. "Conceptualizing Fathers' Roles: Playmates and More." Human Development 47, 4.

Thoburn, June, A. Chand, and J. Procter. 2005. *Child Welfare Services for Minority Ethnic Families: The Research Reviewed.* London: Jessica Kingsley Publishers.

Tilbury, Clare. 2009. "The Over-Representation of Indigenous Children in the Australian Child Welfare System." *International Journal of Social Welfare* 18.

Trocmé, Nico, Barbara Fallon, Bruce MacLaurin, Joanne Daciuk, Caroline Felstiner, Tara Black, Lil Tonmyr, Cindy Blackstock, Ken Barter, Daniel Turcotte, and Richard Cloutier. 2005. *Canadian Incidence Study of Reported Child Abuse and Neglect — 2003: Major Findings.* Ottawa: National Clearinghouse on Family Violence.

Trocmé, Nico, Barbara Fallon, Bruce MacLaurin, Vandna Sinha, Tara Black, Elizabeth Fast, Caroline Felstiner, Sonia Hélie, Daniel Turcotte, Pamela Weightman, Janet Douglas, and Jill Holroyd. 2010. *Canadian Incidence Study of Reported Child Abuse and Neglect — 2008: Major Findings.* Ottawa: National Clearinghouse on Family Violence.

Trocmé, Nico, Della Knoke, Barbara Fallon and Bruce McLaurin. 2006. *CIS-2003: Understanding the Case Substantiation Decision.* Ottawa: Canada: Public Health Agency.

United Kingdom. 1989. *Children Act*, c. 41.

United Kingdom, Department of Children, Schools and Families. 2010. *Working Together to Safeguard Children: A Guide to Inter-Agency Working to Safeguard and Promote the Welfare of Children.* DCFS-00305-2010.

United States. 1997. *Adoption of Safe Families Act*, P.L. 105-89.

United States, Department of Health and Social Services. 2003. *The Child Abuse Prevention and Treatment Act*, P.L. 93-247 as amended by the *Keeping Children and Families Safe Act of 2003*, P.L. 108-36, 6/25/03.

2. Neither Shaken Nor Stirred

The Persistence of Maternal Failure to Protect in Cases of Child Sexual Abuse

Rosemary Carlton and Julia Krane

The sexual abuse of children has a regrettably long history but its rise to public attention and its consideration as a social problem requiring state intervention are relatively recent. "Whereas children's allegations of sexual abuse were once commonly dismissed as the product of a ... rich fantasy or as acts of maliciousness, today's helping professionals are more prone to listen, believe, act, and prevent" (Krane 2003: 38). In particular, professionals in the field of child protection are charged with this mandate. Anglo-American child protection systems are legally responsible to prevent further acts of sexual abuse by determining risk to children of re-abuse and establishing their immediate and long-term protection. Legal statutes dictate professional practice such that determining risk due to child sexual abuse hinges not only on investigations into the acts of the alleged offender but also the alleged failures of a caregiver or parent to protect when s/he is thought to have known or should have known of the sexual abuse. This legislative framework, as was seen in Chapter 1, reveals the emergence of "failure to protect" as a concept wielding powerful influence on CPS practice with non-offending caregivers, usually mothers, in situations of child sexual abuse.

The legislative framework in which child sexual abuse is identified as a category of risk requiring CPS assessment and intervention stems from a particular conceptualization of failure to protect that has distinct impacts on daily practice. Historically, non-offending mothers have been centrally placed in the problem and resolution of child sexual abuse, although recently the focus on mothers as blameworthy has shifted to mothers as responsible for protection. Taken together, these trends reinforce and reproduce dominant ideologies of White, Western, middle-class maternal perfection that then shape research on and practices with non-offending mothers of sexually abused children. In this chapter we show how failure to protect emerges in CPS legislation and practices in situations of suspected or actual child sexual abuse. We take the position that failure-to-protect policies and practices are neither purely beneficial, nor even benign, as will be elaborated in the chapters by Bolen and Krane (Chapter 4), Carlton and Krane (Chapter 5) and Bernard (Chapter 6). These chapters show how failure-to-protect policies and practices rely on homogeneous notions of motherhood, which have resulted in the placement of expectations on non-offending mothers. They highlight the need for a different kind of approach to research and practice in this area that takes into account mothers' variable circumstances, social locations, or processes of coming to terms with their children's disclosures of sexual abuse.

Legislative Context: Child Sexual Abuse as a Circumstance of Risk

Child protection statutes define, amongst other concepts and with varying degrees of precision, the circumstances according to which a child may be deemed to be in need of protection. Child sexual abuse as a category of maltreatment requiring protective intervention is commonly included in these statutes.

In the United States, categories of child abuse and neglect are defined in both federal and state laws. As noted in the introduction to this book, at the federal level, the *Child Abuse Prevention and Treatment Act (CAPTA)* (2003) defines child abuse and neglect as "any recent act or failure to act on the part of a parent or caretaker, which results in death, serious physical or emotional harm, sexual abuse or exploitation, or an act or failure to act which presents an imminent risk of serious harm" (section 111.2). According to *CAPTA* (2003), sexual abuse includes:

> A. the employment, use, persuasion, inducement, enticement, or coercion of any child to engage in, or assist any other person to engage in, any sexually explicit conduct or simulation of such conduct for the purpose of producing a visual depiction of such conduct; or
> B. the rape, and in cases of caretaker or inter-familial relationships, statutory rape, molestation, prostitution, or other form of sexual exploitation of children, or incest with children." (section 111.4)

Although failure to protect is not specified in the definition of sexual abuse, the overarching definition of child abuse and neglect encompasses parental or caregiver failure to act to prevent sexual abuse or the imminent risk of sexual abuse that leads to a determination of a child being in need of protection. Just as state child protection laws provide definitions of sexual abuse that range from very general descriptions to lists of specific acts, similarly, they vary significantly with respect to how failure to protect emerges in relation to sexual abuse. For example, the *Abused and Neglected Child Reporting Act* (2007) in Illinois refers to a sexually abused child as "a child whose parent, immediate family member, person responsible for the child's welfare, individual residing in the same home as the child, or paramour of the child's parent … commits or allows to be committed any sex offense against such child" (section 3). Likewise, New York's *Care and Protection of Children Law*

(2006) states that an "abused child ... means a child less than eighteen years of age whose parent or other person legally responsible for his [sic] care ... (iii) commits, or allows to be committed, an act of sexual abuse against such child as defined in the penal law" (section 4-b). In these examples, the expectation of parental protection from child sexual abuse is explicit. More subtle approaches are seen across other states in the U.S. that refer to parental omissions or supervisory neglect as circumstances indicating risk. For example, the *District of Columbia Official Code* (2008) defines the "neglected child" as one "whose parent, guardian, or custodian has failed to make reasonable efforts to prevent the infliction of abuse upon the child," whereby abuse includes any form of sexual abuse or exploitation. Chapter 26-44 of the *Revised Code of Washington* (2011) defines the "negligent treatment or maltreatment" of a child as a category of abuse and neglect, with "negligent treatment or maltreatment" meaning "an act or a failure to act, or the cumulative effects of a pattern of conduct, behavior, or inaction, that evidences a serious disregard of consequences of such magnitude as to constitute a clear and present danger to a child's health, welfare, or safety" (section 14). Thus, although failure to protect from sexual abuse is not explicitly referenced in Washington's state legislation, decisions that a child is in need of protection due to such failures fall within the category of negligent maltreatment.

The United Kingdom's *Working Together to Safeguard Children* policy document (2010: paragraph 1.35) defines sexual abuse as follows:

> [It] involves forcing or enticing a child or young person to take part in sexual activities, not necessarily involving a high level of violence, whether or not the child is aware of what is happening. The activities may involve physical contact, including assault by penetration (for example, rape or oral sex) or non-penetrative acts such as masturbation, kissing, rubbing and touching outside of clothing. They may also include non-contact activities, such as involving children in looking at, or in the production of, sexual images, watching sexual activities, encouraging children to behave in sexually inappropriate ways, or grooming a child in preparation for abuse (including via the internet). Sexual abuse is not solely perpetrated by adult males. Women can also commit acts of sexual abuse, as can other children.

As can be seen, failure to protect is not explicit but, as noted in the introduction to this book, both the *Children Act* (1989) and *Working Together to Safeguard Children* (2010) present risk to children as arising from parental failure to act to prevent harm. As well, failure to protect from sexual abuse can also be interpreted as a form of neglect which may involve the failure of a parent or caregiver to "protect a child from physical and emotional harm or danger" (*Working Together to Safeguard Children* 2010: paragraph 1.36).

In Canada, the notion of failure to protect in situations of sexual abuse is particularly visible in child protection legislation from province to province. A perusal of CPS legislation in Alberta (2000) and British Columbia (1996) reveals that a child may be deemed to be in need of protection should her/ his parent be "unwilling or unable to protect the child" from sexual abuse. Similarly, in Newfoundland and Labrador, Yukon, and Quebec, a child is considered to have been sexually abused or at risk of being sexually abused should her/his parent "not protect" or "fail to take the necessary steps to protect" the child. In the Northwest Territories, Nova Scotia, Nunavut, Ontario, and Prince Edward Island, the notion of failure to protect is taken even further to include the understanding that if a parent "knew or should have known" of the sexual abuse or the risk of sexual abuse, then that child is in need of protection. While not explicit in Manitoba, New Brunswick, and Saskatchewan, in these jurisdictions legislation leaves ample room for determinations of parental failure to protect from sexual abuse. In all three provinces, legislation recognizes the potential for child endangerment based on caregiver acts and omissions. In addition, each provincial statute states that a child is in need of protection when s/he is in the care of someone "who is unable or unwilling to provide adequate care, supervision or control of the child" (Manitoba 1985, article 12.2(a.i); New Brunswick 1983, article 31.1(c)). Accordingly, in Canada, the U.S., and the U.K., a determination of risk due to child sexual abuse may result not only from the acts of the alleged offender but also as a result of the alleged failures of a caregiver or parent to protect when s/he is thought to have known of the sexual abuse or to have had reasonable cause to suspect the sexual abuse.

Protecting Children from Sexual Abuse

Today's child protection workers are deeply committed to accepting and supporting children's disclosures of sexual abuse with the least disruption to their care. Workers most often deal with cases of child sexual abuse in which the offenders, overwhelmingly male, are known and trusted individuals or relatives often with care-giving responsibilities. In the United States and Canada, for example, retrospective surveys found that between 25 and 29 percent of perpetrators were relatives, about 60 percent were known to the victims but unrelated, and between 11 and 16 percent were total strangers (Badgley 1984; CCJS 1998; Russell 1986). A recent U.S. survey, the *National Incidence Studies of Missing, Abducted, Runaway and Throwaway Children (NISMART–2)*, found that the vast majority of child sexual abuse perpetrators are known to their victims. Based on a household survey over a twelve month period in 1999 from a nationally representative sample of caretakers and youth, almost three-fourths (71 percent) of the 285,400 sexually assaulted children "were assaulted by someone they were acquainted with or knew by sight; 18 [percent] were assaulted by a complete stranger [and] 10 [percent] by a family member" (Finkelhor, Hammer, and Sedlak 2008: 2). The *Fourth National Incidence Study of Child Abuse and Neglect (NIS–4)* in the U.S. found that biological parents were identified as the perpetrators in 37 percent of sexual abuse cases and non-biological parents or partners in 23 percent of the cases. Details of the relationship between the perpetrator and victim in the remaining 40 percent of the sample were not provided; however, at least 60 percent — and likely far more — of the sample of sexually abused children knew the offender (Sedlak et al. 2010). The *Canadian Incidence Study on Reported Abuse and Neglect - 2003 (CIS-2003)* identified non-parental relatives as the largest group of perpetrators (35 percent), followed by children's friends (15 percent), stepfathers (13 percent), biological fathers (9 percent), other acquaintances (9 percent), and boyfriends and girlfriends of the parents (5 percent). Another 5 percent of cases where sexual abuse was the primary substantiated maltreatment involved biological mothers as perpetrators (Trocmé et al. 2005). No comparable categorization of perpetrator was made in the latest *CIS-2008* (Trocmé et al. 2010). These studies confirm that child protection authorities are more likely to become involved in situations of child sexual abuse in which the perpetrator is well-known to or carries caregiving responsibilities for the child. We argue that this skewed client population reproduces, without contestation, maternal failure to protect as justifiable cause for intervention.

In Canada, child protection investigations into situations of alleged child sexual abuse tend to be guided by protocols designed to ensure consistent and thorough handling of these complex situations. Such protocols provide agreements between child protection authorities and law enforcement that establish reciprocal reporting and joint investigation procedures that aim to enhance the likelihood of confirming or refuting allegations of child sexual abuse and ensuring the protection of child victims. Typically, a police detective interviews the child and the alleged offender in order to gather evidence necessary for criminal proceedings. The child protection worker may observe the police interview with the child, interview the non-offending parent(s), and re-interview the child to confirm the child's current safety and assess parental capacity to prevent the recurrence of sexual abuse. Despite ongoing partnerships between law enforcement and child protection authorities, reliance on police involvement to ensure the protection of child victims is rare. According to Bolen (2001), most offenders are not prosecuted in cases of substantiated sexual abuse, and even fewer serve sentences. In fact, Bolen (2001) found that only about 7 percent of offenders in cases of substantiated child sexual abuse spend more than one year in jail. Such marginal prosecution, conviction, and incarceration rates result in increased risk that offenders will continue to have access to their child victims. thus leaving child protection authorities with the burden of ensuring children's protection.

Given the potential for offenders to have ongoing proximity to child victims, protection workers are called upon to act quickly — usually within a few days — to put into place measures that separate alleged offenders from children in order keep them with their primary caregivers, usually non-offending mothers. As noted in the introduction to this book, despite the use of gender-neutral language throughout child protection legislation, gendered practices that concentrate scrutiny and intervention efforts on mothers rather than fathers tend to prevail (Risley-Curtiss and Heffernan 2003; Scourfield 2003; Swift 1995). Findings from the *Canadian Incidence Study of Reported Child Abuse and Neglect-2008* (Trocmé et al. 2010) concur: the almost 1,800 child protection workers surveyed identified females to be the primary caregivers in 90 percent of the cases substantiated for child abuse and neglect. Overwhelmingly, biological mothers were identified as the primary caregiver (86 percent of the cases). In almost half of the cases of substantiated sexual abuse in the *Canadian Incidence Study of Reported Child Abuse and Neglect — 2003*, children were residing with two parental figures; the tendency to focus attention on mothers thus appears persistent in child protection practice.

Investigating, assessing, and responding to allegations of child sexual abuse are driven by the absolute need to ensure that children are protected from further harm. While conscientious workers may recognize the emotional and material difficulties facing families, particularly mothers, in the thick of investigation and its aftermath, children's safety remains at the forefront of interventions. Despite any understanding of and empathy for the shock, disbelief and confusion experienced by non-offending mothers — emotional fallout that is not atypical, as will be seen later — workers must assess their capacities to ensure that the child not be revictimized. In this way a non-offending mother's emotional well-being becomes an important factor in assessing her capacity to provide care and protection. The challenge facing workers is to recognize that non-offending mothers may need time and support in order to come to terms with their child's disclosure, while simultaneously understanding that the child's safety is likely best achieved through the non-offending mothers' ability to be strong and supportive, knowing full well that the last resort is to separate the child from her/his family.

Compounding the emotional distress often experienced by mothers in the wake of their child's disclosures, are the material consequences mothers face, which typically include "relationship losses, reduced income, increased dependence on government programs, employment disruption, and change of residence" (Massat and Lundy 1998: 378). These consequences are significant given that families coming to the attention of child protection authorities tend to be already living in precarious circumstances. "The clients of child welfare agencies are often poorly educated, living in or near poverty, and not infrequently members of a racial minority group and living in a family led by a single parent, usually the mother" (Bala 2004: 24). These women are known to struggle with domestic violence, drug or alcohol abuse, a lack of social supports, mental health issues, and psychological issues resulting from maltreatment as a child (Trocmé et al. 2005, 2010).

With the growing influence of attachment theory regarding the emotional damage caused by separating children from their caregivers at the time of investigation and beyond, few children are now removed from parental care. In 2003, for example, only 6 percent of children were removed from their families in substantiated cases of child sexual abuse at the time of initial investigation (Trocmé et al. 2005). In 2008, only 8 percent of children were removed from their families in substantiated cases of all forms of child maltreatment (Trocmé et al. 2010). While workers strive to minimize the potentially disruptive effects of the disclosure and its aftermath by maintaining children under the care of their non-offending mothers, they are fearful of making decisions that could inadvertently result in repeated sexual abuse. When all is said and done, child protection workers must err on the side of child safety. If the non-offending mother is unable to provide protection, the worker has few other options than to remove the child from parental care. In the context of the urgent mandate and the need to respond quickly, these current practice trends shift the gaze over to the capacity of non-offending mothers to offer immediate and long-term protection to the child.

The Historical Roots of Mother-Blame and Maternal Responsibility for Protection

Child sexual abuse has existed for centuries and across countries and cultures. According to Bolen (2001: 3), "perhaps the single most influential person in the history of the professional literature on child sexual abuse is Sigmund Freud." In the late 1800s, Freud proposed seduction theory, in which he posited that the "hysterical" and "neurotic" symptoms expressed by his adult female patients derived from their attempts to cope with traumatic experiences of childhood sexual abuse. Freud grew increasingly uneasy with incriminating fathers and came to publicly recant his own theory. Later, driven by public pressure, Freud recast his patients' distress as resulting not from actual sexual assault but rather from the projection and sometimes acting out of internal sexual fantasy (Olafson, Corwin, and Summit 1993).

Well into the 1960s, the dominant explanation of child sexual abuse was influenced by Freud's later works and thus focused on girls' alleged seduction of their fathers (Hooper 1992). This analysis was gradually challenged by a family systems approach wherein all family members were thought to somehow contribute to father-daughter incest. Significantly, the mother was allotted a key role in the development and perpetuation of the abuse.

For example, a 1966 study identified the mother as the "cornerstone" in the "pathological family system"; she was said to have set up and sanctioned the sexual abuse by consciously or unconsciously relinquishing her spousal obligations and delegating her daughter to "satisfy" the father's "needs" (Lustig et al. 1966).

Although thinking about child sexual abuse in the context of the family has evolved since the 1960s, the centrality of mother as villain or victim has prevailed (Elbow and Mayfield 1991; Krane and Davies 1996). Mother has been identified as a colluder or accessory through her physical or emotional absence and inadequacies or through actions that suggest she orchestrates, unwittingly or not, the abuse (Krane 2003). For example, Zuelzer and Reposa (1983) viewed mothers as pivotal in incestuous abuse. Said to be needy, demanding and lacking sufficient psychological investment in their children, mothers in incestuous families may "unconsciously" use illness or absence (or even death) to escape their maternal responsibilities (Zuelzer and Reposa 1983: 105). They were thought to ignore or deny "blatantly inappropriate and provocative sexual behavior" or to ignore, deny or react punitively toward girls' attempts to disclose the abuse (Zuelzer and Reposa 1983: 104–105). The incestuous father, on the other hand, was portrayed as a passive recipient of the mother's abdication of her marital and sexual duties. The authors described the mother as abandoning her sexual responsibility to her husband by "forcing" the daughter "to take over [mother's] … role sexually and [function] as family caretaker" (Zuelzer and Reposa 1983: 105).

Krane's (2003: 70) analysis of this persistent focus on mother's role revealed a shift in emphasis from the actions of the alleged offender to the inadequacies and "in/actions of women as mothers [and wives]," particularly when it comes to having known and having failed to protect. This theme was seen in the influential *Handbook of Clinical Intervention in Child Sexual Abuse*:

> Mothers can perhaps be most generally described as failing to protect the child victim…. Sometimes the mother is physically absent on a regular and predictable basis, thereby affording the opportunity for incest to occur. The classic example of this situation involves a mother who works a night or evening shift. Sometimes mother is psychologically absent, often ignoring overt seductive behavior between the incest participants that she should be curbing and redirecting and setting limits on at a very early stage. Some mothers fail to protect in a very direct fashion by deliberately setting up situations in which the incest participants are encouraged to engage in sexual behavior. (Sgroi, Blick, and Porter 1982: 28)

While Sgroi et al. (1982: 29) recognized that not all mothers deliberately set the conditions for incest, they held firm that "most mothers of incest victims are aware, consciously or unconsciously, that the incest exists." Like other scholars at that time, Sgroi et al. (1982: 29) claimed that mothers frequently responded to their daughters' disclosures with "hostility and disbelief," inaction or ineffectual action. Ultimately, mothers failed to protect. Sgroi et al. did give some attention to incestuous fathers. Described as dominating and self-absorbed, these men isolated their families from the "hostile" outside world and maintained "sole authority" over all family decisions (Sgroi et al. 1982: 27). Taking into account this portrayal of the sexually offending father, it is virtually impossible to imagine how a mother, observed by Sgroi et al. (1982: 28) to "usually" occupy "a subordinate position" within the incestuous family, might be able to act in a protective manner.

Between the 1980s and 1990s, efforts were made to broaden family systems approaches by examining the histories and personalities of family members and exploring the couple's intimate relationship (Bolen 2001; Krane 2003). This complexity is seen in Finkelhor's (1984) four preconditions framework for understanding how child sexual abuse comes about. The first precondition, motivation to sexually abuse, included individual factors such as the offender's emotional congruence with a child, sexual arousal to a child or the unavailability of alternative sources of sexual gratification. At the social level, factors included male dominance, child pornography, and the sexualization of male needs. The second precondition centred on factors that might disinhibit the offender such as alcohol, psychosis, impulse disorder, and "failure of incest inhibition mechanism in family dynamics" (Finkelhor 1984: 56). Tolerance of sexual interest in children, weak criminal sanctions, beliefs in the patriarchal rights of fathers and "male inability to identify with needs of children" (Finkelhor 1984: 57) operate at the social level. The third and fourth preconditions delineated factors that enable the sexual abuse to occur by overcoming any external constraints and subduing any resistance by the child. Individual factors were said to include an ill, absent, unprotective, distant or dominated mother; social isolation of family; improper child supervision; unusual sleeping conditions; an emotionally insecure or deprived or unusually trusting child; and/or a child who lacks knowledge about sexual abuse and coercion. Proposed social level factors were lack of social networks and supports for mothers; barriers to women's equality; ideology of family sanctity; and social powerlessness and inadequate sexual education for children. The four preconditions model grasped the multi-faceted nature of child sexual abuse perpetrated by both family and non-family members against girls or boys. It included attention to the psychodynamics of the offender and family system dynamics, and took seriously mother's failure to protect and children's vulnerability as potential factors that come into play only after the offender is motivated to abuse and has overcome his own internal constraints. Although due attention was directed at social factors, in child protection practice, individual factors related to both mother and child are likely to take precedence as a result of risk and safety concerns.

On the front lines of practice, ways of understanding and responding to child sexual abuse continue to be influenced by family systems theory (Bolen 2003; Krane 1994). As Hooper and Humphreys (1998: 566) put it, a family systems analysis allows the father's actions to be "perceived as secondary," as a "response to shared problems such as poor communication," leading to the minimization or denial of his responsibility for his own actions. In contrast,

> anything mothers (and in some cases children) did until the abuse was stopped implicated them in it. In relation to women, this [mother-blame] applied whether or not they knew about the abuse, and whatever they might have tried to do to stop it. (Hooper and Humphreys 1998: 566)

Shifting the Gaze onto Mothers as Protectors

More recently efforts have been made to challenge the ways in which women as mothers have been implicated in the problem of child sexual abuse. Largely feminist in orientation, these critiques have sought to better understand mothers' knowledge of and responses to disclosures of child sexual abuse (Alaggia 2001; Johnson 1992; Myer 1985); mothers' experiences of child protection interventions (Bernard 2001; Krane 1994, 2003); the impact of interventions by child protection agencies and other institutions on mothers of sexually abused children (Carter 1999); and how mothers survive their children's disclosures of sexual abuse (Hooper 1992). Emerging from this research are more complex understandings of mothers vis-à-vis the sexual abuse of their children. Myer's (1985) study was one of the first to examine how mothers respond to disclosures. While some women were initially ambivalent, the majority of mothers accepted the allegations, showed empathy to the child, expressed anger about the abuse and toward the abuser and took some form of action. A few mothers denied the allegations, were passive and took no action. Myer also described some mothers as showing more concern for themselves than their children. Her research revealed that these women were emotionally and financially dependent on partners who dominated, battered, and frightened them. Myer's research thus challenged homogeneous assumptions of mothers as collusive and unprotective and made room for maternal ambivalence in the process of coming to terms with a child's disclosure of sexual abuse. Nearly two decades later, Pintello and Zuravin's (2001) survey of non-offending mothers' responses to their children's disclosures of sexual abuse revealed a similar understanding. Of 435 non-offending mothers, 41.8 percent believed and protected, 13.3 percent believed but did not protect, 14 percent protected but did not believe, and 30.8 percent neither believed nor protected. The authors found that having their first child prior to adulthood, being the sexual partner of the offender, having had knowledge of the sexual abuse prior to the child's disclosure, and having a child who exhibited sexualized behaviour negatively influenced mothers' belief and protection. This research suggests that a broad range of factors ought to be taken into account when intervening with non-offending mothers.

Taken a step further, feminists have proposed that maternal responses to and support of children who were sexually abused ought to be understood as fluid and changing (Alaggia 2001; Hooper and Humphreys 1998) rather than static and binary. A mother's belief and support of her sexually abused child occurs

> against a backdrop of intense and conflicting relationships involving the child, the offender and other members of the immediate and extended family, and of the major material, emotional and legal consequences which mothers [have] to tackle as part of the aftermath of discovery. (Hooper and Humphreys 1998: 569–570)

As Bolen and Lamb (2004: 185) put it, non-offending mothers' potential vacillation or ambivalence in belief and support now tends to be seen as a "normal circumstance of the chaos and impact of the child's disclosure." The implications of this understanding, with its developing empirical base, are tackled by Bolen and Krane in Chapter 4 of this volume.

Understanding that learning of the sexual abuse of a child is likely to be highly stressful and disruptive, researchers might expect non-offending mothers to experience significant distress in the aftermath of this event (Elliot and Carnes 2001). For example, in comparison to mothers of children without a history of sexual abuse, Lewin and Bergin (2001) found that non-offending mothers of sexually abused children showed signs of heightened levels of depression and anxiety as well as diminished maternal attachment behaviours. Similarly, Cyr, McDuff, and Wright (1999) found that of 118 non-offending mothers whose children were followed by child protection services in Quebec following disclosures of sexual abuse, over two-thirds of the mothers exhibited clinical levels of psychological distress, not to mention heightened financial and social disadvantage when compared to the norm of women in the province. The authors suggested that financial and social disadvantage might reflect the circumstances of mothers coming to the attention of child protective services. More recently, Hébert et al. (2007) found that more than half of 149 non-offending mothers reported clinical levels of psychological distress following the sexual abuse of their children. The authors noted that those mothers who expressed a low sense of empowerment were more likely to experience clinical levels of psychological distress. They concluded that a woman's "perceived sense of control and self-efficacy as a parent facing the needs of her sexually abused child or her perceptions of her own abilities to take care of her child are important factors related to her own sense of psychological well-being" (Hébert et al. 2007: 809).

Joyce's (2007) interviews with professional social workers engaged in treatment related to child sexual abuse revealed a depth of sensitivity to non-offending mothers:

> Unlike past literature and practice, which blamed mothers via the collusion hypothesis, these workers saw mothers as unfairly blamed by social actors (police, child welfare, or judges) … and then secondarily, as deprived of the treatment, the social supports, and the economic supports they believed mothers needed to cope effectively with incest's aftermath. (Joyce 2007: 10)

Workers spoke about the dearth of funding and organizational supports that limited their options for engagement with mothers. They also spoke of their fear of public scrutiny, arising in the aftermath of publicized tragedies involving children suffering at the hands of their parents:

> While experiencing that outside actors were subjecting them to ever-heightened observations, second guessing, and culpability, the workers also believed they exercised little control over ultimate outcomes. This combination of pessimism and fatalism reflected clinician beliefs that their interventions did not control much of what occurred in the families they worked with. Workers viewed their clients' lives as chaotic and disorganized; they believed that outside actors asked them to "control the uncontrollable." They felt their professional practice was unfairly dissected. In a passing down of the victimization, there was a parallel process in which outside agencies and actors scrutinized workers, who then scrutinized mothers. (Joyce 2007: 7)

There is little room for maternal ambivalence, psychological distress, or chaotic life circumstances in the expectations to protect children. Krane's (2003) case study of a Canadian child protection agency uncovered how the expectation to protect children from sexual abuse was shifted from caseworkers to women as mothers in families. This shift was seen in casework practices wherein workers encouraged mothers to express their belief and support for their victimized child. They expected mothers to assume the protection of their children as an immediate priority by denouncing the alleged offender's actions and, if need be, separating from him (Krane 2003). With seemingly ambivalent or unprotective mothers, workers compelled mothers to "choose" between supporting the child or alleged offender. The responsibility for mothers to protect often resulted in heightened stresses from adhering to the dictates of protection, loss of significant relationships, including those with intimate partners, loss of paid employment and/or income, and loss of voice and say. Ultimately, because mothers experienced this process as "intrusive, unsettling and costly," (Krane 2003: 186) it led to unintended and unhelpful alienation from their workers.

Given that non-offending mothers are expected to carry out intervention plans in response to child sexual abuse, "the mother's ability to comply with all the provisions of the plan and to enhance her young child's psychological well-being and safety can be impaired if she is experiencing depression, anxiety, and diminished maternal attachment behaviours" (Lewin and Bergin 2001: 373). These reflections speak to the widespread understanding that non-offending mothers' involvement is a crucial mediator, related not only to children's safety in the aftermath of abuse, but also their emotional or psychological recovery (Corcoran 2004; Lovett 2004). As described by Elliott and Carnes (2001: 321), "children's emotional and behavioral adjustment following victimization is associated with the reactions and support they receive from parental figures" — the overwhelming majority being mothers. Indeed, reliance on mothers' emotional support and protective action is in keeping with dominant expectations of women as mothers. This nexus of issues — belief, support, and protection — comes under critical scrutiny in the chapters that follow. It is embedded, however, in a long tradition of dominant ideologies on mothering.

Dominant Ideologies of Mothering

Mothering has been the subject of rapidly developing theoretical and empirical scholarships in the last quarter century, driven in large part by feminists, who have sought to disrupt notions and practices of mothering as expected, universal, and unchanging (Arendell 2000). At the centre of feminist efforts to portray the broad landscape of mothering has been an interrogation of motherhood ideology:

> The prevailing ideology in North America is that of intensive mothering. This motherhood mandate declares that mothering is exclusive, wholly child-centred, emotionally involving, and time-consuming…. The mother portrayed in this ideology is devoted to the care of others; she is self-sacrificing and not a subject with her own needs and interests…. She is the good mother. (Arendell 2000: 1194)

Indeed, since the nineteenth century, motherhood has been exalted as women's chief preoccupation — an experience in which the caring bonds between mother and child have been glorified, "and traits of nurturance and selflessness have been defined as the essence of the maternal, and hence, of the womanly" (Thorne 1992: 15). Intensive mothering ideology assumes that children not only require full-time maternal care but that mothers are understood to be willingly available and best equipped to provide that care despite any other obligations or conditions. According to this model, the child's needs take precedence over the mother's, and she is expected to be all-knowing and thus able to anticipate and respond to her child's every need (Krane and Davies 2000).

Featured in this concept of mothering have been efforts to unpack what it is that mothers actually do, that is, the "work" of mothering. Ruddick (1989, 1994) and Levine (1985) are amongst those who have exposed the heretofore invisible work involved in mothering and the conditions of such work; they point out that mothering has no fixed hours or schedule, no sick leave, vacation, pension, collective bargaining or unionization. As Ruddick (1994: 34) observed, "mothers are identified not by what they feel but by what they try to do." Arendell (2000: 1194) elaborated on the relational work of mothering:

> Maternal practice involves intimate relationships as well as skill. Through dynamic interaction with their children, mothers foster and shape a profound affectional relationship, a deeply meaningful connection.... In this relationship of care, the child has physical, emotional, and moral claims on the mother.

Challenges to a universal and homogeneous model of mothering that is devoid of social location have surfaced through feminist discourses on mothering. Feminists have drawn attention to the Eurocentric, White, middle-class norm upon which the idealized construction of motherhood seemed to rest. As Arendell (2000: 1194–95) observed, "cultural and economic contexts variously shape mothers' activities and understandings. Mothering takes place within 'specific historical contexts framed by interlocking structures of race, class, and gender'" (Collins 1994, cited in Arendell 2000). Collins' (1992, 1994) reflections on the history of Black mothering, for example, revealed collective forms of mothering that included blood mothers and other mothers. McMahon's (1995) study of middle- and working-class women's understandings and experiences of motherhood found that conceptualizations of motherhood and ways of mothering were deeply influenced by socio-economic contexts and prevailing notions of "womanliness" and "motherhood." For example, while middle-class mothers spoke of choosing to delay motherhood until they had achieved a stable, heterosexual relationship, developed a career, and gained a personal sense of maturity, working-class mothers saw little benefit to deferring motherhood and spoke of achieving maturity through having a child. McMahon noted, however, that becoming a mother without the apparent supports of a stable partner and/or career served not only to reproduce social inequalities and complicate the experience of mothering, but also to reinforce negative public perceptions of working-class motherhood.

Not surprisingly, women's experiences of mothering can and do stand in stark contrast to the prevailing, pervasive, and persistent ideologies of mothering and motherhood. Drawing on the works of previous scholars, Arendell (2000: 1196) demonstrated how the experience of mothering is brimming with dialectical tensions. She elaborated as follows:

> "Mothering can confer both maternal power and an immense burden of responsibility" (Oberman and Josselon 1996: 344). Mothering is a font of personal fulfillment, growth, and joy, on the one hand, and one of distress, depression, and anxiety, on the other (e.g., Ross 1995). Child raising may bring personal development but also increased work and economic stress; it brings feelings of liberation but also of oppression and subordination.

Mothering has come to be understood as emotional work with varying and shifting experiences of maternal satisfaction, distress, and ambivalence that are shaped by social location. According to Arendell's reviews of research, married and employed mothers with young children who meet up with difficulties in securing affordable child care and who bear the brunt of child rearing without support prove to be distressed and stressed if not depressed. "Mothers having preschool-aged or multiple children and living in crowded conditions feel more overburdened than other mothers" (Arendell 2000: 1197). The complex feelings associated with mothering have been the subject of Parker's works (1995, 1997). She was instrumental in theorizing and normalizing feelings of maternal ambivalence that range from love, adoration, joy, passion, and delight to the darker, often unspoken and guilt-ridden feelings of hate, rage, frustration, hopelessness, and despair. Parker also problematized maternal ambivalence, bringing to light how its expression may vary according to culture, historical period and social location, as well as the level of support available to women.

Although feminists have drawn attention to the impossibility of achieving and maintaining maternal perfection, intensive mothering ideology persists. Feminists have argued that this ideology and the structures that support and reproduce it exclude the possibilities that the involvement of partners or fathers in the daily care of children might present. It imposes the maternal facet of a woman's identity as her sole character. At the same time, it renders invisible the emotional and material conditions around which mothering occurs. Women's struggles as mothers are thus silenced: it is assumed that "normal mothers cope" (Krane and Davies 2000: 39).

Arendell (2000: 1202) concluded her analysis on mothering with a call to focus "on mothers' identities, experiences, and activities, and their understandings of each" in order to "secure far more realistic and less normative portrayals of mothers' lives than those afforded by sweeping images." Contributors to this book take to heart Arendell's call to embrace mothers' identities, experiences, and activities as a starting point from which to deconstruct notions of failure to protect in practices related to child sexual abuse and to offer insights into alternative practices on the front lines.

References

Alaggia, Ramona. 2001. "Cultural and Religious Influences in Maternal Response to Intrafamilial Child Sexual Abuse: Charting New Territory for Research and Treatment." *Journal of Child Sexual Abuse* 10, 2.

Alberta. 2000. *Child, Youth and Family Enhancement Act*, R.S.A. 2000, c. C-12.

Arendell, Terry. 2000. "Conceiving and Investigating Motherhood: The Decade's Scholarship." *Journal of Marriage and Family Therapy* 62, 4.

Badgley, Robin. 1984. *Report of the Committee on Sexual Offences Against Children and Youths. Sexual Offences against Children In Canada: Summary*. Ottawa: Canadian Government Publishing Centre, Supply and Services Canada.

Bala, Nicholas. 2004. "Child Welfare Law in Canada: An Introduction." In Nicholas Bala, Michael K. Zapf, R. James Williams, Robin Vogl and Joseph P. Hornick (eds.), *Canadian Child Welfare Law: Children Families and the State*. Second edition. Toronto: Thompson Education Publishing.

Bernard, Claudia. 2001. *Constructing Lived Experiences: Representations of Black Mothers in Child Sexual Abuse Discourses*. Aldershot: Ashgate Publishing.

Bolen, Rebecca M. 2003. "Nonoffending Mothers of Sexually Abused Children: A Case of Institutionalized Sexism?" *Violence Against Women* 9, 11.

____. 2001. *Child Sexual Abuse: Its Scope and our Failure*. New York: Kluwer Academic/Plenum.

Bolen, Rebecca M., and Jan Leah Lamb. 2004. "Ambivalence of Nonoffending Guardians after Child Sexual Abuse Disclosure." *Journal of Interpersonal Violence* 19, 2.

British Columbia. 1996. *Child, Family and Community Service Act*, BC Reg 533/95

Carter, Betty. 1999. *Who's to Blame? Child Sexual Abuse and Non-Offending Mothers*. Toronto: Toronto University Press.

CCJS (Canadian Centre for Justice Statistics). 1998. *Statistics Canada. References 203 Uniform Crime Reporting Survey*.

Collins, Patricia Hill. 1994. "Shifting the Center: Race, Class, and Feminist Theorizing About Motherhood." In Donna Bassin, Margaret Honey and Meryle M. Kaplan (eds.), *Representations of Motherhood*. New Haven: Yale University Press.

____. 1992. "Black Women and Motherhood." In Barrie Thorne and Marilyn Yalom (eds.), *Rethinking the Family*. Boston: Northeastern University Press.

Corcoran, Jacqueline. 2004. "Treatment Outcome Research with the Non-offending Parents of Sexual Abuse Children: A Critical Review." *Journal of Child Sexual Abuse* 13, 2.

Cyr, Mireille, Pierre McDuff and John Wright. 1999. "Le profil des mères d'enfants agressés sexuellement: santé mentale, stress et adaptation." *Santé Mentale au Québec* 24, 2.

District of Columbia. 2008. *District of Columbia Official Code.*

Elbow, Margaret, and Judy Mayfield. 1991. "Mothers of Incest Victims: Villains, Victims, or Protectors?" *Families in Society: The Journal of Contemporary Human Services* 72, 2.

Elliot, Ann N., and Connie N. Carnes. 2001. "Reactions of Nonoffending Parents to the Sexual Abuse of Their Child: A Review of the Literature." *Child Maltreatment* 6, 4.

Finkelhor, David. 1984. *Child Sexual Abuse: New Theory and Research.* New York: Free Press.

Finkelhor, David, Heather Hammer, and Andrea J. Sedlak. 2008. *Second National Incidence Studies of Missing, Abducted, Runaway, and Thrownaway Children (NISMART–2) — Sexually Assaulted Children: National Estimates and Characteristics.* Washington: Office of Juvenile Justice and Delinquency Prevention, U.S. Department of Justice.

Hébert, Martine, Isabelle Daigneault, Delphine Collin-Vézina, and Mireille Cyr. 2007. "Factors Linked to Distress in Mothers of Children Disclosing Sexual Abuse." *Journal of Nervous and Mental Disease* 195, 10.

Hooper, Carole-Ann. 1992. *Mothers Surviving Child Sexual Abuse.* London and New York: Tavistock/Routledge.

Hooper, Carole-Ann, and Catherine Humphreys. 1998. "Women Whose Children Have Been Sexually Abused: Reflections on a Debate." *British Journal of Social Work* 28, 4.

Illinois. 2007. *Abused and Neglected Child Reporting Act,* 325 ILCS 5/.

Johnson, Janis. 1992. *Mothers of Incest Survivors: Another Side of the Story.* Bloomington: Indiana University Press.

Joyce, Patricia A. 2007. "The Production of Therapy: The Social Process of Construction of the Mother of a Sexually Abused Child." *Journal of Child Sexual Abuse* 16, 3.

Krane, Julia. 1994. "The Transformation of Women into Mother Protectors: An Examination of Child Protection Practices in Cases of Child Sexual Abuse." Unpublished doctoral dissertation, University of Toronto, Toronto.

___. 2003. *What's Mother Got to Do with It? Protecting Children from Sexual Abuse.* Toronto: University of Toronto Press.

Krane, Julia, and Linda Davies. 2000. "Rethinking Risk Assessment in Mothering and Child Protection Practice." *Child and Family Social Work* 5, 1.

___. 1996. "Mother-Blame in Child Sexual Abuse: A Look at Dominant Culture, Writings, and Practices." *Textual Studies in Canada* 7.

Levine, Helen. 1985. "The Power Politics of Motherhood." In L. Emery and J. Turner (eds.), *Perspectives on Women in the 1980s.* Winnipeg: University of Manitoba Press.

Lewin, Linda, and Christi Bergin. 2001. "Attachment Behaviors, Depression, and Anxiety in Nonoffending Mothers of Child Sexual Abuse Victims." *Child Maltreatment* 6, 4.

Lovett, Beverly. 2004. "Child Sexual Abuse Disclosure: Maternal Response and Other Variables Impacting the Victim." *Child and Adolescent Social Work Journal* 21, 4.

Lustig, Noel, John Spellman, Seth Dresser, and Thomas Murray. 1966. "Incest." *Archives of General Psychiatry* 14.

Manitoba. 1985. *The Child and Family Services Act*, C.C.S.M. c. C80.

Massat, Carol R., and Marta Lundy. 1998. "'Reporting Costs' to Nonoffending Parents in Cases of Intrafamilial Child Sexual Abuse." *Child Welfare* 77, 4.

McMahon, Martha. 1995. *Engendering Motherhood: Identity and Self-Transformation in Women's Lives*. New York: Guilford.

Myer, Margaret. 1985. "A New Look at Mothers of Incest Victims." *Feminist Perspectives on Social Work and Human Sexuality* 3.

New Brunswick. 1983. *Family Services Act*, S.N.B. 1980, c. F 2-2.

New York. 2006. *New York Code — Laws: Social Services: (371–391) Care and Protection of Children*.

Newfoundland and Labrador. 2010. *Children and Youth Care and Protection Act*, S.N.L. 2010, c.C-12.2.

Northwest Territories. 1997. *Child And Family Services Act*, S.N.W.T. 1997, c 13.

Nova Scotia. 2002. *Children and Family Services Act*, S.N.S. 1990, c.5.

Nunavut. 1997. *Child And Family Services Act*, S.N.W.T. (Nu) 1997, c 13.

Oberman, Yael, and Ruthellen Josselson. 1996. "Matrix of Tensions: A Model of Mothering." *Psychology of Women Quarterly* 20.

Olafson, Erna, David Corwin, and Roland Summit. 1993. "Modern History of Child Sexual Abuse Awareness: Cycles of Discovery and Suppression." *Child Abuse and Neglect* 17, 1.

Ontario. 1990. *Child and Family Service Act*, R.S.O. 1990, c. C.11.

Parker, Rozsika. 1997. "The Production and Purposes of Maternal Ambivalence." In Wendy Holloway and Brid Featherstone (eds.), *Mothering and Ambivalence*. London: Routledge.

_____. 1995. *Torn in Two: The Experience of Maternal Ambivalence*. London: Virago.

Pintello, Denise, and Susan Zuravin. 2001. "Intrafamilial Child Sexual Abuse: Predictors of Postdisclosure Maternal Belief and Protective Action." *Child Maltreatment* 6, 4.

Prince Edward Island. 2003. *Child Protection Act*, R.S.P.E.I. 1988, c. C-5.1.

Quebec. 2007. *Youth Protection Act*, R.S.Q., c P-34.1.

Risley-Curtiss, Christina, and Kristin Heffernan. 2003. "Gender Biases in Child Welfare." *Affilia* 18, 4.

Ross, Ellen. 1995. "New Thoughts on 'The Oldest Vocation:' Mothers and Motherhood in Recent Feminist Scholarship." *Signs: Journal of Women in Culture and Society* 20.

Ruddick, Sara. 1989. *Maternal Thinking: Towards a Politics of Peace*. Boston: Beacon.

_____. 1994. "Thinking Mothers/Conceiving Birth." In Donna Bassin, Margaret Honey, and Meryle M. Kaplan (eds.), *Representations of Motherhood*. New Haven: Yale University Press.

Russell, Diana. 1986. *The Secret Trauma: Incest in the Lives of Girls and Women*. New York: Basic Books.

Saskatchewan. 1989–1990. *Child and Family Services Act*, S.S. 1989-1990, c. C-7.2.

Scourfield, Jonathan. 2003. *Gender and Child Protection*. London: Palgrave MacMillan.

Sedlak, Andrea, Jane Mettenburg, Monica Basena, Ian Petta, Karla McPherson,

Angela Greene and Spencer Li. 2010. *Fourth National Incidence Study of Child Abuse and Neglect (NIS–4): Report to Congress.* Washington, DC: U.S. Department of Health and Human Services, Administration for Children and Families.

Sgroi, Suzanne, Linda Blick, and Frances Porter. 1982. "A Conceptual Framework for Child Sexual Abuse." In Suzanne Sgroi (ed.), *Handbook of Clinical Intervention in Child Sexual Abuse.* Toronto: Lexington Books, D.C. Heath.

Swift, Karen. 1995. *Manufacturing "Bad Mothers": A Critical Perspective on Child Neglect.* Toronto: University of Toronto Press.

Thorne, Barrie. 1992. "Feminism and the Family: Two Decades of Thought." In Barrie Thorne and Marilyn Yalom (eds.), *Rethinking the Family.* Revised edition. Boston: Northeastern University Press.

Trocmé, Nico, Barbara Fallon, Bruce MacLaurin, Joanne Daciuk, Caroline Felstiner, Tara Black, Lil Tonmyr, Cindy Blackstock, Ken Barter, Daniel Turcotte, and Richard Cloutier. 2005. *Canadian Incidence Study of Reported Child Abuse and Neglect — 2003: Major Findings.* Ottawa: National Clearinghouse on Family Violence.

Trocmé, Nico, Barbara Fallon, Bruce MacLaurin, Vandna Sinha, Tara Black, Elizabeth Fast, Caroline Felstiner, Sonia Hélie, Daniel Turcotte, Pamela Weightman, Janet Douglas, and Jill Holroyd. 2010. *Canadian Incidence Study of Reported Child Abuse and Neglect — 2008: Major Findings.* Ottawa: National Clearinghouse on Family Violence.

United Kingdom. 1989. *Children Act,* c. 41.

United Kingdom, Department of Children, Schools and Families. 2010. *Working Together to Safeguard Children: A Guide to Inter-Agency Working to Safeguard and Promote the Welfare of Children.* DCFS-00305-2010.

United States, Department of Health and Social Services. 2003. *The Child Abuse Prevention and Treatment Act,* P.L. 93-247 as amended by the *Keeping Children and Families Safe Act of 2003*, P.L. 108-36, 6/25/03.

Washington State. 2011. *Revised Code of Washington.* Chapter 26-44.

Yukon. 2008. *Child and Family Services Act,* S.Y. 2008, c.1.

Zuelzer, Margot, and Richard Reposa. 1983. "Mothers in Incestuous Families." *International Journal of Family Treatment* 5, 2.

3. Asking the Impossible of Mothers
Child Protection Systems and Intimate Partner Violence
Susan Strega and Caitlin Janzen

Peter Lee had many times assaulted his wife Sunny in the presence of their son, Christian, although only one of those incidents, a car accident in which Peter attempted to kill Sunny, resulted in a criminal charge. Peter had also warned Sunny that he would kill her rather than agree to a divorce. The police who investigated the car accident believed that Peter posed a serious risk to Sunny. Because they believed that he would not abide by court-imposed conditions to have no contact with her, they hoped he might be remanded in custody. When Peter was released on bail, the police reported their concerns to child protection services (CPS). The worker assigned to the case met with Sunny and expressed her concern about Christian's exposure to the intimate partner violence. The worker assessed Sunny as being able and willing to protect Christian at that moment, but warned her that if Christian was exposed to further intimate partner violence that child protective services would take more intrusive measures possibly including apprehending Christian, if Sunny was unable or unwilling to protect him from being exposed. The worker made no attempt to meet with Christian's father. On September 4, 2007, six-year-old Christian Lee was supposed to walk into his Grade 1 classroom for the first time. Instead, in the early hours that morning, Christian, his mother and his grandparents were murdered by his father, Peter Lee.[1]

The story of the Lee family is far from unique. Over the last quarter-century, failure-to-protect policies and practices have proliferated in Anglo-American child protection systems, ostensibly in an effort to safeguard children caught up in these situations and to act in their best interests. While exposure to intimate partner violence can never be characterized as a benign situation for children, we argue that intervening in it through failure-to-protect policies and practices increases — rather than reduces — the likelihood of harm to children and contravenes — rather than supports — their best interests. As the previous chapter explained, child protection in particular and Anglo-American societies in general have long held mothers responsible for violations against their children even when identifiable others, usually men and frequently male relatives, are the actual abusers. This gendered and inequitable approach has most recently been applied in situations of intimate partner violence. In this chapter, we illustrate the myriad ways in which failure-to-protect policies and practices add to the burdens and challenges faced by victimized women, fail to support their attempts to mother in difficult circumstances, and do little to ameliorate the negative sequelae of male-perpetrated intimate partner violence. These policies and practices hold mothers solely responsible for creating and maintaining safety in the home and absolve men — even when they are fathers or father-figures — from the responsibility of protecting children. By asking women to do the impossible, that is, to control and manage men's violence, child protection systems ultimately fail to protect children.

We focus on male violence as it is by far the most common type of intimate partner violence encountered in child protection. A review of Canadian child welfare incidence data found that fathers were the perpetrators in 73 percent of substantiated intimate partner violence incidents and stepfathers or common-law male partners in another 14.9 percent (Black et al. 2008). From 1991–2003, 97 percent of Canadian spousal homicides involved a male perpetrator and a female victim (Danvergne and Li 2006). Recent U.K. research reports that 93.8 percent of intimate violence perpetrators were men (Radford et al. 2011). The percentage of male perpetrators is lower in the U.S. and Australia, but the gender pattern holds. In the U.S., Maguire (2007) noted that men killed women in 78 percent of intimate partner violence homicides committed in 2005. Similarly, recent U.S. survey data identified men as perpetrators in 78 percent of all intimate partner violence incidents and 88 percent of the most violent (kicking, choking, or beating) incidents (Hamby et al. 2010). Fathers (biological and non-biological) were the most commonly reported perpetrators. In Australia, 76.9 percent of intimate partner homicides involved a male offender and a female victim (Australian Domestic and Family Clearinghouse 2003), and recent statistics from the state of New South Wales indicate that men were the perpetrators in 82.1 percent of intimate partner violence situations (Grech and Burgess 2011).

As this chapter explains, there are several reasons that failure-to-protect policies and practices continue to be widely deployed despite their demonstrated ineffectiveness. Underlying each of these reasons, however, are institutionalized discourses connecting failure to protect to taken-for-granted "truths" about women, men, and violence. For example, Adrian Howe (2008) documents the ongoing propensity to hold women (girlfriends, partners, wives or mothers) responsible when men commit violence. In their analyses of discourses related to divorce and child custody, Smart, Neale, and Wade (2001) document how women are constructed as having responsibilities to protect their children while men are constructed as having rights to custody or visitation. Although a central role for fathers beyond the "good provider" stereotype has been widely promoted by some child development theorists (see, for example, Lamb 2010), this idea has made little impact in either the popular parenting literature or in child welfare education. In studies of popular parenting literature in the United States and Britain, mothers were consistently portrayed as primary caregivers while fathers, when they appeared at all, were relegated to peripheral roles as helpers or playmates (Fleming and Tobin 2005; Sunderland 2004). Hodgins' (2007) content analysis of program materials in formal parent education programs offered in B.C. found that fathers were usually depicted as having only a minor role in parenting. Walmsley et al.'s (2009) survey of Canadian undergraduate social work curriculum documented overwhelming attention to women as mothers and little if any inclusion of men as fathers. Despite the significant role of fathers in child maltreatment, there is little attention to men in the child psychopathology literature (Cassano et al. 2006; Phares et al. 2005).

These approaches reinforce race, class, and gender disproportionalities in child protection practice. We argue that the way forward from this ineffective and dangerous situation is contained in the practices of workers who resist blaming mothers and absenting fathers and in promising policy and practice innovations implemented some jurisdictions.

Failure-to-Protect Policies

As noted in the introductory chapter, Canadian child welfare is legislated at the provincial or territorial level. As a result, there are some discrepancies in how failure to protect is designated across the country. In some jurisdictions, failure to protect is designated as a specific category of child maltreatment. In other jurisdictions, it is encompassed either specifically or by inference in other child maltreatment categories such as "neglect" or "emotional abuse." In recent years, a child's exposure to intimate partner violence has found its way into child protection statutes as a category of child maltreatment. For example, seven Canadian provinces (Alberta, Saskatchewan, New Brunswick, Nova Scotia, Prince Edward Island, Quebec, and Newfoundland and Labrador) and one territory (Northwest Territories) include a specific reference to exposure or witnessing or living in a situation where there is violence as grounds for child protection intervention. In the remaining Canadian jurisdictions, failure to protect is alluded to but not specified in legislation or policy. In the U.S., Minnesota has a specific statutory reference to exposure to domestic violence while other states subsume maltreatment because of exposure to intimate partner violence under other categories, most often neglect. Some Australian states specify that intimate partner violence is a form of child abuse, while other states categorize it as a form of emotional abuse; in most jurisdictions, police and other professionals are required to report incidents where children are present during intimate partner violence to child protection services (Bromfield and Higgins 2005). In the U.K., definition of categories of child abuse and vulnerabilities expanded in the *Children Act* in 2002 to include a reference to failure to protect children from exposure to any form of danger, clearing the way for CPS intervention in intimate partner violence cases (Humphreys and Stanley 2006). The U.K. policy document *Working Together to Safeguard Children* now includes "witnessing domestic violence" as a form of emotional abuse (DCFS 2010). Finally, in 2011, New Zealand criminalized the "failure to protect" a child or vulnerable adult from harm and specifically designated exposure to intimate partner violence as a harm.

These jurisdictional variations make the exact extent and nature of failure-to-protect statutes, policies, and practices difficult to track (Kaufman Kantor and Little 2003). Alternatively, including "failure to protect" as a specific child maltreatment category causes substantial and sometimes overwhelming increases in child protection reports. Incidence data for 2008 reveals that exposure to intimate partner violence has become the single largest maltreatment category in Canada, representing 34 percent of all substantiated child welfare investigations (Trocmé et al. 2010). Minnesota introduced and then later repealed a statute defining "failure to protect" as a category of child maltreatment after a flood of complaints swamped its child protection system. Intimate partner violence notifications were the main contributor to a doubling of the number of child protection notifications in Australia between 2001–02 and 2005–06 (Potito et al. 2009). In one Australian state (Queensland), from 1980 to 2005, referrals relating to intimate partner violence increased 867 percent compared with 247 percent for emotional abuse, 128 percent for neglect, 77 percent for physical abuse, and 8 percent for sexual abuse (Faulkner 2008). In Canada, the 2003 *Canadian Incidence Study of Reported Child Abuse and Neglect (CIS)* documented a 259 percent increase in substantiated intimate partner violence reports from 1998 to 2003 (Trocmé et al. 2005).

These increases may in part reflect a progressively broadening definition of what constitutes "exposure." Once narrowly defined as a child seeing and/or hearing a man (father, father-figure, mother's boyfriend) assaulting her/his mother, other experiences, such as seeing mother's injuries, hearing post-incident conversations about the violence, participating in police or child protection interviews or accompanying mother to a hospital or shelter, are now routinely defined as "exposure." Legislation in New Brunswick, Newfoundland and Labrador, Northwest Territories, Nova Scotia, Prince Edward Island, and Saskatchewan explicitly name exposure to intimate partner violence as a form of maltreatment requiring protective intervention; in

Alberta and Quebec, it is contained within the category of emotional abuse. The *Youth Protection Act* (2007: article 38 (c)) in Quebec asserts:

> Psychological ill-treatment refers to a situation in which a child is seriously or repeatedly subjected to behaviour on the part of the child's parents or another person that could cause harm to the child, and the child's parents fail to take the necessary steps to put an end to the situation. Such behaviour includes in particular indifference, denigration, emotional rejection, isolation, threats, exploitation … and exposure to conjugal or domestic violence.

In all other provinces and territories in Canada, legislation implicitly requires protective intervention for a child who is exposed to intimate partner violence through wording that refers to parental behaviour as endangering a child's well-being. For example, in British Columbia, a child is deemed to be in need of protection "if the child is emotionally harmed by the parent's conduct." (British Columbia, *Child, Family and Community Service Act* 1996: article 13.1 (e)). In the Yukon, a child is in need of protection if the child "is, or is likely to be, emotionally harmed by the conduct of the child's parent … [or] is, or is likely to be, emotionally harmed by a person's conduct and the child's parent does not protect the child" (*Child and Family Services Act* 1996: article 28.1 (c) and (f)).

Child protection authorities commonly respond to intimate partner violence situations by engaging primarily or solely with victimized women, while male perpetrators of violence are largely ignored, even when they are fathers or father-figures (Baynes and Holland 2010; Radhakrishna et al. 2001). The failure-to-protect implication is that women are seen as neglectful, even abusive, because their actions or inactions in response to the violence inflicted on them either directly harmed their children or placed them at risk for harm (Bragg 2003). Workers are usually required by legislation or policy to assess whether the non-offending parent is "able and willing" to protect her children, an instruction that fails to take into account that it is someone else's violence that may be creating problems in her ability to do so (Bancroft and Silverman 2004; Lapierre 2010). The focus on a woman's response to the violence enacted against her (as it is almost always women who are non-offending parents) has the corollary effect of absolving the offending parent from responsibility for the care and protection of children.

Perhaps the most dangerous implication of failure-to-protect policies is the implicit assumption that women can, hence should, control men's violence. While, on the face of it, such a demand seems absurd, it accords with persistent and widespread beliefs about women's responsibility for male violence (Howe 2008). Enshrining women's responsibility to manage men's violence in child welfare statutes and policies is congruent with dominant and widely circulated discourses about women's culpability when men are violent (Flood and Pease 2009). A study conducted by Terrance, Plumm, and Little (2008) offers a telling example: Undergraduate psychology students were presented with two scenarios of physical child abuse by fathers — one in which the father had previously assaulted the mother, and one in which he had not. Participants held the assaulted mother more responsible for the perpetrator's abuse towards the child than the mother who had not been abused. In Doherty's (2002) Canadian survey, more participants (54 percent) were concerned about children's negative psychological effects from witnessing family violence than from actually experiencing it (44 percent). Notably, while one Canadian province (British Columbia) and the U.K. have statutes in place allowing child protection services to exclude domestically violent men from contact with children, these statutes are rarely used (Strega 2004). Research from all Anglo-American jurisdictions clearly documents that even when law or policy direct them to do otherwise, CPS intervenes with women rather than perpetrators (Hughes, Chau, and Poff 2011; Strega et al. 2008). As the following sections document, if the intent of failure-to-protect statutes and policies is to increase child safety and reduce child endangerment, their enactment in practice clearly demonstrates that they fail to do so.

Failure-to-Protect Practices

As noted earlier, while failure to protect is only specifically defined in policy in some jurisdictions, it is such a powerful and hegemonic concept in child protection that it is enacted in similar ways in all Anglo-American CPS systems. For example, the Canadian CPS workers interviewed by Navid (2009) told her that they investigated women for failing to protect because policy required them to do so, even though no failure-to-protect statute or policy existed in their jurisdiction. Theoretically, the requirement to protect and the corollary allegation of failing to protect could be applied equally to women and to men, particularly to fathers and father-figures. Indeed, the gender-neutral language employed in most Anglo-American CPS legislation and policy would seem to support equal treatment of parents. But research demonstrates conclusively that, when intimate partner violence occurs, CPS workers are preoccupied with the reactions and behaviours of mothers and not the violence of perpetrators (see Bourassa et al. 2006; Hughes et al. 2011; Humphreys 2000; Johnson and Sullivan 2008; Landsman and Copps Hartley 2007; Strega et al. 2008). Black's (2010) analysis exploring the unusually high substantiation rate for Canadian intimate partner violence investigations noted that risk factors attributed to non-offending mothers, but not those related to perpetrators, were significant in CPS decisions to substantiate child maltreatment.

Yet, research about mothering in the context of intimate partner violence demonstrates that mothers routinely take action to safeguard their children from its effects (see Cavanagh 2003; Hollander 2002; Lapierre 2010; Levendosky, Lynch, and Graham-Bermann 2000). But while a woman may act in ways that she believes are protective in the face of intimate partner violence, her protective attitudes and behaviours will receive CPS support only if she acts in ways prescribed by child protection authorities. In order to be seen as acting protectively, women are routinely required to monitor and manage the behaviour of violent men and ameliorate the consequences of violence (Hughes et al. 2011; Scourfield 2003). Child protection supervision orders may require that a woman control the perpetrator's access to children. Mothers who choose to remain with violent partners, especially in the face of multiple violent incidents, are often considered, based on that evidence, to be unwilling or unable to protect their children (DeVoe and Smith 2003; Kaufman Kantor and Little 2003). Should mothers fail to engage in particular actions that CPS defines as protective, they risk losing their children (Johnson and Sullivan 2008), whether the men involved are fathers or father-figures or connected to children primarily through their involvement with the children's mother (Radhakrishna et al. 2001). Workers routinely use the possible apprehension of children as a threat or incitement to force a woman to leave an abusive partner (Hughes et al. 2011; Humphreys 2007; Lessard and Chamberland 2003). These gendered practices inappropriately transform women who are victims of violence into child abusers, while exculpating and absenting the actual perpetrators of violence.

The challenge to have one's protective moves legitimized is confounded at the intersection of gender and class. Mothers who are financially dependent upon abusive intimate partners face losing the ability to adequately house, feed and clothe their children. When child protection strategies are punitive, women are reluctant to disclose their victimization, thus making them and their children more vulnerable to violence. Not surprisingly, when mothers fear losing custody of their children, it significantly increases their reluctance to seek help, either for themselves or their children. Take, for example, the case review with which we opened this chapter, where the following interaction was reported:

> The social worker advised the mother [Sunny] that if Christian were exposed to further domestic violence or if he were in his father's sole care, the ministry would need to reassess his safety and consider taking more intrusive measures. She explained to Sunny that she had the authority to remove a child, but [would] consider other measures first. This alarmed Sunny, and was reported to Peter by Sunny's sister. The next day Peter phoned the social worker and expressed concern about this possibility. (RCY 2009: 26)

Sunny Park's fears were based in reality. Research demonstrates that significant numbers of women lose custody of their children as a result of investigations initiated because of intimate partner violence (DeVoe and Smith 2003; Holt 2003; Neilson 2001). Several studies (see DeVoe and Smith 2003; English, Edleson and Herrick 2005; Holt 2003; Kaufman Kantor and Little 2003) report that children in intimate partner violence situations are more likely to end up in out-of-home placement. Bala, Jaffe, and Crooks (2007) documented several Canadian cases in which child protection authorities took children into permanent state care when a mother allegedly "allowed" a father to have contact with her children or when she failed to terminate a relationship with a man who was assaulting her. Workers are particularly likely to remove children when exposure to intimate partner violence coexists with any other form of maltreatment (Black et al. 2008). A U.S. study (Kohl et al. 2005) found that children were ten times more likely to be removed from families where intimate partner violence coincided with another form of maltreatment; however, intimate partner violence alone was not strongly associated with removal.

Parents caught up in child protection processes commonly experience ongoing uncertainty about exactly what CPS workers are looking for in terms of behaviour changes (Brown 2006; Dumbrill 2006): this seems to be especially true for intimate partner violence victims (Hughes et al. 2011). In a Canadian study, Alaggia et al. (2007) demonstrated, through several research methods (key informant interviews with intimate partner violence service providers and mothers who had been investigated by CPS; focus groups with service providers and with mothers who had been investigated by CPS in relation to intimate partner violence; and statistical analysis), that CPS workers kept intimate partner violence cases open for lengthy periods. Mothers underwent prolonged scrutiny and experienced ongoing uncertainty and anxiety about whether or not their children would be apprehended. In her secondary analysis of data collected in the 2003 *Canadian Incidence Study of Reported Child Abuse and Neglect* (*CIS*-2003), Black (2010) notes that cases were kept open for lengthy periods when intimate partner violence occurred concurrently with any other form of maltreatment. Black also reported that these cases were particularly likely to result in child apprehension. Beeman, Hagemeister, and Edleson's (2001) quantitative review of American file data indicated results similar to those reported by Alaggia at al. (2009) and Black (2010). As we describe in the next section, mothers victimized by intimate partner violence contend not only with a blaming rather than supportive response from CPS, but with many additional challenges.

Revictimizing Mothers

When child protection systems take up intimate partner violence situations by focusing on the parenting of non-offending mothers, they operationalize erroneous and dangerous assumptions: that a woman has some control over her partner's violence; that reporting the violence or leaving the perpetrator will reduce violence; that victimized mothers receive swift and supportive response from the criminal justice system if they choose to report; and that drawing attention to men's violence results in greater safety for children.

It is problematic to construct a woman's decision to stay with a violent partner as child endangerment because perpetrators often threaten, and in some cases do, kill women and children precisely because women leave or indicate their intention to do so (Campbell et al. 2003). This was Peter Lee's primary motivation. Indeed, men's violence not only continues, but may even intensify post-separation (Fleury, Sullivan, and Bybee 2000). Citing U.S., Australian, and Canadian research, Bala et al. (2007) noted that separation sharply increases the likelihood that a man will kill his former partner: about 50 percent of women killed in all three countries were murdered in the first two months after separation, and 87 percent were killed within the year. A U.K. study found that men who killed an intimate partner were ten times more likely to have been recently divorced or separated than those who committed non-lethal violence against an intimate partner (Dobash, Dobash, and Medina-Ariza 2000). Children are also in grave danger from domestically violent men. Research covering the period 1991–2003 shows that in Canada, biological fathers and stepfathers were responsible for 68 percent of murders of children and youth; the vast majority of these killings took place post-separation (Hotton 2005).

A woman's attempts to comply with CPS directives are also complicated by the separate and often contradictory rules, expectations, and enforcement mechanisms of child protection, criminal justice, and family law systems. Although the official position of the criminal justice system is that it takes male violence against women seriously, in practice it frequently fails to provide a protective response to victims: ineptness, ineffectiveness, and victim-blaming are well-documented. Recent Canadian research found that even though most women who called the police did so because they needed immediate protection, police responded to only about half of those calls (Barrett, St. Pierre, and Vaillancourt 2011). When police did respond, they left the perpetrator in the home about 75 percent of the time (Barrett et al. 2011). A recent U.K. study noted that only 26 percent of reported intimate partner violence incidents resulted in arrest of the perpetrator, and only 7 percent resulted in charges (Home Affairs Select Committee 2008). Similarly, Canadian research found that police only removed perpetrators from the home 27.3 percent of the time (Barrett et al. 2011). Even if men are charged, they rarely remain in custody. A Canadian study reported that "stay of proceedings" was the most frequent disposition for intimate partner violence cases (Beckstead 2006). In the U.S., the intimate partner violence victims surveyed by Belknap et al. (2009) rated criminal justice system personnel (including prosecutors, legal advisors, and the police) as the most unsupportive of all potential social or institutional supporters. A particular concern voiced in the study was that women who reported higher levels of violence also reported lower levels of support from the police. Research into the criminal justice system response to victimized women in Australia found that those seeking help in the courts not only received little assistance or protection, they were frequently deemed responsible for the violence inflicted on them (Meyer 2011).

Other remedies ostensibly available through the criminal justice system often fail to support women who are trying to protect themselves and their children. Although women can apply for restraining or protection orders, the process is complicated and orders are difficult to obtain (Adams 2009). Even when "victim-friendly" procedures and forms are introduced, women who cannot mobilize legal representation are significantly less likely to have their requests for orders granted (Durfee 2009). Police and courts may also be slow or entirely fail to enforce restraining orders or peace bonds. In their review of statistics in one Canadian jurisdiction (Alberta), Tutty et al. (2005) note that the criminal justice system reported that 20–25 percent of men breached their peace bond conditions, often within a few days of an order being issued. In their meta-review of research on the effectiveness of restraining orders and peace bonds in the U.S., Fleury-Steiner, Fleury-Steiner, and Miller (2011) concluded that peace bonds and restraining orders are violated about half the time. In stark contrast to the considerable focus on the failure of individual mothers to protect children from exposure to intimate partner violence, the failures of the criminal justice system to support women's protective efforts appear to be largely invisible to child protection authorities. This is particularly troubling, given the prevalence of both research and media accounts, such as the one appearing at the beginning of this chapter, documenting the murders of mothers and children by domestically violent men who are well-known to the criminal justice system.

Another problematic reality is that while CPS often requires mothers to restrict men's access to their children, these instructions are frequently directly contradicted by family court orders that require women to facilitate children's contact with violent men. Family law courts in all Anglo-American jurisdictions routinely order high levels of contact despite documented intimate partner violence (Brown and Alexander 2007; Harrison 2006; Hunter 2006). In the U.K., women have been both imprisoned and threatened with the loss of their children through CPS proceedings when they refused to facilitate their children's contact with a violent ex-partner (Women's Aid Federation

England 2007). Violent men are granted not only access, but sometimes custody of children (Smart et al. 2005; Trinder, Firth, and Jenks 2010), with terrible consequences for women and children. For example, in England and Wales between 1994 and 2004, twenty-nine children in thirteen families were killed by their fathers or father-figures during court-ordered contacts; it was evident in five of these cases that the father killed the children in order to take revenge on his ex-partner for leaving him (Saunders 2004). Yet women must be wary of even mentioning their experiences of violence in family court settings, lest they be accused of making false allegations or alienating children from their fathers — accusations that can and do result in violent men being granted access or custody (Hester 2001; Kernic et al. 2005).

These difficulties are compounded for poor, racialized, or otherwise marginalized women. For example, a U.S. study documented a variety of legal, economic, and social barriers to safety for immigrant women, notably legal and financial dependence on the abuser, who may also be their sponsor (Erez, Adelman, and Gregory 2009). Abused immigrant women in Canada justifiably fear deportation if they separate from a violent partner (Alaggia, Regehr, and Rishchynski 2009). In the U.K. there is a demonstrable lack of support for abused South Asian women, whether they are citizens or immigrants (Anitha 2008; 2010). Australian research notes that both Australian Aboriginal and overseas-born women are reluctant to call the police for help in intimate partner violence situations and that both immigrant and Aboriginal women must deal with magistrates and judges mistakenly attributing violent acts to culture (Hunter 2006). A review of the conduct and comments of Australian magistrates and judges notes that these officials seem to take intimate partner violence in non-White cultures and poor communities less seriously, with some asserting that poor or working-class women "don't mind being roughed up" (Hunter 2006: 772).

It is clear that women typically face difficulties in seeking to separate from violent men and/or to restrict the access that a violent intimate partner has to their children. Given that in many cases leaving a domestically violent partner demonstrably elevates risk for women and increases child endangerment, is the damage or potential damage that might result when children are exposed to intimate partner violence so great that mothers should place themselves and their children at risk to avert it? While we have detailed how current CPS policies and practices are ineffective at reducing (and may even increase) men's violence towards mothers and children, are they effective in reducing the harms that these children may experience? In the next section, we address these important questions.

But What About the Children?

The literature on the effects of exposure to, or witnessing of, intimate partner violence is vast; it is beyond the scope of this chapter to review or critique it in detail. Instead, we turn to recent meta-analyses conducted in Anglo-American jurisdictions that effectively summarize the evidence. Sety's (2011) Australian review contends that children exposed to intimate partner violence are more likely than non-exposed children to experience a variety of problems, including behavioural and cognitive problems, higher rates of depression and anxiety, and, in some cases, trauma symptoms. In New Zealand, the WAVES (2010) review notes that exposed children not only experience emotional and psychological difficulties, but are more likely than their non-exposed peers to engage in crimes against property, to misuse substances, and to live with physical health problems. In the U.K., Holt, Buckley, and Whelan (2008) conducted a comprehensive search of databases over an eleven-year period (1995–2006) and concluded that children and adolescents living with intimate partner violence are at increased risk of being subjected to other forms of abuse and of experiencing emotional and behavioural problems, though they also highlight protective factors that mitigate against these impacts. American researchers reached similar conclusions. In their meta-analysis, Evans, Davies, and DiLillo (2008) reviewed sixty studies and found a moderate relationship between exposure and children's behavioural difficulties and trauma symptoms. A meta-analysis focused specifically on preschool children (Sternberg et al. 2006) suggests that exposed children may be at the same risk for developing behavioural problems as children who are direct victims of abuse. In their review of recent research, Hungerford et al. (2012) note that, while exposure sometimes poses significant risks to children, there is also considerable variability in children's responses. Similarly, Howell's (2011) review of literature specific to preschool children reveals that, while many children experience problems, others appear to function well in behavioural, cognitive, and socio-emotional domains.

In other words, although there is now a very extensive research database on children's exposure to intimate partner violence, no direct causal relationship between exposure and either short- or long-term harm has been clearly established. While some children who have been exposed to such violence may experience severe consequences, others may be unaffected. By defining exposure to intimate partner violence as child maltreatment in its own right or as emotional abuse or neglect, CPS confounds cause with effect (Kaufman Kantor and Little 2003). Thus, children are at risk of being removed from their homes and their mothers on the false premise that their exposure to intimate partner violence equals maltreatment or the risk of maltreatment. As Black (2010: 97) contended,

The unusually high substantiation rate for investigations involving only exposure to intimate partner violence appears to be partially due to an important conceptual difference: the occurrence of intimate partner violence rather than child maltreatment due to exposure may be the driving factor in the decision to substantiate. That is, child welfare workers are not considering whether this child was harmed, only if he or she was exposed to potentially harming circumstances.

In order to ensure the best possible CPS interventions, decisions about whether or not children have been or may be harmed by exposure to intimate partner violence must take into consideration factors that mediate, mitigate, and moderate the effects of exposure. For example, Bedi and Goddard (2007) and Clements, Oxtoby, and Ogle (2008) demonstrate that factors such as children's age, gender, coping abilities, social supports and socio-economic status mediate the nature and extent of harm suffered by children exposed to violence. Retrospective research with adults exposed to intimate partner violence as children document children's ability to resist negative sequelae and implement positive and adaptive coping strategies (Anderson and Danis 2006; Suzuki, Geffner, and Bucky 2008). Kitzmann et al.'s (2003) meta-analysis reports that the type, frequency, and severity of violence impact the nature and extent of consequences for children. In her review of research, Humphreys (2007) notes that high levels of extended familial and social support have been demonstrated to enhance children's coping capacity. In Howell's (2011) consolidated review, she notes that children's well-being is enhanced when they are able to appropriately ascribe responsibility for violence.

Of particular significance for CPS practice and policy is the extensive empirical evidence that maternal functioning is the key factor in children's ability to cope with and recover from exposure to intimate partner violence (Graham-Bermann et al. 2011). The research reviews conducted by Howell (2011) and Hungerford et al. (2012) detail some of these: maternal emotional and psychological well-being; mothers' ability to effectively establish limits and boundaries; and maternal social competence. Humphreys et al. (2006) link children's ability to cope with the abilities of their mothers to maintain caregiving functions and to model assertive and nonviolent responses to abuse. Sullivan, Egan, and Gooch (2004) note that conjoint therapeutic work with children and mothers is noticeably effective in reducing trauma symptoms in children exposed to intimate partner violence. Similarly, in their study of the effectiveness of interventions with exposed children, Graham-Bermann et al. (2011) note that while children benefit from receiving individual treatment, they also benefit when their mothers receive support services.

The above studies demonstrate that removing children from the care of their mothers, or threatening to remove them without providing opportunities and resources to support victimized mothers, perpetuates rather than ameliorates the effects on children of exposure to intimate partner violence. It also inappropriately severs the "best interests" of children from those of their mothers. Because mothers' ability to engage in caregiving is impacted by the behaviour of the men who assault them, CPS assessments of these abilities must take these influences into account. Interventions that support rather than blame, coerce or frighten mothers are essential for reducing harm to children. But first and foremost, CPS assessments and interventions must take into account the substantial danger that domestically violent men pose to children.

Violent Men and Child Endangerment

The notion that CPS should intervene directly with violent men is certainly not new; in 1997, Einat Peled pointed out the necessity of working directly with domestically violent fathers, and her call has been repeated regularly since then (see, for example, Rivett 2009; Scourfield 2003; Strega et al. 2008). Yet CPS continues to avoid men in general and, in particular, avoids holding men responsible for the intimate partner violence they perpetrate. For example, in their investigation of child protection practices in northern England, Gilligan, Manby, and Pickburn (2012) document marginal engagement with fathers even when they are central to the family's difficulties. In their qualitative studies of Canadian child protection practices, Hughes et al. (2011) and Profitt (2008) found that workers focused almost exclusively on mothers while ignoring perpetrators. These practices persist even though the failure to engage directly with men's violence increases danger for women and children (Casanueva et al. 2008; Letourneau, Fedick, and Willms 2007; Lapierre 2011). Although the overlap between intimate partner violence and physical child abuse by male partners is well-documented, as Salisbury, Henning, and Holdford (2009: 233) note, "men's role in this child abuse is grossly under-evaluated." A study examining 126 profiles of perpetrators of fatal child assault in United States found that men were three times more likely than women to fatally assault their children (Yampolskaya, Greenbaum, and Berson 2009). A U.K. report noted intimate partner violence as a commonly recurring feature in case reviews of child deaths (Jenkins and Dunne 2007). A recent U.K. review of deaths of children involved with CPS found that men who had previously committed intimate partner violence were responsible for more than half of child deaths (Ofsted 2010). Previous intimate partner violence was a factor in sixteen of the twenty-nine child death cases reviewed in Victoria, Australia, in 2010–11 (Victorian Child Death Review Committee 2011). A U.S. study noted the substantial overlap between intimate partner violence and the most severe forms of child maltreatment, including the killing of a child (Brandon et al. 2008). Based on their re-examination of a decade-long study of child murderers, Pritchard, Davey, and Williams (2012) conclude that men with previous convictions for violence, including intimate partner violence, pose the greatest risk to kill children. Rather than avoid domestically violent men, CPS should be alert to the likelihood that they will inflict other forms of child maltreatment, some of them fatal.

Children in families that are characterized by intimate violence directed against their mothers are more likely than children in non-violent families to experience other forms of victimization, with physical abuse being the most prevalent form of maltreatment (Terrance et al. 2008). The co-occurrence rate between intimate partner violence and child maltreatment has been variously reported but is always significant. Kaufman Kantor and Little (2003) found that intimate partner abuse and physical child abuse co-occur in at least 30 percent and up to 60 percent of U.S. cases. A meta-analysis of international co-occurrence studies concluded that between 30 percent and 70 percent of children exposed to intimate partner violence are also physically or sexually abused by the batterer (Rothman, Mandel, and Silverman 2007). A review of Canadian incidence data documented a 43 percent co-occurrence rate (Black et al. 2008). Two different studies of Australian children who experienced physical or sexual abuse and exposure to intimate partner violence estimated the co-occurrence rate at 55 percent and 40 percent (Bedi and Goddard 2007). Canadian researchers have also pointed to strong associations between intimate partner violence and child neglect, as well as between intimate partner violence and emotional and physical abuse (Lavergne et al. 2003). In other words, a man who assaults his intimate partner is at an elevated and perhaps extremely elevated risk of also harming her children. This provides a persuasive though as yet largely unheeded argument for CPS to engage directly with violent men in order to best protect children.

When CPS focuses on women and ignores perpetrators, it is reinforcing dangerous beliefs held by many men: that they have a right to be violent, including in the presence of children, and that their violence is justifiable or excusable. Many of the domestically violent men in Wood's (2004) study blamed women for their violence and, worryingly, some men in Harne's (2004) research with violent fathers blamed their children. Researchers also note that many perpetrators elicit children's direct participation in violence against their mothers, for example by engaging the child in spying on her/his mother or encouraging the child to participate in verbally abusing or denigrating her/his mother (Bancroft and Silverman 2004; Kaufman Kantor and Little 2003; Thomison 2000). A focus on women to the exclusion of domestically violent men supports an inappropriately gendered approach to child protection practice, one in which men have rights to violence as well as to access, visitation, and sometimes custody, while women have wide-ranging responsibilities not only for the primary care of children but also for stopping men's violence and ameliorating its effects. When CPS workers instruct women to end relationships with violent men, they are taking little account of the fact that these men are likely to remain in their children's lives and, even if they do not, may go on to establish new relationships in which they perpetrate abuse. In a large-scale American study of men convicted of intimate partner assault, 77.6 percent had a fathering role with a child or children less than eighteen years of age prior to (and in most cases following) their arrests (Salisbury et al. 2009). More than half of these men expected to continue these family relationships after their release. Notably, the men in this study were not particularly concerned about the effects of their violence on the children with whom they were involved.

Alternatively, Rothman et al. (2007) found that about half of the violent men they surveyed, including both biological and social fathers, were concerned about the effects of their violence on their children. Almost two-thirds stated they would stop their violence if they knew that they harmed their children by assaulting the children's mother. Even though these sentiments may reflect aspirations rather than actions, they suggest that the CPS failure to engage directly with violent men represents a missed opportunity to end violence and ameliorate its consequences for children. The most salient reasons that failure-to-protect practices and policies must be abandoned is that they not only absolve men of responsibility for the violence they enact, but they negate men's responsibilities for the care and protection of children.

The Way Forward

As we have demonstrated, intervening in intimate partner violence under the aegis of failure to protect, whether or not failure to protect is formally codified in statute or policy, not only fails to effectively protect children, but actually contributes to increased endangerment for children — and for women. Thus, while we take as our starting position that failure-to-protect statutes and policies, where they exist, must be eliminated, we recognize that these changes alone will not effectively transform dominant CPS approaches to intimate partner violence, given the hegemony of failure to protect in child protection. Reforming current CPS practices requires destabilizing dominant discourses of gendered parenting that are widely circulated in Anglo-American jurisdictions.

It is important to note that despite the dominance of these discourses within society in general and child protection in particular, some CPS workers already practise in ways that more effectively protect children, support women and engage violent men. A study of CPS practices in England and Quebec that found a dominant pattern of mother-blaming and father exculpation, also detailed four positive practices: recognizing that both children *and women* are victims; building a trusting relationship with victimized women; providing both emotional and practical support; and balancing risk and safety (Lapierre and Côté 2011). Another Canadian study (Emerson 2011) documented increased child safety when CPS workers intentionally challenged their existing beliefs and practices regarding intimate partner violence through a number of strategies, including studying the book *The Batterer as Parent* (Bancroft and Silverman 2002) and training in response-based approaches (Todd and Wade 2003; Richardson and Wade 2009; Wade 2007). The response-based intervention, "Islands of Safety," described in Chapter 8 of this book, has demonstrated success with intimate partner violence in Indigenous families involved with CPS (Richardson and Wade 2009).

Returning to the case we opened this chapter with, we can only speculate about how the tragic murder of five people might have been prevented if the CPS workers involved had engaged directly with Christian's father, Peter Lee. What we do know is that sole responsibility for safety planning resided with Christian's mother, Sunny Park, making her both the messenger and enforcer of state directives. While Peter Lee exercised his rights to be updated to any changes to custody decisions, Sunny was responsible for keeping Christian safe from violent attacks by his father and from exposure to violent attacks perpetrated against her. The Lee case echoes a dominant theme in child protection: men have many rights but few responsibilities; women have many responsibilities but few rights.

We recommend legislative and policy changes that would mandate CPS workers to speak with fathers, stepfathers or father-figures in heterosexual relationships. Intervening and imposing conditions on male perpetrators of violence, rather than on mothers, should be a routine CPS requirement and considered a "best practice" in child protection work. The failure of child protection workers to engage with Peter Lee in any substantive way was highlighted in the report issued by B.C.'s Representative for Children and Youth, the body charged with reviewing the death of Christian Lee. Their report (RCY 2009: 57) states: "Peter was central to the domestic violence situation but was not included in any assessment or safety plan because neither MCFD nor the justice system is institutionally organized to intervene effectively with male perpetrators of violence."

Research with fathers involved with CPS indicates that some workers already expect domestically violent fathers to take responsibility for their violent acts as well as for the care and protection of children (Strega et al. 2009). Many of the fathers in Strega et al.'s research had participated in a program specifically designed to encourage domestically violent men to take responsibility for their violence, understand its impact on their children (and the children's mothers) and learn parenting skills. Similarly, Scott and Crooks

(2006) described the success of the Caring Dads program, a seventeen-week group intervention for men who have abused their children's mother and/or maltreated their children. These and other programs designed specifically for domestically violent fathers, rather than for abusive men, are a promising new intervention (Brown et al. 2009), but as Rivett (2009) pointed out, the diversity of men who engage in intimate partner violence means that interventions must also be diverse. Like most parents who come to the attention of child protection authorities, domestically violent fathers are likely to be disproportionately poor, racialized or otherwise marginalized; consequently, interventions that engage with these factors are likely to be more useful than those that ignore them (Ferguson and Hogan 2004). The Massachusetts Department of Social Services Domestic Violence Unit developed a comprehensive child protection response to foster accountability and connection with domestically violent men while also challenging race, class, and gender stereotypes (Mederos 2004), and New Hampshire and Oregon have adopted similar approaches. While these practices are promising, research conducted with domestically violent fathers recommends that men demonstrate significant progress in stopping their violence before returning to any fathering role (Peled and Perel 2007; Perel and Peled 2008).

We contend that it is only when intimate partner violence is understood as behaviour deeply embedded in gender and other inequalities, and not seen simply a matter of individual dysfunction, that failure-to-protect approaches will be effectively abandoned. So long as CPS workers define a good mother as a mother who leaves her abusive partner, they will continue to play a role in increasing women and children's vulnerability. Alternatively, contextual and gendered analysis can expose men's choice and responsibility in enacting violence, the protective actions that women are already taking, complicating and contributing factors such as poverty or racism, and the mitigating circumstances that may reduce harmful effects on children (Richardson and Wade 2009). We believe that CPS practice in intimate partner violence investigations is likely to be positively impacted once workers come to fully appreciate, document, and take into account the dilemmas faced by non-offending mothers. Similarly, in order to provide an accurate foundation for intervention, workers need to elicit and record detailed accounts of violent acts and avoid the sanitized and mutualizing descriptions that so often appear in case files (Baynes and Holland 2010). When CPS workers hold violent men accountable, cooperation and collaboration between CPS workers and mothers increases dramatically (Shim and Haight 2006). But effective engagement with violent men involves more than accountability. It requires that workers actively engage with both positions that many domestically violent men occupy: abuser and father.

While statutory and policy changes that would more explicitly require

CPS engagement with perpetrators might support practice changes, long-established traditions of mother-blame and father-invisibility in child welfare are resistant to change. In Ireland, Ferguson and Hogan (2004) published extensive recommendations, based on their research, for engaging marginalized fathers, including those who had been violent to their intimate partners. The following year, Northern Ireland launched a new national strategy for interventions in intimate partner violence situations, including direct engagement with perpetrators. But six years later, *County Kildare Practice Handbook* instructs CPS workers to practise solely with non-offending mothers in cases of intimate partner violence (County Kildare Health Service Executive 2011). This underlines that changes in law or policy will be ineffective without parallel efforts to educate and train CPS workers to intervene effectively with violent men and to support mothers rather than revictimizing them and endangering their children. In this regard, it is important to note that CPS is not solely culpable in focusing on women and ignoring men who perpetuate violence. Our cultural preoccupation with why women stay in abusive relationships, rather than why men assault women, is well-documented, as is the tendency to blame women, predominantly partners and mothers, when men are violent (Howe 2008). Failure-to-protect policies and practices reflect and enact these preoccupations.

As we noted at the outset, intimate partner violence is never a benign event for children. When a man assaults their mother, children will suffer, whether or not they witness or are directly exposed to the violence. But if our intent is truly to protect children, then all of us — and not only child protection workers and systems — must insist that violent men, including violent fathers, accept responsibility and accountability for their actions.

Notes

1. The full report of the investigation into this matter, conducted by the Representative for Children and Youth (B.C., Canada), is available at <crvawc.ca/documents/RCYChristianLeeReportFINAL.pdf>.

References

Adams, Jill. 2009. "The Civil Restraining Order Application Process: Textually Mediated Institutional Case Management." *Ethnography* 10, 2.

Alaggia, Ramona, Allison Jenney, Josephine Mazzuca, and Melissa Redmond. 2007. "In Whose Best Interest? A Canadian Case Study of the Impact of Child Welfare Policies in Cases of Domestic Violence." *Brief Treatment and Crisis Intervention* 7, 4.

Alaggia, Ramona, Cheryl Regehr, and Giselle Rishchynski. 2009. "Intimate Partner Violence and Immigration Laws in Canada: How Far Have We Come?" *International Journal of Law and Psychiatry* 32, 6.

Anderson, Kim, and Fran Danis. 2006. "Adult Daughters of Battered Women:

Resistance and Resilience in the Face of Danger." *Affilia: Journal of Women and Social Work* 21, 4.

Anitha, Sundari. 2010. "Neither Safety nor Justice: The U.K. Government Response to Domestic Violence Against Immigrant Women." *British Journal of Social Work* 40, 2.

___. 2008. "No Recourse, No Support: State Policy and Practice Towards South Asian Women Facing Domestic Violence in the U.K." *Journal of Social Welfare and Family Law* 30, 3.

Australian Domestic and Family Clearinghouse. 2003. *Australian Statistics on Domestic Violence*. Canberra: Author.

Bala, Nicholas, Peter Jaffe, and Claire Crooks. 2007. "Spousal Violence and Child-Related Cases: Challenging Cases Requiring Differentiated Responses." *Canadian Family Law Quarterly* 27, 1.

Bancroft, Lundy, and Jay Silverman. 2004. "Assessing Abusers' Risks to Children." In Peter G. Jaffe, Linda L. Baker and Alison J. Cunningham (eds.), *Protecting Children from Intimate Partner Violence: Strategies for Community Intervention*. York: Guildford Publications.

___. 2002. *The Batterer as Parent*. Thousand Oaks: Sage.

Barrett, Betty Jo, Melissa St. Pierre, and Nadine Vaillancourt. 2011. "Police Response to Intimate Partner Violence in Canada: Do Victim Characteristics Matter?" *Women and Criminal Justice* 21 1.

Baynes, Polly, and Sally Holland. 2010. "Social Work with Violent Men: A Child Protection File Study in an English Local Authority." *Child Abuse Review* 21. <onlinelibrary.wiley.com/doi/10.1002/car.1159/full>.

Beckstead, Lori. 2006. "Violence, Policy and the Law: An Exploratory Analysis of Crown Counsel Domestic Violence Policy in British Columbia." Unpublished master's thesis, Simon Fraser University.

Bedi, Gullinder, and Chris Goddard. 2007. "Intimate Partner Violence: What Are the Impacts on Children?" *Australian Psychologist* 42, 1.

Beeman, Sandra K., Annelies K. Hagemeister, and Jeffrey Edleson. 2001. "Case Assessment and Service Receipt in Families Experiencing Both Child Maltreatment and Woman Battering." *Journal of Interpersonal Violence* 16, 5.

Belknap, Joanne, Heather Melton, Justin Denney, Ruth Fleury-Steiner and Chris Sullivan. 2009. "The Levels and Roles of Social and Institutional Support Reported by Survivors of Intimate Partner Abuse." *Feminist Criminology* 4, 4.

Black, Tara. 2010. "Children's Exposure to Intimate Partner Violence (IPV): Challenging Assumptions About Child Protection Practices." Unpublished doctoral dissertation, University of Toronto.

Black, Tara, Nicholas Trocmé, Barbara Fallon, and Bruce MacLaurin. 2008. "The Canadian Child Welfare System Response to Exposure to Domestic Violence Investigations." *Child Abuse and Neglect* 32.

Bourassa, Chantal, Chantal Lavergne, Dominique Damant, Genevieve Lessard, and Pierre Turcotte. 2006. "Awareness and Detection of the Co-occurrence of Interparental Violence and Child Abuse: Child Welfare Worker's Perspective." *Children and Youth Services Review* 28, 11.

Bragg, H. Lien 2003. *Child Protection in Families Experiencing Domestic Violence*. Washington: U.S. Dept. of Health and Human Services, Administration for Children and

Families, Children's Bureau, Office on Child Abuse and Neglect. <childwelfare. gov/pubs/usermanuals/domesticviolence/domesticviolence.pdf >.

Brandon, Marian, Pippa Belderson, Catherine Warren, David Howe, Ruth Gardner, Jane Dodsworth and Jane Black. 2008. *Analysing Child Deaths and Serious Injury through Abuse and Neglect: What Can We Learn? A Biennial Analysis of Serious Case Reviews 2003–5*. London: Department for Children, Schools and Families.

British Columbia. 1996. *Child, Family and Community Service Act 1996*. <bclaws.ca/ EPLibraries/bclaws_new/document/ID/freeside/00_96046_01>.

Bromfield, Leah, and Daryl Higgins. 2005. "National Comparison of Child Protection Systems. Child Abuse Prevention Issues (no. 22)." Melbourne: Australian Institute of Family Studies. <aifs.gov.au/nch/pubs/issues/issues22/ issues22.pdf>.

Brown, Debra. 2006. "Working the System: Re-thinking the Institutionally Organized Role of Mothers and the Reduction of 'Risk' in Child Protection Work." *Social Problems* 53, 3.

Brown, Leslie, Susan Strega, Marilyn Callahan, Lena Dominelli and Christopher Walmsley. 2009. "Manufacturing Ghost Fathers: The Paradox of Father Presence and Absence in Child Welfare." *Child and Family Social Work* 14, 1.

Brown, Thea, and Renata Alexander. 2007. *Child Abuse and Family Law: Understanding the Legal Issues Facing Human Service and Legal Professionals*. Sydney: Allen and Unwin.

Campbell, Jacquelyn, Daniel Webster, Jane Koziol-McLain, Carolyn Block, Doris Campbell, Mary Ann Curry, Faye Gary, Nancy Glass, Judith McFarlane, Carolyn Sachs, Phyllis Sharps, Yvonne Ulrich, Susan A. Wilt, Jennifer Manganello, Xiao Xu, Janet Schollenberger, Victoria Frye, and Kathryn Laughon. 2003. "Risk Factors for Femicide in Abusive Relationships: Results from a Multisite Case Control Study." *American Journal of Public Health* 93, 7.

Casanueva, Cecelia, Sandra Martin, Desmond Runyan, Richard Barth, and Robert Bradley. 2008. "Quality of Maternal Parenting Among Intimate-Partner Violence Victims Involved with the Child Welfare System." *Journal of Family Violence* 23, 6.

Cassano, Michael, Molly Adrian, Gina Veits, and Janice Zeman. 2006. "The Inclusion of Fathers in the Empirical Investigation of Child Psychopathology: An Update." *Journal of Clinical Child and Adolescent Psychology* 35, 4.

Cavanagh, Kate. 2003. "Understanding Women's Responses to Domestic Violence." *Qualitative Social Work* 2, 3.

Clements, Caroline, Claire Oxtoby, and Richard Ogle. 2008. "Methodological Issues in Assessing Psychological Adjustment in Child Witnesses of Intimate Partner Violence." *Trauma, Violence and Abuse* 9, 2.

County Kildare Health Service Executive. 2011. *Child Protection and Welfare Practice Handbook*. Dublin: Author.

Danvergne, Mia, and Geoffrey Li. 2006. "Homicide in Canada." *Juristat* 26, 5.

DCSF (Department for Children, School and Families). 2010. *Working Together to Safeguard Children: A Guide to Inter-agency Co-operation*. <education.gov.uk/publica-tions/eOrderingDownload/00305-2010DOM-EN.pdf>.

DeVoe, Ellen R., and Erica L. Smith. 2003. "Don't Take My Kids: Barriers to Service Delivery for Battered Mothers and their Young Children." *Journal of*

Emotional Abuse 3, 3–4.

Dobash, Rebecca, Russell Dobash, and Juan Medina-Ariza. 2000. *Lethal and Non-Lethal Violence Against an Intimate Partner: Risks, Needs and Programs.* Manchester, England: Economic and Social Research Council.

Doherty, Diane. 2002. *Health Effects of Family Violence.* Ottawa: National Clearinghouse on Family Violence.

Dumbrill, Gary. 2006. "Parental Experience of Child Welfare Intervention: A Qualitative Study." *Child Abuse and Neglect* 30, 1.

Durfee, Alesha. 2009. "Victim Narratives, Legal Representation, and Domestic Violence Civil Protection Orders." *Feminist Criminology* 4, 1.

Emerson, Darcie. 2011. "Taking Care in Child Protection: A Descriptive Account of Practices with Women Who Have Experienced Violence by Their Domestic Partners." Unpublished master's thesis, University of Victoria.

English, Diana J., Jeffrey L. Edleson, and Mary E. Herrick. 2005. "Domestic Violence in One State's Child Protective Caseload: A Study of Differential Case Dispositions and Outcomes." *Children and Youth Services Review* 27, 11.

Erez, Edna, Madelaine Adelman, and Carol Gregory. 2009. "Intersections of Immigration and Domestic Violence: Voices of Battered Immigrant Women." *Feminist Criminology* 4, 1.

Evans, Sarah, Corrie Davies, and David DiLillo. 2008. "Exposure to Domestic Violence: A Meta-Analysis of Child and Adolescent Outcomes." *Aggression and Violent Behavior* 13.

Faulkner, Melissa. 2008. "Understanding Child Maltreatment Trends: Reflections on 25 Years of Data from the Royal Children's Hospital Suspected Child Abuse and Neglect Team." *Child Abuse Prevention Newsletter* 16, 2.

Ferguson, Harry, and Fergus Hogan. 2004. *Strengthening Families through Fathers: Developing Policy and Practice in Relation to Vulnerable Fathers and their Families.* Waterford: The Centre for Social and Family Research, Waterford Institute of Technology.

Fleming, Linda M., and David J. Tobin. 2005. "Popular Child-Rearing Books: Where Is Daddy?" *Psychology of Men and Masculinity* 6, 1.

Fleury, Ruth E., Cris M. Sullivan, and Deborah I. Bybee. 2000. "When Ending the Relationship Doesn't End the Violence: Women's Experiences of Violence by Former Partners." *Violence Against Women* 6, 12.

Fleury-Steiner, Ruth. E., Benjamin D. Fleury-Steiner, and Susan L. Miller. 2011. "More Than a Piece of Paper? Protection Orders as a Resource for Battered Women." *Sociology Compass* 5, 7.

Flood, Michael, and Bob Pease. 2009. "Factors Influencing Attitudes to Violence Against Women." *Trauma, Violence and Abuse* 10, 2.

Gilligan, Philip, Martin Manby, and Carole Pickburn. 2012. "Fathers' Involvement in Children's Services: Exploring Local and National Issues in 'Moorlandstown'." *British Journal of Social Work* 42, 3: 500–18.

Graham-Bermann, Sandra, Kathryn Howell, Michelle Lilly, and Ellen DeVoe. 2011. "Mediators and Moderators of Change in Adjustment Following Intervention for Children Exposed to Intimate Partner Violence." *Journal of Interpersonal Violence* 26, 9.

Grech, Katrina and Melissa Burgess. 2011. *Trends and Patterns in Domestic Violence Assaults: 2001 to 2010.* Sydney: NSW Crime Statistics Bureau.

Hamby, Sherry, David Finkelhor, Heather Turner, and Richard Ormrod. 2010. "The Overlap of Witnessing: Partner Violence with Child Maltreatment and Other Victimizations in a Nationally Representative Survey of Youth." *Child Abuse & Neglect* 34.

Harne, Lynne. 2004. "Childcare, Violence and Fathering: Are Violent Fathers Who Look After Their Children Likely to Be Less Abusive?" In Renate Klein and Bernard Wallner (eds.), *Conflict, Gender and Violence*. Vienna: Studien-Verlag.

Harrison, Christine. 2006. "Damned If You Do and Damned If You Don't." In Cathy Humphreys and Nicky Stanley (eds.), *Domestic Violence and Child Protection: Directions for Good Practice*. London: Jessica Kingsley Publications.

Hester, Marianne. 2001. "Violent Men as Good Enough Fathers? A Look at England and Sweden." *Violence Against Women* 7, 7.

Hodgins, B. Denise. 2007. "Father Involvement in Parenting Young Children: A Content Analysis of Parent Education Programs in B.C." Unpublished master's project, University of Victoria.

Hollander, Jocelyn A. 2002. "Resisting Vulnerability: The Social Construction of Gender in Interaction." *Social Problems* 49, 4.

Holt, Stephanie. 2003. "Child Protection Social Work and Men's Abuse of Women: An Irish Study." *Child and Family Social Work* 8.

Holt, Stephanie, Helen Buckley, and Sadhbh Whelan. 2008. "The Impact of Exposure to Domestic Violence on Children and Young People: A Review of Literature." *Child Abuse & Neglect* 32.

Home Affairs Select Committee. 2008. "Domestic Violence, Forced Marriage and 'Honour'-Based Violence." London: Author.

Hotton, Tina. 2005. "Family Violence in Canada: A Statistical Profile." *Juristat* 21, 7.

Howe, Adrian. 2008. *Sex, Violence and Crime*. New York: Routledge-Cavendish.

Howell, Kathryn. 2011. "Resilience and Psychopathology in Children Exposed to Family Violence." *Aggression and Violent Behavior* 16.

Hughes, Judy, Shirley Chau, and Deborah C. Poff. 2011. "They're Not My Favorite People": What Mothers Who Have Experienced Intimate Partner Violence Say About Involvement in the Child Welfare System." *Children and Youth Services Review* 33, 7.

Humphreys, Cathy. 2000. *Social Work, Domestic Violence and Child Protection: Challenging Practice*. Bristol: Policy Press.

____. 2007. *Domestic Violence and Child Protection: Challenging Directions for Practice. Issues Paper 13*. Sydney: Australian Domestic and Family Violence Clearinghouse.

Humphreys, Cathy, Audrey Mullender, Ravi Thiara, and Agnes Skamballis. 2006. "'Talking to My Mum': Developing Communication Between Mothers and Children in the Aftermath of Domestic Violence." *Journal of Social Work* 6, 1.

Humphreys, Cathy, and Nicky Stanley. 2006. "Introduction." In Catherine Humphreys and Nicky Stanley (eds.), *Domestic Violence and Child Protection: Directions for Good Practice*. London: Jessica Kingsley.

Hungerford, Anne, Sierra Wait, Alyssa Fritz, and Caroline Clements. 2012. "Exposure to Intimate Partner Violence and Children's Psychological Adjustment, Cognitive Functioning, and Social Competence: A Review." *Aggression and Violent Behavior* 17.

Hunter, Rosemary. 2006. "Narratives of Domestic Violence." *Sydney Law Review* 28.

Jenkins, Tracey, and Jennifer Dunne. 2007. *Domestic Abuse, the Facts: A Secondary Research Report*. London: Equal Opportunities Commission.

Johnson, Susan P., and Cris Sullivan. 2008. "How Child Protection Workers Support or Further Victimize Battered Mothers." *Journal of Women and Social Work* 23, 3.

Kaufman Kantor, Glenda, and Liza Little. 2003. "Defining the Boundaries of Child Neglect: When Does Domestic Violence Equate with Parental Failure to Protect?" *Journal of Interpersonal Violence* 18, 4.

Kernic, Mary A., Daphne J. Monary-Ernsdorff, Jennifer K. Koepsell, and Victoria L. Holt. 2005. "Children in the Crossfire: Child Custody Determinations Among Couples with a History of Intimate Partner Violence." *Violence Against Women* 11, 8.

Kitzmann, Katherine, Noni Gaylord, Aimee Holt, and Erin Kenny. 2003. "Child Witnesses to Domestic Violence: A Meta-analytic Review." *Journal of Consulting and Clinical Psychology* 71.

Kohl, Patricia L., Jeffery L. Edleson, Diana J. English, and Richard P. Barth. 2005. "Domestic Violence and Pathways into Child Welfare Services: Findings from the National Survey of Child and Adolescent Well-Being." *Children and Youth Services Review* 27, 11.

Lamb, Michael. 2010. *The Role of the Father in Child Development*. Fifth edition. New Jersey: John Wiley & Sons.

Landsman, Miriam J., and Carolyn Copps Hartley. 2007. "Attributing Responsibility for Child Maltreatment when Domestic Violence Is Present." *Child Abuse and Neglect* 31, 4.

Lapierre, Simon. 2010. "More Responsibilities, Less Control: Understanding the Challenges and Difficulties Involved in Mothering in the Context of Domestic Violence." *British Journal of Social Work* 40, 5.

___. 2011. "Are Abused Women 'Neglectful' Mothers? A Critical Reflection Based on Women's Experiences." In Brid Featherstone, Carol-Ann Hooper, Jonathan Scourfield, and Julie Taylor (eds.), *Gender and Child Welfare in Society*. Chichester, UK: John Wiley & Sons.

Lapierre, Simon, and Isabelle Côté. 2011. "I Made Her Realise that I Could Be There for Her, That I Could Support Her": Child Protection Practices with Women in Domestic Violence Cases." *Child Care in Practice* 17, 4.

Lavergne, Chantal, Claire Chamberland, Lise Laporte, and Rosanna Baraldi. 2003. "Domestic Violence: Protecting Children by Involving Fathers and Helping Mothers." CECW Information Sheet #6E. <cecw-cepb.ca/sites/default/files/publications/en/DomesticViolence6E.pdf>.

Lessard, Gillian, and Claire Chamberland. 2003. "Agir auprès des familles où il y a de la violence conjugale et de la violence parentale." In Claire Chamberland (ed.), *Violence Parentale et Violence Conjugale. Des Réalités Plurielles, Multidimensionnelles et Interreliées*. Sainte-Foy, Quebec: Presses de l'Université du Québec.

Letourneau, N., C. Fedick, and D. Willms. 2007. "Mothering and Domestic Violence: A Longitudinal Analysis." *Journal of Family Violence* 22, 8.

Levendosky, Alytia, Shannon Lynch, and Sandra Graham-Bermann. 2000. "Mothers'

Perceptions of the Impact of Woman Abuse on their Parenting." *Violence Against Women* 6, 3.

Maguire, Kathleen (ed.). 2007. *Sourcebook of Criminal Justice Statistics*. <albany.edu/sourcebook/pdf/t31312005.pdf>.

Mederos, Frederick. 2004. *Accountability and Connection with Abusive Men: A New Child Protection Response to Increasing Family Safety*. <thegreenbook.info/documents/Accountability.pdf>.

Meyer, Silke. 2011. "Seeking Help for Intimate Partner Violence: Victims' Experiences When Approaching the Criminal Justice System for IPV-related Support and Protection in an Australian Jurisdictions." *Feminist Criminology* 6, 4.

Navid, Carla. 2009. "Fathers in the Frame: Protecting Children by Including Men in Cases of Violence Against Women." Unpublished master's thesis, University of Manitoba.

Neilson, Linda C. 2001. *Spousal Abuse, Children and the Legal System: Final Report for Canadian Bar Association*. Fredericton, NB: Muriel McQueen Fergusson Centre for Family Violence Research, University of New Brunswick. <unb.ca/fredericton/arts/centres/mmfc/_resources/pdfs/team2001.pdf >.

Ofsted. 2010. *Learning Lessons from Serious Case Reviews 2009-2010*. <ofsted.gov.uk/resources/learning-lessons-serious-case-reviews-2009-2010>.

Peled, Einat. 1997. "The Battered Women's Movement Response to Children of Battered Women: A Critical Analysis." *Violence Against Women* 3, 4.

Peled, Einat, and Guy Perel. 2007. "Duality in Practice: A Conceptual Framework for Intervening with Abusive Men as Parents." In J. Edleson and O. Willimas (eds.), *Parenting of Men Who Batter: New Directions for Assessment and Intervention*. Oxford: Oxford University Press.

Perel, Guy, and Einat Peled. 2008. "The Fathering of Violent Men: Constriction and Yearning." *Violence Against Women* 14, 4.

Phares, Vicky, Elena Lopez, Sherecce Fields, Demy Kamboukos, and Amy Duhig. 2005. "Are Fathers Involved in Pediatric Psychology Research and Treatment?" *Journal of Pediatric Psychology* 30, 8.

Potito, Christine, Andrew Day, Ed Carson, and Patrick O'Leary. 2009. "Domestic Violence and Child Protection: Partnerships and Collaboration." *Australian Social Work* 62, 3.

Pritchard, Colin, Jill Davey, and Richard Williams. 2012. "Who Kills Children? Re-examining the Evidence." *British Journal of Social Work*. <http://bjsw.oxford-journals.org/content/early/2012/05/03/bjsw.bcs051.short?rss=1>.

Profitt, Norma Jean. 2008. *In the Best Interests of Women and Children: Exploring the Issue of "Failure to Protect" in the Acadian Peninsula*. Fredericton: Department of Social Work, St. Thomas University.

Quebec. 2007. *The Youth Protection Act 2007*.

Radford, Lorraine, Susana Corral, Christine Bradley, Helen Fisher, Claire Bassett, Nick Howat, and Stephan Collishaw. 2011. *Child Abuse and Neglect in the U.K. Today*. London: NSPCC.

Radhakrishna, Aruna, Ingrid E. Bou-Saada, Wanda M. Hunter, Diane J. Catellier, and Jonathan B. Kotch. 2001. "Are Father Surrogates a Risk Factor for Child Maltreatment?" *Child Maltreatment* 6, 4.

RCY (Representative for Children and Youth). 2009. *Honouring Christian Lee — No Private*

Matter: Protecting Children Living With Domestic Violence. Victoria, British Columbia: Office of the Representative for Children and Youth.

Richardson, Cathy, and Allan Wade. 2009. "Taking Resistance Seriously: A Response-Based Approach to Social Work in Cases of Violence Against Indigenous Women." In Susan Strega and Jeannine Carriere (eds.), *Walking this Path Together: Anti-Racist and Anti-Oppressive Child Welfare Practice*. Winnipeg: Fernwood Publishing.

Rivett, Mark. 2009. "Working with Violent Male Carers (Fathers and Stepfathers)." In Brid Featherstone, Carol-Ann Hooper, Jonathan Scourfield, and Julie Taylor (eds.), *Gender and Child Welfare in Society*. Chichester, UK: Wiley-Blackwell.

Rothman, Emily F., David G. Mandel and Jay Silverman. 2007. "Abusers' Perceptions of the Effect of their Intimate Partner Violence on Children." *Violence Against Women* 13, 11.

Salisbury, Emily J., Kris Henning, and Robert Holdford. 2009. "Fathering by Partner-Abusive Men." *Child Maltreatment* 14, 3.

Saunders, Hilary. 2004. *Twenty-Nine Child Homicides: Lessons Still to Be Learnt on Domestic Violence and Child Protection*. London: Women's Aid.

Scott, Katreena, and Claire V. Crooks. 2006. "Intervention for Abusive Fathers: Promising Practices in Court and Community Responses." *Juvenile and Family Court Journal* 57, 3.

Scourfield, Jonathan. 2003. *Gender and Child Protection*. Basingstoke, UK: Palgrave MacMillan.

Sety, Megan 2011, *The Impact of Domestic Violence on Children: a Literature Review*. Sydney, NSW: Australian Domestic and Family Violence Clearinghouse and Benevolent Society.

Shim, Woochan S., and Wendy Haight. 2006. "Supporting Battered Women and Their Children: Perspectives of Battered Mothers and Child Welfare Professionals." *Children and Youth Services Review* 28, 6.

Smart, Carol, Vanessa May, Amanda Wade, and Clare Furniss. 2005. "Residence and Contact Disputes in Court, Volume 2." Department of Constitutional Affairs (London, UK) Research Series 4/05.

Smart, Carol, Bren Neale, and Amanda Wade. 2001. *The Changing Experience of Childhood: Families and Divorce*. Oxford: Polity Press.

Sternberg, Kathleen J., Laila P. Baradaran, Craig B. Abbott, Michael E. Lamb, and Eva Guterman. 2006. "Type of Violence, Age, and Gender Differences in the Effects of Family Violence on Children's Behavior Problems: A Mega-analysis." *Developmental Review* 26, 1.

Strega, Susan. 2004. "The Case of the Missing Perpetrator: A Cross-national Study of Child Welfare Policy, Practice and Discourse when Men Beat Mothers." Unpublished doctoral dissertation, University of Southampton, UK.

Strega, Susan, Leslie Brown, Marilyn Callahan, Lena Dominelli, and Christopher Walmsley. 2009. "Working with Me, Working at Me: Fathers' Narratives of Child Welfare." *Journal of Progressive Human Services* 20, 1.

Strega, Susan, Claire Fleet, Leslie Brown, Lena Dominelli, Marilyn Callahan, and Christopher Walmsley. 2008. "Connecting Father Absence and Mother Blame in Child Welfare Policies and Practice." *Children and Youth Services Review* 30, 7.

Sunderland, Jane. 2004. *Gendered Discourses*. New York: Palgrave Macmillan.

Sullivan, Michael, Marcia Egan, and Michael Gooch. 2004. "Conjoint Interventions for Adult Victims and Children of Domestic Violence: A Program Evaluation." *Research on Social Work Practice* 14, 3.

Suzuki, Staci, Robert Geffner, and Steven Bucky. 2008. "The Experiences of Adults Exposed to Intimate Partner Violence as Children: An Exploratory Qualitative Study of Resilience and Protective Factors." *Journal of Emotional Abuse* 8, 1/2.

Terrance, Cheryl, Karyn Plumm, and Betsi Little. 2008. "Maternal Blame: Battered Women and Abused Children." *Violence Against Women* 14, 8.

Thomison, Adam. 2000. "Exploring Family Violence: Links Between Child Maltreatment and Domestic Violence." Issues in Child Abuse Prevention, Paper No. 13. Melbourne: Australian Institute of Family Studies.

Todd, Nick, and Allan Wade. 2003. "Coming to Terms with Violence and Resistance: From a Language of Effects to a Language of Responses." In Thomas Strong and David Paré (eds.), *Furthering Talk: Advances in the Discursive Therapies*. New York: Kluwer Academic.

Trinder Liz, Alan Firth, and Christopher Jenks. 2010. "'So Presumably Things have Moved on Since Then?' The Management of Risk Allegations in Child Contact Dispute Resolution." *International Journal of Law, Policy and the Family* 24, 1.

Trocmé, Nico, Barbara Fallon, Bruce MacLaurin, Joanne Daciuk, Caroline Felstiner, Tara Black, Lil Tonmyr, Cindy Blackstock, Ken Barter, Daniel Turcotte, and Richard Cloutier. 2005. *Canadian Incidence Study of Reported Child Abuse and Neglect — 2003: Major Findings*. Ottawa: National Clearinghouse on Family Violence.

Trocmé, Nicho, Barbara Fallon, Bruce MacLaurin, Vandna Sinha, Tara Black, Elizabeth Fast, Caroline Felstiner, Sonia Hélie, Daniel Turcotte, Pamela Weightman, Janet Douglas, and Jil Holroyd. 2010. *Canadian Incidence Study of Reported Child Abuse and Neglect — 2008: Major Findings*. Ottawa: Public Health Agency of Canada.

Tutty, Leslie, Jennifer Koshan, Deborah Jesso, and Kendra Nixon. 2005. *Alberta's Protection Against Family Violence Act: A Summative Evaluation*. Calgary: RESOLVE Alberta.

Victorian Child Death Review Committee. 2011. *Annual Report of Inquiries into the Deaths of Children Known to Child Protection*. Melbourne: Office of the Child Safety Commissioner.

Wade, Allan. 2007. "Despair, Resistance, Hope: Response-Based Therapy with Victims of Violence." In Carmel Flaskas, Imelda McCarthy, and Jim Sheeban (eds.), *Hope and Despair in Narrative and Family Therapy: Adversity, Forgiveness and Reconciliation*. New York: Routledge/Taylor and Francis Group.

Walmsley, Christopher, Susan Strega, Leslie Brown, Lena Dominelli, and Marilyn Callahan. 2009. "More than a Playmate, Less than a Co-parent: Fathers in the Canadian BSW Curriculum." *Canadian Social Work Review* 26, 1.

WAVES (Waitakere Anti-violence Essential Services). 2010. "Children and Family Violence: A Review of Recent Literature." <waves.org.nz/media/Children_and_FV_Lit_Review.pdf>.

Women's Aid Federation England. 2007. "Statistics: Domestic Violence." <womensaid.org.uk/domestic_violence_topic.asp?section=0001000100220036&sectionTitle=Statistics>.

Wood, Julia T. 2004. "Monsters and Victims: Male Felons' Accounts of Intimate

Partner Violence." *Journal of Social and Personal Relationships* 21, 5.

Yampolskaya, Svetlana, Paul E. Greenbaum, and Ilene R. Berson. 2009. "Profiles of Child Maltreatment Perpetrators and Risk for Fatal Assault: A Latent Class Analysis." *Journal of Family Violence* 24, 5.

Yukon. 1996. *Child and Family Services Act 1996.*

4.　What Do We Really Know About Maternal Failure to Protect in Cases of Child Sexual Abuse?

Rebecca Bolen and Julia Krane

The scholarship on failure to protect in cases of child sexual abuse reveals that while assumptions abound regarding maternal ambivalence and support in the aftermath of child sexual abuse, these assumptions have their own inherent failings that must be questioned. Despite the gender-neutral facade of failure-to-protect policy and practice, this chapter shows that its application in the real world is very much gendered. Moreover, the complexity and contradictions in failure-to-protect policy have been eclipsed by the prevailing perceptions of and responses to non-offending mothers involved with child protection services. Our analysis is intended to compel CPS practitioners and policy makers to revisit their assumptions. Specifically, we urge CPS to recognize the breadth and depth of notions of ambivalence and support, which inform assessments, interventions, and determinations of failure to protect in cases of child sexual abuse.

Incidence and Prevalence

In the United States, as in other Anglo-American child protection systems, parents and caregivers can face criminal or civil charges because "they did not act towards their children when, or in the manner that, a trier of fact determined that they ought to have acted" (Fugate 2001: 273). Although failure-to-protect statutes could apply to any parent or caregiver, mothers are disproportionately charged with this offence, when compared to fathers, in relation to harms perpetrated against their children (Fugate 2001). To elaborate, we turn now to the first *National Incidence Study of Child Abuse and Neglect (NIS-1)* of maltreated children, which was completed in 1981 in the United States (Finkelhor and Hotaling 1984). This review of all cases of child maltreatment known by professionals to occur in nationally representative counties found that female caregivers, almost all of whom were mothers or mother-figures, were reported to be sexual offenders in 46 percent of the cases of sexual abuse. In the 1998 annual *National Child Abuse and Neglect Data System* incidence study, the percentage of mothers and mother-figures reported to be sexual offenders dropped only slightly to 44 percent (U.S. Department of Health and Human Services 2000). Furthermore, mothers were categorized as sexual offenders in 27 percent of all cases of sexual abuse and in 53 percent of all cases of parental abuse. Finkelhor and Hotaling (1984) concluded that most of these mothers were categorized as sexual offenders for their purported failure to protect. These findings suggest that failure to protect had indeed worked its way into CPS practices in cases of child sexual abuse. It is impossible to determine whether this trend continues today since the *NIS-4* (Sedlak et al. 2010) changed the manner in which non-offending parents were classified as sexual offenders. In this latest incidence survey, only those who physically perpetrated the sexual abuse were identified and categorized as sexual offenders. Using this more narrow definition, the percentage of female caregivers categorized as sexual offenders dropped to 22 percent, still strikingly high when compared to prevalence studies.

Prevalence studies, based on retrospective surveys aimed at determining the percentage of individuals reporting sexual abuse in childhood, stand in stark contrast to incidence studies with respect to the gendered nature of child sexual abuse offenders. Time and again, these studies reveal that the overwhelming majority of perpetrators of sexual abuses are males, whether the victims are boys or girls. In fact, a series of rigorous prevalence studies undertaken in the U.S. has consistently found that females commit 5 percent or less of all sexual abuses against children and youths (Finkelhor et al. 1990; Russell 1983; Vogeltanz et al. 1999; Wyatt 1985; Wyatt et al. 1999). In their capacity as mothers, women commit 1 percent or less of all sexual abuses against girls (Russell 1983; Bolen 2001), although one national prevalence study cautions that the rate of child sexual abuse perpetrated by women, primarily against boys, might well be underestimated (Briere and Elliott 2003). In this study, based on a randomly selected sample of 935 adults, half of whom were male, the gender breakdown for female victims was consistent with the figures in circulation through the sexual abuse scholarship (93 percent had been abused by at least one male, and 9 percent had been abused by at least one female). Briere and Elliott (2003) offered new insights on perpetrators against male victims. They found that among the abused males, 39 percent reported sexual abuse by at least one female, and 70 percent by at least one male. This supports the claim that the vast majority of child sexual abusers are male but shows that the rate of child sexual abuse perpetrated by women against boys might be underestimated.

Making Sense of Incidence and Prevalence Research: Mother-Blame

How might the discrepancy between findings from incidence and prevalence studies be explained? Mothers' failure to protect, we suggest, speaks to a breach of expectations of maternal perfection, including clairvoyance, that is, to be all-knowing when it comes to the maltreatment of their children from acts of sexual abuse by others (Krane 2003). As discussed elsewhere in this volume, mothers have long been implicated through their actions or inactions, and their alleged knowledge, tolerance or denial of incestuous abuse. Early writings offered a blatantly harsh view of mothers that has waned over time, but its influence continues to surface in the beliefs voiced by helping professionals about the rightful site of blame and responsibility in situations of child sexual abuse.

The earliest known study on attributing blame in sexual abuse situations was undertaken by Dietz and Craft (1980) and was based on insights from child protection workers. The researchers found that 65 percent of CPS workers believed the non-offending mother was as responsible for the sexual abuse as was the offending father, and they also believed that 85 percent of non-offending mothers somehow gave consent, albeit unconsciously, to the abuse. A decade later, 70 to 86 percent of helping professionals (social workers, psychologists, psychiatrists, teachers, and counsellors) reported believing that mothers were partially responsible for not only paternal abuse, but also sexual abuse committed by a neighbour (Johnson et al. 1990; Kelley 1990; Reidy and Hochstadt 1993). In a recent study (Rogers, Davies, and Cottam 2010), non-offending mothers were scored in the "moderate range" of responsibility for child sexual abuse. The extent to which mothers are blamed for sexual abuses perpetrated against their children has been observed by Bolen in her university level child maltreatment courses at both Boston University and the University of Tennessee over the past thirteen years. Responding to questions about case vignettes with a seven-point scale, Bolen's students consistently rated the offenders as responsible for the sexual abuse and the children as not being at fault for their victimization. Students' rating of the non-offending mother's culpability has been neither consistent nor clear-cut. About 40 percent of Bolen's students scored maternal blame at the lower end of the scale, meaning they did not seem to blame mothers. However, the remaining students scored mother-blame evenly across the scale, all the way up to being completely blameworthy. This range suggested ambivalence regarding mothers' role in child sexual abuse. Thus, the past thirty years of research, both published and anecdotal, shows continued blame ascribed to non-offending mothers, and arguably reflects beliefs that permeate CPS and other professional practice.

Mother-blaming assumptions are further seen in a study based on CPS case records of abuse by any relative (Ryan, Warren, and Weincek 1991). The study revealed that child protection workers often assumed that mothers colluded with the perpetrator to maintain the sexual abuse; indeed, 81 percent of mothers were assessed as having known about the abuse before its official report. Of those mothers presumed to have knowledge of the ongoing abuse, 42 percent were considered mostly or very protective; the remaining 58 percent of mothers were considered to be poorly supportive of the child prior to the official disclosure. This study exposed the assumption that mothers knew of the sexual abuse of their children and the belief that over half were unsupportive or ambivalent in support.

Maternal Belief, Support, and Protection

Efforts to understand mothers' alleged contributions to the dynamics of child sexual abuse have been accompanied by attempts at documenting non-offending mothers' responses to disclosure, especially in the context of CPS practice. During the1980s and 1990s, inquiries sought to assess the support of non-offending parents (almost always mothers) in terms of their belief in the veracity of the abuse allegations, their supportive or nonsupportive actions towards the victim and their emotional experiences, including ambivalence. This research yielded little agreement on the definition of support after disclosure. Bolen's (2002) analysis of twenty-seven published studies of post-disclosure responses of non-offending guardians examined how "guardian support" in response to child sexual abuse had been defined. Overwhelmingly, these studies focused on non-offending mothers' support. The analysis was able to determine the percentage of supportive and unsupportive non-offending mothers as rated by different types of professionals. Across all twenty-seven studies, 44 percent of non-offending mothers were rated by professionals as fully supportive, 31 percent were rated as ambivalent and somewhat supportive, and 25 percent were rated as not supportive of the child. These percentages suggest that professionals perceive non-offending mothers to be mostly supportive, as compared to perceptions by CPS that non-offending mothers are mostly unsupportive (Dietz and Craft 1980).

Bolen (2002) further argued that rather than interpreting maternal ambivalence as a lack of support, CPS authorities might consider support as dynamic and changing over time. "Whereas this latter approach evokes a strengths orientation, the first approach evokes a deficits orientation. Regretfully, this deficit orientation … resonates most clearly within the child protection system in which most children are removed from their homes" (Bolen 2002: 55) when maternal support vacillates or is considered ambivalent (Everson et al. 1989). With respect to the woefully inadequate conceptualization and operationalization of guardian support in research, Bolen theorized that guardian support, a fundamental factor in determining whether children remain in the care of their non-offending mothers following disclosure and investigation, has been defined in a way that meets CPS needs. As Bolen (2002: 54) stated, "it appears that anything less than full support may be a significant risk factor for removal of the child. Thus, a final profound implication of having a system-driven construct is that doing so leads [yet again] to a deficits interpretation of supportive behaviors." Full support in this context is typically considered the expression, without ambivalence, of belief in the child's allegations and concern for the child's well-being while taking immediate steps to separate the child from the perpetrator and comply with all CPS requests to maintain distance from the perpetrator both emotionally and materially.

Supportive responses to children's disclosures of sexual abuse are thought to enhance children's well-being after disclosure. Studies over time (De Jong 1988; Everson et al. 1989; Thériault, Cyr, and Wright 2003; Bolen and Lamb 2007) have, once again, focused almost exclusively on non-offending mothers when establishing the relationship between their support and reduced negative consequences for children (see Elliott and Carnes 2001 for a review). Bolen and Lamb's (2004, 2007) research has begun to unravel the complexities of support, with an emphasis on non-offending mothers who vacillate between supporting the perpetrator and the victim. In this research, they defined support on a continuum from less to more support of the child. As well, they presented ambivalence in two different ways: (a) positive feelings (affective), thoughts (cognitive) or actions (behaviour) towards the victim, and (b) positive feelings (affective), thoughts (cognitive) or actions (behaviour) towards the perpetrator. Greater ambivalence occurred when positive thoughts for both the victim and perpetrator were high, reflecting the tension experienced when non-offending mothers have positive feelings for both the child and perpetrator. Therefore, they captured support and ambivalence as two separate concepts.

Bolen and Lamb (2004, 2007) took this conceptualization one step further by considering ambivalence as a normative response to the stresses and confusions arising from a disclosure of child sexual abuse, especially when the non-offending mother had deep feelings for both the child and perpetrator. They also suggested that non-offending mothers could express ambivalent feelings towards the perpetrator while taking supportive actions with their children. In other words, ambivalence and supportive behaviours could coexist. Based on responses from twenty-nine non-offending mothers whose children were seen at an outpatient clinic for a sexual abuse medical or forensic examination, Bolen and Lamb examined the relationship between non-offending maternal support and ambivalence. They found that maternal ambivalence increased as emotional costs (the loss of a relationship with the perpetrator, for example) and financial costs (income instability, possible loss of home or automobile) of the disclosure increased. If the non-offending mother experienced intrusive and/or avoidant symptoms of post-traumatic stress disorder, she was also at risk to experience greater affective ambivalence. Bolen and Lamb concluded that ambivalence was related to attachment to the child and/or perpetrator, length of the relationship with the perpetrator, presence of intimate partner violence, total relationship stressors, and partner income. However, the presence of maternal ambivalence did not negate maternal support. The theoretical and practice implications are stark: a mother can certainly be ambivalent about her child's disclosure of sexual abuse and about what to do about it but this ambivalence does not therefore mean that this mother cannot or will not be supportive of her child post-disclosure.

Also related to non-offending mothers' support has been the notion of "belief," or the extent to which the non-offending mother believes that the sexual abuse occurred, that the alleged perpetrator committed the abuse, and that the victim was abused by the perpetrator. According to Elliott and Carnes (2001), it is rather difficult to evaluate non-offending parental belief because belief, support and protection are interrelated but not necessarily synonymous (though very few studies have examined these factors separately); second, these concepts are not static and, as such, ought to be evaluated at several points in time; and finally, belief, support and protection have been measured in research studies in so many different ways — most often with voluntary participants — that thematic conclusions cannot be reliably drawn.

Several trends, however, can be identified from Elliott and Carnes' review. It appears that the majority of non-offending mothers believed their children's allegations of sexual abuse and were supportive. While belief did not necessarily "ensure supportive or protective responses," many non-offending mothers who exhibited ambivalence were "nonetheless able to take actions to protect their children" (Elliott and Carnes 2001: 316). In addition, supportive and protective non-offending mothers might also exhibit inconsistency and ambivalence. Elliott and Carnes stated that the most inconclusive results were seen in efforts to identify factors that predict belief, support and protection; they therefore called for more empirical research on the intersection of belief, support, protection, and outcomes for children and their non-offending mothers.

Very recently, based on insights from seventeen non-offending guardians, almost all mothers, Bolen, Dessel, and Sutter (2011, under review) categorized seven dimensions of parental support. These include, for example: instrumental parenting (taking actions to elicit some type of support for the sexually abused child); protection and safety (taking action to make sure no harm comes to the sexually abused child and the child feels safe); active parenting (discipline, guidance, and boundaries); and availability (physical and emotional) to talk with the child. Rather than action-oriented support, non-offending guardians offered a more cognitive conception of belief. They talked about the evidence, supportive or not, that the abuse occurred and that the offender was the one to have abused the child. This dimension of parental support was labelled "decision-making." Just as professionals weigh the available evidence to figure out what had happened in terms of the allegations of sexual abuse, so did non-offending mothers, each in their own ways: confronting the offender, talking to the child, refraining from talking to the child, searching for physical evidence on the child's body, or taking time to think about the allegations. Few mothers stated they believed the child immediately and unconditionally, and those who did typically had taken their children to the hospital for an evaluation. What was striking was that all mothers engaged in at least some protective behaviours even as they reconciled the evidence regarding the abuse.

How non-offending mothers came to believe that sexual abuse occurred can be a complex and non-linear process (see for example, Hooper 1992, 1997). Hooper and Humphreys (1998: 508–509) discussed this process:

> While previous research had tended to describe women as either knowing or not knowing, believing or disbelieving, protecting or not protecting, our research suggested that these states were frequently not either/or, but often both/and, and that women's position in relation to them was often not fixed and stable but fluctuating.... While professionals speak of "disclosure," women spoke of "finding out." This could take place over varying timespans, and was an interpretative process ... in which information was often ambiguous, limited and/or conflicting.... The ability to believe that child sexual abuse had occurred was inextricably linked with this process of "finding out." Women spoke of a multi-layered state in which quite contradictory positions could be held simultaneously, and where the certainty of belief held one day could not be predictably held on to the next. Within this multi-layered experience there appeared to be both cognitive and emotional aspects to believing that a child had been sexually abused. Most mothers spoke of their initial responses in terms of belief and disbelief, with the latter occurring as a spontaneous, emotional reaction — a natural defense against traumatic news.

That is, the process of believing that the abuse occurred is complex. Dichotomizing this process as simply belief or disbelief disregards ample evidence that belief is a process, which may or may not be related to the support the child receives from the non-offending mother.

Maternal Support and Well-Being of Children

Non-offending mothers are also scrutinized because of the assumption that their post-disclosure support is closely and strongly related to how well children do after disclosure. Several decades of research argue that when parents are more supportive, their children have fewer symptoms from the abuse and are emotionally healthier (Elliott and Carnes 2001). However, a meta-analysis of the twenty-seven known empirical studies on this topic (Bolen and Gergely 2011) unearthed little evidence of a relationship between parental support

and the post-disclosure effects on the children of the abuse. In these studies, only a few post-disclosure mental health symptoms and other effects of
the sexual abuse were related to the mother's level of support; however, this
statistical relationship was for the most part very weak. For CPS workers, it
is important to point out that there is not sufficient evidence at this point to
suggest that the support of non-offending parents to their victimized children
after the disclosure of the abuse is related to the children's adjustment and
well-being after disclosure.

There are other concerns within these twenty-seven studies. First, these
studies defined and captured support in sixteen different ways, suggesting
that there is not yet an agreed-upon definition of parental support. Secondly,
some of these studies analyzed multiple post-disclosure child symptoms.
Yet, as long as at least one relationship was statistically significant, the study
authors tended to conclude that there was a significant relationship between
parental support and sequelae in children. This conclusion reproduces the
lore that support by non-offending mothers after sexual abuse disclosure is
closely related to how well their children fare. It is built around the actions
of non-offending mothers while virtually ignoring non-offending fathers.
Until there is a single definition of post-disclosure parental support and an
understanding of the complexity of how it is defined and measured, including
ways to determine non-offending fathers' support, the relationship between
parental support and child well-being after disclosure remains truly unknown.
This has significant implications for a different practice today.

Failure to Protect

Amid the thousands of studies on child sexual abuse, it is truly amazing that
only a handful specifically focus on failure to protect (Berkowitz 1997; Coohey
2006; Coohey and O'Leary 2008; Malloy and Lyon 2006; Shadoin and
Carnes 2006; Vieth 2006). One that stands out (Coohey 2006) used a sample
of child maltreatment reports in a single county in the U.S. over a four-year
period to compare thirty-one mothers with a substantiated case of failure to
protect in cases of sexual abuse and sixty-two mothers for whom failure to
protect was not substantiated. Responding to the widespread belief that child
protection caseworkers are inconsistent in their decisions and might interject
their own values into the case, the overall purpose was to determine how CPS
workers substantiated failure to protect. Variables that were reviewed included
the worker's perception of the length of time the mother purportedly knew
about the abuse and how she knew; consistent belief, support, and protection;
actions taken for the benefit of the child and against the offender; cooperation
with CPS; the relationship of the non-offending mother with the perpetrator;
characteristics of the abuse and of the investigator; and maternal capacity to
protect, based on assessments of substance abuse, mental health problems,

use of prescription drugs for anxiety, depression or psychosis, and intimate partner violence. From the perceptions of caseworkers "every mother who was substantiated knew about the abuse before the investigation began, and 96.7 percent (thirty out of thirty-one) of these mothers did not consistently act protectively" (Coohey 2006: 78). Knowing and acting protectively were sometimes overlooked if other insights suggested that the child was not at immediate high risk. In these situations, "consistently believing, supporting, and not having a personal challenge, such as a drug or alcohol problem, could have influenced [the CPS] decision to not substantiate some mothers" (Coohey 2006: 78). Workers' perceptions of mothers having knowledge of the abuse were taken at face value. Given that only very few mothers know about the sexual abuse before it is disclosed (Faller 1990; Margolin 1992; Myer 1985), it seems rather incredible that *all* mothers were thought to know about the abuse in *all* substantiated cases. An accurate presentation would explicitly state that it was actually the perception of CPS workers that "every mother who was substantiated knew about the abuse before the investigation began" (Coohey 2006: 78).

Building on Coohey (2006), Shadoin and Carnes (2006) further elaborated on four broad issues warranting more detailed consideration in order to better inform policy decisions:

> One area in which more knowledge is needed is that of how decisions on substantiation for … failure to protect … are influenced at the levels of agency policy and individual cases by variations in statutory definitions of child abuse and neglect and in published guidance for CPS investigators. (Shadoin and Carnes 2006: 85)

A second issue is "how much and what type of education, training, and experience is needed by the average CPS investigator and CPS supervisor in order to make reasonably accurate substantiation decisions" (Shadoin and Carnes 2006: 86). Training varies substantially by state and county in the U.S. as it does in other Anglo-American CPS jurisdictions. Third, the state of knowledge regarding risk assessment measures of failure to protect needs consideration. "A fourth area of interest … entails determining what is known about nonoffending caregivers that can help to inform the CPS substantiation decision process and what remains to be learned about the … [nonoffending caregiver] that may be relevant to making … failure to protect decisions" (Shadoin and Carnes 2006: 91). As of yet, there is very little material to guide decisions on failure to protect. Decisions based on discrete categorizations of "protective" or "not protective" belie the complexity of parenting and culpability, and clearly, as Shadoin and Carnes (2006: 94) conclude, "children and their nonoffending caregivers deserve a more sophisticated, nuanced conceptualization" of failure to protect.

Coohey and O'Leary's (2008) study elaborated on understanding why some non-offending mothers consistently protected their children following disclosure of sexual abuse. Based on analyses of CPS investigators' reports from one county in a mid-western U.S. state, the authors compared forty-eight cases randomly selected from 144, in which non-offending mothers offered consistent protection, to thirty-seven cases in which non-offending mothers did not consistently protect. Seven variables explained between 47 and 63 percent of the variance in consistent protection: believing the child was sexually abused; not being a victim of intimate partner violence herself; asking her child about the sexual abuse; not having directly seen or heard the abuse; refraining from asking the abuser about the sexual abuse; attributing responsibility to the abuser; and having had knowledge of the abuse for one year or less. While these results cannot be generalized, this study contributes to an understanding of CPS workers' views of the factors related to non-offending mothers' protective efforts and actions while highlighting some of the complexities that need to be accounted for in both research and practice.

Bolen's (2007, 2010) secondary analyses of the *National Survey of Child and Adolescent Wellbeing* (NSCAW) also sought to determine the factors predicting failure to protect. The NSCAW is a random national survey of over 5,000 children across the U.S. In this survey, approximately 700 children had a report of sexual abuse, came into the system over a one-year period, and were followed for five years. Data were collected via questionnaires and interviews with CPS workers, non-offending guardians (mostly mothers) and children regarding the level of protection and failure to protect. Non-offending mothers were more likely to be considered to have failed to protect when the following factors were present: their children were categorized as "Other" (mostly Native American) versus Caucasian; previous reports of maltreatment had been made; and the caseworker was Latino, or to a lesser extent Caucasian, as compared to Black. When variables regarding CPS workers' perceptions of the non-offending mother were also considered, a determination of failure to protect was more likely to occur when CPS workers held a bachelor degree (rather than a master's) and when they believed the caregiver had unrealistic expectations of the child. This finding suggests that racial discrimination and educational achievement likely infiltrate failure-to-protect decisions.

Moving Forward

Notwithstanding the mandate of CPS, responsibility for protecting children and youths from sexual abuse continues to fall on the shoulders of non-offending guardians, most often their mothers. As we have shown, protection is not a benign activity; indeed, failure to adequately protect, in the U.S. and in many other jurisdictions, is cause for civil or criminal charges, scrutiny of these non-offending mothers, and possible loss of guardianship of one's children. The practice of ensuring the protection of children, it seems, is deeply embedded within the fabric of CPS but has questionable assumptions about non-offending maternal belief and the relationship between postdisclosure support and children's well-being. We set out to shake up these assumptions by highlighting what we know about the area even though this complex, incomplete, and inconsistent knowledge base has evaded practice consciousness. Though still inadequate, what we do know ought to compel us to understand belief, support, and protection as processes that are variable rather than fixed or static, and certainly far from simple to define or categorize. As has been discussed, supportive and protective non-offending mothers may at the same time be hesitant, inconsistent, and confused, but such ambivalence does not necessarily equate to failure to protect, inaction, or lack of support.

To regard the protection process as multi-layered with possible contradictory positions is to enter into child protection practice in a dramatically different way. CPS practices ought to begin with a more sophisticated, nuanced understanding of protection and its corollary, failure to protect. This approach takes as its starting point an explicit recognition of belief and support as processes through which individual non-offending mothers take in, evaluate, and reconcile evidence of risk to their children in the context of sexual abuse, even if such evidence is contradictory. It asks workers to consciously challenge a dichotomous conception of protection, that is, either protective or having failed to protect, because such a conception conceals the "figuring it out" process for many mothers and denies the reality that most non-offending mothers are or become supportive.

We contend that children who have experienced sexual abuse ought to remain under the care of their non-offending mothers even when these women are struggling to be supportive. This idea of struggling to believe and support, and hence protect, asks CPS workers to let go of mythical assumptions of immediate and full support and to embrace the concept of "supportive enough," "good enough," or developing protection. This approach builds on research that reveals widespread maternal support when room is made for ambivalence, and accepting non-offending maternal responses of ambivalence and uncertainty after disclosure as normal. This approach also contests the underlying notion of maternal perfection when it comes to protection, with the implication being that, if non-offending mothers can act in a supportive enough manner, even when they feel ambivalent, then removal of their children from their care may not be necessary as a protective practice. This implies, however, that CPS works with law enforcement to remove the offender from the home. If that cannot occur, then it behooves CPS to seek safe housing for the mother and her children, just as CPS might for intimate partner violence victims and their families.

Ambivalence is predicted by factors including maternal distress, style of attachment, preoccupation with the abuse, relationship with the perpetrator, partner income, total relationship stressors, and stressors since disclosure. Those factors associated with the mother's partner are of particular interest because they suggest that ambivalence is more typical or normative when the mothers' costs of disclosure increase. Caseworkers need to be especially vigilant to the losses and costs related to disclosure, as well as to the stressors upon the non-offending mother. It has been shown, for example, that providing resources has an impact independent of lessening stressors (Ganzel, Morris, and Wethington 2010). Recognizing that the aftermath of disclosure for non-offending mothers "is like a tsunami washing over me," as one mother in Bolen's research put it, may increase workers' empathy and sensitivity to the experiences of non-offending mothers. In turn, as non-offending mothers are provided needed material resources (food, shelter, income support) that reduce some of the more tangible costs of the disclosure to them and their families, are offered emotionally supportive resources (peer support groups), and are made to feel more competent and empowered, it is likely that maternal ambivalence will decrease. Finally, if workers become more aware of the potential factors that contribute to a mother's post-disclosure ambivalence, they could be incited to ask more questions about her circumstances and be better able to respond to her particular challenges and needs without judgment.

In essence, what is required is a shift in focus from assessing failures to protect to assessing protective behaviours. This approach means explicitly taking into account what mothers do to safeguard their children even if their actions do not coincide with institutionally constructed, if not predetermined, expectations of protection. This suggestion asks that CPS workers view the non-offending mother as protective and supportive, rather than assuming that she either knew of, or colluded with, the abuse and did nothing. This should compel practitioners to let go of the persistent assumptions that all mothers knew and failed to protect.

To date, supportive responses from the non-offending parent are considered fundamental to determining risk and developing protection plans. Supportive responses, that is, protection, are also thought to mediate the effects of sexual abuse, its disclosure, investigation, and treatment on children. Nonetheless, this area raises many questions and needs further clarification. What are supportive responses? What specific symptoms are reduced as a result of support? Under what conditions is protection maintained? In CPS practice, maternal support should be seen as complex and changing; this dynamic ought to be taken into account in workers' conceptualization and assessment. Similarly, workers should understand that ambivalence is a normal response to what is a typically horrific time for non-offending mothers, while also realizing that it can and does occur side-by-side with protective and supportive behaviours of the non-offending mother.

We end with a final observation. Without doubt, the concept of non-offending guardians or non-offending caregivers used so often in research and practice really means non-offending mothers. Yet only 7 to 8 percent of all child sexual abuse is perpetrated by a father or father-figure (Bolen 2001; Krane 1994, 2003; see also Chapter 2 of this book), which means that non-offending fathers are potentially available as supportive resources for their children and their partners. This potential needs to be tapped in CPS practice, but to do so would further challenge the expectations of mothers and open up protective possibilities that contest the assumptions upon which practice has unfolded.

References

Berkowitz, Carol D. 1997. "Failure to Protect: A Spectrum of Culpability: A Commentary." *Journal of Child Sexual Abuse* 6, 1.

Bolen, Rebecca M. 2001. *Child Sexual Abuse: Its Scope and Our Failure*. New York: Kluwer Academic/Plenum Press.

____. 2002. "Guardian Support of Sexually Abused Children: A Definition in Search of a Construct." *Trauma, Violence, & Abuse* 3, 1.

____. 2007. *Final Report: What Happens to Children after Their Sexual Abuse Is Substantiated?* Washington, DC: Department of Health & Human Services, Administration for Children & Families (Grant No. 90PH0005/01).

____. 2010. *Failure to Protect in Cases of Child Sexual Abuse: Findings from a National Random Longitudinal Sample of Cases of Reported Maltreatment. Failing to Protect: Moving beyond Gendered Responses.* University of Victoria, School of Social Work. Victoria, British Columbia, Canada.

Bolen, Rebecca M., Adrienne Dessel, and Julie Sutter. 2011 under review. *Parents Will Be Parents: How Nonoffending Parents and Other Guardians Define Protection, Safety and Decision-Making Following Disclosure of Sexual Abuse.* Manuscript Under Review.

Bolen, Rebecca M., and Kellie Gergely. 2011. *A Critical Review of Caregiver Support and Postdisclosure Impairment in Sexually Abused Children: Are We Ready for a Meta-Analysis?* Manuscript submitted for publication.

Bolen, Rebecca M., and J. Leah Lamb. 2004. "Ambivalence in Nonoffending Guardians after Child Sexual Abuse Disclosure." *Journal of Interpersonal Violence* 19, 2.

____. 2007. "Can Nonoffending Mothers of Sexually Abused Children be Both Ambivalent and Supportive?" *Child Maltreatment* 12, 2.

Briere, John, and Diana Elliott. 2003. "Prevalence and Psychological Sequelae of Childhood Physical and Sexual Abuse in a General Population Sample of Men and Women." *Child Abuse & Neglect* 27.

Coohey, Carol. 2006. "How CPS Investigators Decide to Substantiate Mothers for Failure-to-Protect in Sexual Abuse Cases." *Journal of Child Sexual Abuse* 15, 4.

Coohey Carol, and Patrick O'Leary. 2008. "Mothers' Protection of Their Children after Discovering They Have Been Sexually Abused: An Information-Processing

Perspective." *Child Abuse & Neglect* 32, 2.

De Jong, Allan R. 1988. "Maternal Responses to the Sexual Abuse of Their Children." *Pediatrics* 81, 1.

Dietz, Christine A., and John L. Craft. 1980. "Family Dynamics of Incest: A New Perspective." *Social Casework: The Journal of Contemporary Social Work* 61, 10.

Elliott, Ann, and Connie Carnes. 2001. "Reactions of Nonoffending Parents to the Sexual Abuse of Their Child: A Review of the Literature." *Child Maltreatment* 6, 4.

Everson, Mark D., Wanda M. Hunter, Desmond K. Runyan, Gail A. Edelsohn, and Martha Coulter. 1989. "Maternal Support Following Disclosure of Incest." *American Journal of Orthopsychiatry* 59, 2.

Faller, Kathleen C. 1990. "Sexual Abuse by Paternal Caretakers: A Comparison of Abusers Who Are Biological Fathers in Intact Families, Stepfathers and Noncustodial Fathers." In Anne L. Horton, Barry L. Johnson, Lynn M. Roundy, and Doran Williams (eds.), *The Incest Perpetrator: A Family Member No One Wants to Treat*. Newbury Park, CA: Sage.

Finkelhor, David, and Gerald T. Hotaling. 1984. "Sexual Abuse in the National Incidence Study of Child Abuse and Neglect: An Appraisal." *Child Abuse & Neglect* 8.

Finkelhor, David, Gerard T. Hotaling, I.A. Lewis, and Christine Smith. 1990. "Sexual Abuse in a National Survey of Adult Men and Women: Prevalence, Characteristics, and Risk Factors." *Child Abuse & Neglect* 14, 9.

Fugate, Jeanne A. 2001. "Who's Failing Whom? A Critical Look at Failure-to-Protect Laws." *New York University Law Review*, 76.

Ganzel, Barbara L., Pamela A. Morris, and Elaine Wethington. 2010. "Allostasis and the Human Brain: Integrating Models of Stress From the Social and Life Sciences." *Psychological Review* 117, 1.

Hooper, Carol. 1997. "Child Sexual Abuse and the Regulation of Women: Variations on a Theme." In Laura L. O'Toole and Jessica R. Schiffman (eds.), *Gender Violence: Interdisciplinary Perspectives*. New York: New York University Press.

___. 1992. *Mothers Surviving Child Sexual Abuse*. New York: Tavistock.

Hooper, Carol, and Catherine Humphreys. 1998. "Women Whose Children Have Been Sexually Abused: Reflections of a Debate." *British Journal of Social Work* 28.

Johnson, Pauline A., Glynn R. Owens, M. Dewey, and Nadine E. Eisenberg. 1990. "Professionals' Attributions of Censure in Father-Daughter Incest." *Child Abuse & Neglect* 14.

Kelley, Susan J. 1990. "Parental Stress Response to Sexual Abuse and Ritualistic Abuse of Children in Day-Care Centers." *Nursing Research* 39, 1.

Krane, Julia. 2003. *What's Mother Got to Do With it?* Toronto: University of Toronto Press.

___. 1994. "The Transformation of Women Into Mother Protectors: An Examination of Child Protection Practices in Cases of Child Sexual Abuse." Doctoral thesis, University of Toronto.

Malloy, Lindsay C., and Thomas D. Lyon. 2006. "Caregiver Support and Child Sexual Abuse: Why Does it Matter?" *Journal of Child Sexual Abuse* 15, 4.

Margolin, Leslie. 1992. "Sexual Abuse by Grandparents." *Child Abuse & Neglect* 16.

Myer, Margaret H. 1985. "A New Look at Mothers of Incest Victims." *Journal of Social Work and Human Sexuality* 3.

Reidy, Thomas J., and Neil J. Hochstadt. 1993. "Attribution of Blame in Incest Cases: A Comparison of Mental Health Professionals." *Child Abuse & Neglect* 17.

Rogers, Paul, Michelle Davies, and Lisa J. Cottam. 2010. "Perpetrator Coercion, Victim Resistance and Respondent Gender: Their Impact on Blame Attributions in a Hypothetical Child Sexual Abuse Case." *Journal of Aggression, Conflict and Peace Research* 2, 3.

Russell, Diana E.H. 1983. "The Incidence and Prevalence of Intrafamilial and Extrafamilial Sexual Abuse of Female Children." *Child Abuse & Neglect* 7, 2.

Ryan, Patricia, Bruce L. Warren, and Peggy Weincek. 1991. "Removal of the Perpetrator Versus Removal of the Victim in Cases of Intrafamilial Child Sexual Abuse." In Dean D. Knudsen and Joan L. Miller (eds.), *Abused and Battered: Social and Legal Responses to Family Violence*. New York: Aldine de Gruyter.

Sedlak, Andrea J., Jane Mettenburg, Monica Basena, Ian Petta, Karla McPherson, Angela Greene, and Spencer Li. 2010. *Fourth National Incidence Study of Child Abuse and Neglect (NIS–4): Report to Congress*. Washington, DC: U.S. Department of Health and Human Services, Administration for Children and Families.

Shadoin, Amy L., and Connie N. Carnes. 2006. "Comments on *How Child Protective Services Investigators Decide to Substantiate Mother for Failure-to-Protect in Sexual Abuse Cases*." *Journal of Child Sexual Abuse* 15, 4.

Thériault, Chantal, Mireille Cyr, and John Wright. 2003. "Facteurs contextuels associés aux symptôms d'adolescentes victimes d'agression sexuelle intrafamiliale." *Child Abuse and Neglect* 27, 11.

U.S. Department of Health and Human Services, National Center on Child Abuse and Neglect. 2000. *Child Maltreatment 1998: Reports from the States to the National Child Abuse and Neglect Data System*. Washington, DC: U.S. Department of Health and Human Services.

Vieth, Victor L. 2006. "Commentary on *Child Protective Service Decide to Substantiate Mothers for Failure-to-Protect in Sexual Abuse Cases*." *Journal of Child Sexual Abuse*. 15, 4.

Vogeltanz, Nancy D., Sharon C. Wilsnack, T. Robert Harris, Richard W. Wilsnack, Stephen A. Wonderlich, and Arlinda F. Kristjanson. 1999. "Prevalence and Risk Factors for Childhood Sexual Abuse in Women: National Survey Findings." *Child Abuse & Neglect* 23, 6.

Wyatt, Gail E. 1985. "The Sexual Abuse of Afro-American and White-American Women in Childhood." *Child Abuse & Neglect* 9.

Wyatt, Gail E., Tamari B. Loeb, Beatriz Solis, Jennifer V. Carmona, and Gloria Romero. 1999. "The Prevalence and Circumstances of Child Sexual Abuse: Changes Across a Decade." *Child Abuse & Neglect* 23, 1.

5. Take a Chance on Me

Rethinking Risk and Maternal Failure to Protect in Cases of Child Sexual Abuse

Rosemary Carlton and Julia Krane

In courts of law, mothers are found guilty of having failed to protect their children from harms perpetrated by the men in their lives. Typical contemporary cyber headlines, such as "Mom accused of letting father beat children" (*Journal Gazette* June 4, 2009) and "Man Charged with Child Rape, Mother for Failure to Protect" (*Daily News Journal* May 18, 2011), attest to public outrage, not only about the abuse of children, but also about the explicit expectation of their mothers to have made the appropriate efforts to protect their children, by taking such measures as recognizing the abuse, understanding its effects on their children and stopping all contact with the abuser. Indeed, this expectation was the focus of two episodes of the *Dr. Phil Show*, on September 1 and 2 of 2011. Entitled "Forgiving the Unforgivable," the two-part series featured sisters Marita and Katrina, now in their late twenties, who were sexually abused by their stepfather when they were children. While it had been sixteen years since he was found guilty and imprisoned, the siblings struggled to find closure on their traumatic childhood. Katrina stated that she could not come to terms with how their "mother allowed me and my sister to be sexually molested by her ex-husband." Their memories of being served wine coolers and watching soft porn with both their mother and stepfather, being asked by their mother to show their developing breasts to their stepfather, and being kissed by their stepfather in front of other family members provided evidence to them that their mother knew what was happening and encouraged their stepfather's inappropriate behaviour. "What type of mother allows this to happen? Why didn't she stand up and say something? It's wrong," "I feel like my mother served me on a platter to a predator," and "why didn't you come in and save me?" stated the tormented sisters, aching for their mother to recognize their pain and suffering. They could not understand how their mother stood by her husband during the trial or why she requested that they apologize to him. Throughout the televised episodes, their mother was challenged to take responsibility for knowing about the abuse and failing to take steps to prevent or stop it. Her daughters sought an admission of, and an apology for, having failed to put their needs ahead of her marriage. A perusal of the well over 1,200 comments made on Dr. Phil's Facebook page following these episodes found not one empathic, sympathetic, or compassionate response about the mother. Despite having virtually no information about her circumstances or experiences, the public criticized this mother for being selfish, sick and ignorant, and clearly having failed to protect. While one would be hard pressed to forgive this mother's unforgivable inaction, in this chapter we suggest that child protection services (CPS) ought to make central an understanding of the emotional and material contexts for any potential protective efforts rather than allowing these factors to remain fully invisible, if not irrelevant.

As we laid out in Chapter 2, this taken-for-granted expectation of non-offending mothers as readily willing, capable, and best suited to protect their children from sexual abuse permeates child protection practices. This expectation is consistent with the principles of child protection legislation that privilege child safety and favour family autonomy, least intrusion, and stability in children's care; it is compatible with Eurocentric dominant ideologies of maternal perfection in terms of clairvoyance, omnipotence, and self-sacrificing nurturance. At the same time, however, the challenges facing non-offending mothers in the aftermath of disclosure of, and investigation into, allegations of child sexual abuse remain on the periphery. The fast-paced, time-bound, highly proceduralized, risk-averse climate in CPS simultaneously leaves non-offending mothers open to intense scrutiny while creating little opportunity for meaningful engagement with, and complex understandings of, them. In this chapter, we advocate for a shift in thinking about child protection practice in situations of sexual abuse and demonstrate the usefulness of inviting risk tolerance with non-offending mothers. By embracing a tolerance for risk as a potential source for an enhanced practice, we explore ways to work with non-offending mothers in the face of disclosure/investigation of child sexual abuse such that we might interrupt hasty and decontextualized assessment that mothers are failing to protect.

Risk Aversion in CPS Practice

We "live in a world saturated with and preoccupied by risk" (Webb 2006: 23). From 9/11 and Al Qaeda, to natural disasters and global warming, from the effects of unhealthy lifestyles to debt crises and global recessions, risk now pervades common parlance, bringing with it uncertainty, insecurity, and fear. Indeed, the field of practice in child protection has been shaped markedly by risk for the last thirty years. As noted in the introduction to this book, public inquiries following the tragic deaths of children under the supervision of local CPS authorities in Anglo-American CPS jurisdictions have spurred risk-avoidant child protection policies, procedures, and practices. Such inquiries revealed a number of thematic concerns with CPS: flawed communication in terms of record-keeping, inter-agency coordination, and information-sharing; inadequate assessments (i.e., integration of available information, recognition of warning signs, basis of decision-taking); limited staffing resources and irregular supervision; and inconsistent and inadequate compliance with policies and procedures and their interpretation on the front lines of practice (Reder and Duncan 2004). According to Reder and Duncan (2004: 97), CPS systems were plagued with all too many "inexperienced and unconfident" practitioners who were mandated to work "with extremely complex cases where the parents were chaotic, violent or suffering from mental health or substance abuse problems." Not surprisingly, the public inquiries following such tragedies contributed to creating an atmosphere of fear, blame, and defensiveness — experienced largely by front-line workers and the families with whom they work — within child protection systems (Ayre 2001; Littlechild 2009; Macdonald and Macdonald 2010; Munro 2004; Parton, Thorpe and Wattam 1997; Swift and Callahan 2009). This "blame culture," as Brown (2010: 1216) put it, is one wherein "social workers can be publicly named, shamed and sacked when mistakes are made."

Inquiries ensuing from child protection tragedies have brought about organizational reforms intended to standardize CPS practice, facilitate quick decision-making, and reduce uncertainty in calculating and managing risk to children. As has been well-documented, child protection systems were "bureaucratized," characterized by "increasingly detailed procedures and guidelines [including prescribed time frames for assessment and intervention], strengthened managerial control to ensure compliance, and steady erosion of the scope for individual professional judgment through use of standardized protocols, assessment frameworks and decision-making aids" that treated risk as identifiable, measurable, quantifiable, and ultimately preventable (Munro 2004: 533). As Rycos and Hughes (2003: 8) put it, risk assessment instruments were intended to "help practitioners more accurately determine the likelihood and potential severity of future occurrences of child abuse or neglect, based upon the presence of certain family characteristics or environmental conditions determined to be highly associated with recurrent child maltreatment." Organizational reforms, driven by a fear of the complexity of risky situations (Brown 2010), translated into procedures for overseeing worker accountability, information sharing, decision-making transparency, and case audit. Parton (2008: 259) concluded that the increased "emphasis on the need to collect, share, classify and store *information*" came at the expense of "coherent causal accounts ... [of clients] in their social context." In other words, CPS systems witnessed a shift in procedures and practices that brought the focus to the collection of forensic data in order to determine the nature and extent of risk to a child and the degree of intrusion by authorities into private families.

CPS practice as it has been transformed — with its emphasis on risk — assumes that parents are what Lupton (1999) and Kemshall (2006, 2010) might call rational actors: capable of weighing and avoiding risks and able to take in information relevant to risk in order to act in acceptable or expected ways;

to do otherwise is to be considered an irrational actor who is vulnerable to blame and likely to be subjected to regulatory interventions. Rational actors are envisioned as "free actors who are constrained only by their ignorance about the threat to which they may be exposed or their lack of self-efficacy in feeling able to do something about a risk" (Lupton 1999: 23). Swift and Callahan (2009: 222) observed that assessments of risk virtually always focus on the individual; as such, CPS interventions aimed at risk reduction have tended to centre on educating individual parents about what is needed in order for their children to be safe, and on charging them "with the responsibility to help themselves through solutions that continually monitor their efforts and extend social control over them." In other words, armed with the necessary information about the circumstances that gave rise to risk and the appropriate responses to resolve it, the parent, as a rational actor, is assumed to be in a position to make the right choice to protect her/his child. The "right choice" for a non-offending mother in the face of a disclosure of and investigation into child sexual abuse involves expressing belief in her child's allegations; choosing to support her child over the alleged abuser regardless of her relationship with him; ensuring no contact between the child and the alleged abuser; and collaborating with police and social work professionals to ensure the best interests and well-being of her child (Krane 2003).

CPS clients, as rational actors, are judged against particular and predetermined norms and ideologies of parenting and protection; they are made responsible for their decision making around risk and are rewarded for protection choices that are socially sanctioned as correct. Non-offending mothers' actions are viewed and scrutinized without consideration of the context within which they negotiate their responses to their children's disclosures. Those who make flawed or risky choices will be viewed as having failed to protect and subjected to further CPS involvement and regulation. As was discussed in Chapter 2 (Carlton and Krane), non-offending mothers in situations of child sexual abuse are expected to embrace White, Western, often middleclass, ideologies of motherhood that reify maternal omniscience, self-sacrifice, and unwavering devotion. Thus, those mothers found to be ambivalent or failing to protect will be scrutinized and closely monitored through formal protection plans that lay out the expectations of and methods for regulating risk that coincide with these dominant ideologies. Lupton (1999) conceptualized compliance as the acceptance and internalization of the objectives of organizational authorities. In the context of CPS, compliance for nonoffending mothers means demonstrating a capacity to immediately take on the expectation to protect one's child from risk — with little, if any, room for ambivalence or confusion and uncertainty — at all costs and irrespective of the social and emotional context of such protection.

The notion of the rational actor has been criticized for its deceptively narrow understanding of individual choice and action; its conception appears devoid of context, power and opportunity in individual experiences and negotiations of risk (Kemshall 2006, 2010; Lupton 1999). Kemshall (2010) argued that choices to address risk are not necessarily free. He suggested that individual decision making and actions related to risk are governed by influential discourses and ideologies as well as through institutional strategies and practices. "Choices, even to act more safely, can be heavily constrained … [and are] embedded in place, time and network" (Kemshall 2010: 1249). These kinds of critiques have led to the recasting of the rational actor as a social actor for whom there is no linear relationship between knowing about risk and freely choosing to act in a risk-taking or a risk-reducing manner. Rather, the decisions made by the social actor are contingent on the social and personal constraints and circumstances of her/his particular situation, social locations, and time. Gender, age, race, ethnicity, or sexual identity, as well as the effects of linguistic constraints, geographic isolation, citizenship status, colonization, cultural or community loyalties, and poverty, for example, can neither be elided nor reduced to a series of risk factors. Instead, these aspects of people's lives shape their understandings of risk, risk decision making, and their experience of risk-regulating interventions. This critique is particularly poignant in the field of child protection in Canada and the U.S., given the over-representation of visible minorities and Indigenous people and the multiple social problems — such as unemployment, poverty, substance misuse, mental health issues, and domestic violence — that figure prominently in the lives of CPS clients (Sedlak, McPherson and Das 2010; Trocmé et al. 2005; Trocmé et al. 2010).

A social actor is not a passive recipient of risk but is instead active in her/his interpretations and experiences of risk. As will be seen, we advocate for an understanding of non-offending mothers as social actors whose protective decisions may fluctuate and are contingent on context, time, and circumstance. Considering non-offending mothers as social actors does not preclude the possibility that they are responsible, to a certain extent, for the parenting choices they make, including seemingly non-protective ones. Swift and Callahan (2009: 228) proposed that, instead of "assigning blame and responsibility for problems that individuals did not create and simply cannot address on their own," CPS practice ought to examine and make efforts to address "imbalances between individual and social capacities and responsibilities for problems" when determining risk to children and deciding upon how best to intervene.

In looking back at the reforms to CPS in the last thirty years that have rendered risk as a central driving force, Macdonald and Macdonald (2010: 1180) aptly point out that they have been built upon "high-profile cases of low-probability events [that distort] decision making." The authors argued that such reforms cannot accurately assess and respond to risk in the vast majority of cases in which abuse or neglect is less obvious, maltreatment likely arises from a range of interacting factors, and there is no imminent risk of harm. In Munro's thorough analysis of CPS policy and practice since the 1970s in England, she remarked that these trends responded to the need to deal with uncertainty and to monitor the work of CPS practitioners. She pointed out that the risk management strategies instituted over the years could not eradicate risk but could contribute to reducing the probability of harm to children (Munro 2010). Given that children's needs are varied and complex, as are family circumstances, predicting and preventing child maltreatment of any sort will always be uncertain. Munro (2011a) saw this process as necessarily fallible, one that may err on the side of either over- or under-estimation of danger to a child. Titterton (2005) earlier noted that promises of risk elimination are misleading in that risk can never be completely removed from people's lives in the context of health and social services. Munro also considered the elimination of risk to be a false hope and asserted that, realistically, serious injury or even the death of a child may result "even when the quality of professional practice is high" (2011b: 38). According to Munro (2011b: 43), in this field, "there is no option of being risk averse since there is no absolutely safe option."

Embracing Risk for Innovation

The latest reviews of CPS in Anglo-American jurisdictions are beginning to call for innovations that engage with the uncertainties surrounding risk to children and the means to safeguard their protection in a more thoughtful way on the front lines of practice. For example, following the brutal beating and subsequent death of ten-year-old Nubia Barahona on February 11, 2011, in the state of Florida, an investigative panel not only ascribed blame to the assigned social workers but were explicitly critical of the Department of Children and Family Services (DCFS) system. The panellists argued that administrative and bureaucratic procedures such as checking off items on a standardized form to assess risk, or "observing children during a brief visit, or conducting a pro forma evaluation without considering all the issues that impact a child do not eliminate the need for reasoned judgment" (Lawrence, Martínez and Sewell 2011: 6). Lawrence et al. suggested, instead, the need to infuse DCFS with the most skilled, well-trained, and caring child protection professionals, capable of engaging in critical thinking and drawing on practice wisdom and common sense. These kinds of sentiments permeated the most recent reviews undertaken in the U.K. (Laming 2009; Munro 2010, 2011a, 2011b), wherein collecting data on abuse and neglect and practising from a technological approach to identify and manage risk were seen to constrict complex understandings of children's circumstances and thus compromise professional judgement. Rather than maintaining the current emphasis on adherence to rules, processes, and procedures, Munro (2011b: 87) argued for the need to elevate direct practice:

> Knowing what data to collect is useful, but it is equally useful to know *how* to collect them; how to get through the front door and create a relationship where the parent is willing to tell you anything about the child and family; how to ask challenging questions about very sensitive matters; and how to develop the expertise to sense that the child or parent is being evasive. Above all, it is important to be able to work directly with children ... and their families to understand their experiences, worries, hopes and dreams, and help them change.

To do so requires, at the minimum, time. In Quebec, for example, CPS workers are required to complete formal decisions about risk in cases of child sexual abuse within four days. However, in urgent cases wherein the child's protection cannot be assured — usually because there is no guarantee that the alleged abuser will have no contact with the child — decisions would be expected to be made within twenty-four hours, if not sooner. Ultimately, this means that the non-offending mother has to step up to the protection plate and do what is expected of her. Munro's most recent review of CPS organizations and practices (2011b) called for revisions of prescribed time frames for assessment in statutory practice to allow for a more thorough and concentrated understanding of child protection concerns and risk to children. She argued that because the underlying principle of timeliness is important, it ought to be applied to "the whole process of helping a child or young person, not just the early stage of assessment" (Munro 2011b: 7). Indeed, Munro's (2011b: 10) recommendations for change highlight a CPS system that "values professional expertise" over adherence to rigid time scales as seen in the following set of suggestions:

- remove the distinction between initial and core assessments and the associated time scales in respect of these assessments, replacing them with the decisions that are required to be made by qualified social workers when developing an understanding of children's needs and making and implementing a plan to safeguard and promote their welfare;
- [give attention] to:
  - timeliness in the identification of children's needs and provision of help;
  - the quality of the assessment to inform next steps to safeguard and promote children's welfare; and

- the effectiveness of the help provided;
- [and] give … [CPS agencies] the responsibility to draw on research and theoretical models to inform local practice. (Munro 2011b: 10)

These suggestions are, in a sense, "a re-professionalisation of social work — a move away from mechanism and rote" (Broadhurst et al. 2010: 1061). Understanding that the needs and circumstances of children and their families are contextual, varied, multi-faceted, and changing, Munro (2011b) suggested a professional practice free from prescriptive procedures and accountable only to the primary mandate of protection and the following principles that underpin good practice: skilful engagement and communication with children and parents; and the ability to make complex interpretations about circumstances, problems and needs, while recognizing the potential impact of personal context, such as the presence of domestic violence, mental illness, or substance misuse, on the security and development of children. Other factors which need recognition and assessment include social context, i.e., poverty, housing, racial discrimination, linguistic or geographic isolation, citizenship status, colonization history, etc.; commitment to developing purposeful relationships with children and their families; capacity to take a comprehensive family history and use this information when making decisions about a child's safety and welfare; knowledge about child development and attachment as well as the potential impact of child abuse or neglect on both; and competence to present and explain the reasoning behind protective interventions and decisions to diverse audiences.

Taking Chances with Mothers to Rethink Failure to Protect

Within today's risk-averse climate, wherein the protection of children is paramount and assessment and intervention tend to be pursued in a bureaucratized, procedurally delineated, fast-paced, and urgent manner, practice with non-offending mothers in situations of child sexual abuse involves a narrow concentration on their abilities and failures to comply with normative and socially sanctioned conceptions of maternal protection. As elaborated in Chapter 2 (Carlton and Krane), the focus on maternal protection of child victims of sexual abuse is well-established in CPS practice. Coupled with organizational fear of making mistakes that could result in further abuse or harm to children, non-offending mothers deemed to be ambivalent or failing to protect their children are, as noted elsewhere in this book, subject to scrutiny and surveillance and are vulnerable to having their children removed from their care. Contrary to the core guiding principles of CPS practice — support for family autonomy, least intrusion, and promotion of children's secure attachments with primary caregivers — this type of scenario likely sets up defensive practices and adversarial relationships with the very women relied upon to protect their children in the aftermath of sexual abuse. Drawing on recent calls for innovation, we propose a practice that diverges from time-bound and proceduralized determinations of non-offending mothers as "protective," "ambivalent," or "failing to protect" and, instead, suggest one that allows for taking risks with non-offending mothers outside the boxes of such discrete categorizations. Borrowing from Munro's recommendations, our approach embraces the notion of "timeliness" and entails engaging in meaningful relationships with non-offending mothers, thereby allowing for more flexibility and fluidity in assessment and decision making. Here we envision a practice that promotes workers' use of professional skills and judgment to generate complex understandings of non-offending mothers not as rational actors but as social actors whose protective efforts are shaped by their social locations and personal contexts.

To elaborate, instead of adherence to strict time frames for meeting procedural requirements, an innovative approach insists upon a commitment to "timeliness." Munro proposed that workers take the time needed to make the appropriate decisions for each specific case at particular moments in time. Timeliness means slowing down the investigation and decision making around a child's safety, placing the emphasis on quality of assessment rather than efficiency in response time. In thinking back to the case illustration in Chapter 1, potential risk of further sexual abuse to Tammy was identified because her mother, Tabatha, was once again in contact with her partner. Slowing down this investigation means figuring what might be going on for Tabatha at this time. While she appeared to take a protective stance at the onset following her daughter's disclosure, her seemingly unprotective choice to have contact with the abuser will be an important point for exploration by her CPS worker. Hence, a worker might ask "what is her experience of her daughter's disclosure?" "What circumstances or obstacles are influencing her protective actions?" "What is her understanding of CPS practices and expectations?" This approach to time is predicated on an understanding of the assessment of protection — or failure to protect — as dynamic and gradual versus static and fixed in the moment. It assumes that the assessment of protection during an initial investigation is a beginning — rather than a final — determination of a mother's capacity to offer protection. As Munro (2004) saw it, assessing protection concerns ought to open opportunities for dialogue and generate working hypotheses over certainty about risk to a child as evidenced by maternal protection or failure.

Borrowing from Munro's vision of reinterpreting risk assessment, we suggest that the results of forensic investigations ought to be subject to constant critical review, again underscoring the possibility of movement from the fixed categorizations of protective or ambivalent or failing to protect.

Exploring protection or failure to protect in this way embraces the possibility of its evolution and endorses an expanded view of protection. Here we imagine workers beginning their investigation with an acknowledgement of the potential for change. A worker might let Tabatha, for example, know that non-offending mothers' experiences of finding their way through their children's disclosures, and the effects on their daily lives and relationships, are likely to change and may well run the gamut between seemingly protective and not protective. This appreciation of protection as a process is based on an understanding that the non-offending mother's circumstances and needs vis-à-vis the protection of her child may vary over time. Recognizing that a non-offending mother protects her child at her own pace means she may need time to come to terms with her child's sexual abuse and all that it entails.

Engaging with non-offending mothers in a timely manner, instead of the current procedurally driven, time-bound approach, includes giving space to deeper understandings of the emotional and material contexts within which mothers are able to protect. Bringing this kind of practice to life encourages workers to use their professional skills, practice wisdom, and critical reflections to work with non-offending mothers in a different way. Drawing on Davies et al.'s (2007) mothering narrative, we suggest inviting non-offending mothers into intense conversations about themselves and their own accounts of their experiences right from the start. At the crucial moment of beginning an investigation, the various facets of the non-offending mother's life ought to be made deeply meaningful in the assessment and development of a protection plan. Here, the worker actively listens for a mother's reactions to her child's disclosure and the sudden involvement of police and child protection authorities in her life, as well as the emotional, relational, and material consequences that unfold in the aftermath. Exploring the effects of the disclosure and ensuing investigation from the non-offending mother's perspective enables the worker to talk with her about where she is at with respect to believing, supporting, and protecting her child. This narrative approach unfolds with a genuine grasp of the uncertainty and confusion that are all too frequently part and parcel of the "normal circumstance of the chaos and impact of [her] child's disclosure" (Bolen and Lamb 2004: 185). In other words, engaging non-offending mothers around protection takes into account a range of maternal reactions — such as the disruption, ambivalence, and distress, already noted in preceding chapters — as expected responses to child sexual abuse. Such an approach provides an understanding of the emotional and material factors that shape her experience of the disclosure and its immediate aftermath, and integrates this complex understanding in assessing the need for protection and initiating immediate protection plans.

Embarking upon a mothering narrative diverges from traditional forensic investigations that aim to identify risk factors as evidence for capacity to protect. Kemshall (2010: 1255) expressed scepticism about risk assessment tools and procedures for investigating and determining risk in that they focus on monitoring and information exchange "at the expense of understanding, problem solving and client engagement"; they transform clients "into repositories of risk factors." Acknowledging this critique, we suggest a practice that treats information garnered through mothering narratives as providing indispensable insights needed to formulate informed protection plans. Thus, rather than evaluating a mother's protective efforts as acceptable and socially sanctioned or risky and flawed, protection planning places her efforts within her particular opportunities and context. Planning requires really knowing a mother in contextual detail. Who is Tabatha? Is she situated in an urban centre or in a remote rural location? What is her citizenship status? Is she reliant on her partner for sponsorship? Is she Indigenous, painfully aware of being seen as fulfilling the stereotype of the neglectful, passive, and non-protective Indigenous mother? How does Tabatha manage with Tammy and maybe her other children? Upon what source of income does she rely, and in what conditions does she live? These questions represent the tip of the iceberg in terms of really getting to know a mother facing decisions around protection. It is not hard to imagine that a mother's world is disintegrating around her when faced with a disclosure of, and investigation into, child sexual abuse. What she may have believed to be stable in her life — her child's safety and innocence, her intimate relationship, and her own parenting — are no longer necessarily secure. Indeed some, if not most, mothers will experience life in the aftermath of child sexual abuse disclosure as worse and not better.

Giving space to a mother's expression of her emotional and material context means not just listening but hearing her without judgment while taking into consideration what supports would assist her in the protection of her child. The worker listens for the details of the mother's actions upon hearing of her child's sexual abuse and explicitly recognizes the efforts she has made to protect her child, whatever they may be. As Bolen and Krane (Chapter 4) demonstrate, most mothers act or come to act protectively. To refrain from really understanding who the mother is and what she needs at this moment in time is to run the risk of alienating her as a needed resource to protect (Krane 2003). On the other hand, involving her deeply in the assessment and development of a protection plan is to live up to the principles of family autonomy and least intrusion.

Committing time to a narrative approach aims to promote realistic, suitable, and attainable protection plans that are flexible and consistent with non-offending mothers' actual contextualized lives. As such, protection plans can be revisited, revised, and renegotiated. This approach might mean tolerating a certain degree of risk and uncertainty. This requires workers to be aware of where they draw the line about risk in each particular situation, recognize that this line may well differ from that which is drawn by the non-offending mother and even her child, and explicitly own this position on risk. The worker might be clear with Tabatha in that she is worried about Tammy's safety. Owning one's position on risk is meant to open dialogue and maybe even negotiation around tolerance for risk and drawing the risk line. This approach is quite different from a worker drawing on CPS legislation to impose a position about risk to the child and hence, a non-offending mother's expectation to act protectively. Other than those instances in which there are obvious and serious protection concerns, protection may be pursued with a mother who is struggling with her child's disclosure and its effects. Instead of scrutinizing non-offending mothers for their willingness and ability to comply with prescribed notions of protection, we propose collaborating with non-offending mothers to make joint decisions around protection that are based on information derived from their narratives. Certainly this route to protection necessitates intensive worker involvement with the hope that supportive planning will not be experienced as coercive intrusion. This type of collaborative practice is by no means easily accomplished, particularly with Indigenous communities, which have historically experienced CPS as enacting a colonial code which brings with it humiliation and oppression. Similarly, as noted by Alaggia (2002), such practice is also complicated by culture and religion with respect to potential differences in belief systems, parenting practices, and cultural loyalties.

Spending time, taking account of complexity, recognizing the potential for protection to be an ongoing, changing process takes to heart the principles upon which CPS practice is founded. Embracing a practice that privileges time for understanding and responding stands in contrast to current CPS practices that do not facilitate the building of helping relationships. In current CPS practice, the emphasis is on identifying and reducing risk to vulnerable children, workers' adherence to specific agency procedures and time frames, narrow interpretations of regulatory frameworks, and a persistent limited access to scarce resources (Brown 2010; Darlington, Healy and Feeney 2010; Maiter et al. 2006; Palmer, Maiter and Manji 2006; Spratt 2001).

Supporting Risk Tolerance versus Risk Aversion

Research tells us time and again that fostering helping relationships — wherein CPS clients feel safe enough to offer honest accounts about their circumstances without fear of being judged as posing a risk or failing to protect — is essential to successful outcomes but is complicated by the reality of the institutional power which can be wielded by CPS. CPS clients, even those who consider their relationships as collaborative, report engaging with their workers with a great deal of caution given the realization that their workers are representatives of an organization believed to hold absolute power

(Dumbrill 2006). Parents' perceptions of CPS as all-powerful are heightened by the prevailing "high-risk, low-probability" framework or what Dale (2004: 144) described as practice driven by "a 'worst scenario' perspective." This kind of practice was experienced as coercion to comply with protection plans that seem to be disproportionate to the nature and seriousness of the incident under investigation. Although CPS is viewed as a powerful entity by parents, they appreciate workers who listen attentively, communicate clearly, encourage cooperation, and demonstrate caring and empathy without judgment (Dale 2004; Maiter et al. 2006; Spratt and Callan 2004). This commitment to developing genuinely helping relationships has been noted by parents to be undertaken by workers who go "beyond the procedural requirements of their work" (Spratt and Callan 2004: 214). An approach such as ours, one that views meaningful relationships as part of — as opposed to going beyond — everyday practice, requires significant organizational change.

Historically, changes to CPS practices have been ruled by fears of making mistakes and a desire to manage risk. Moving away from the safety of formalized procedures and risk assessment strategies to a CPS practice that tolerates — rather than avoids — uncertainties around risk when working with non-offending mothers in situations of sexual abuse cannot be left to individual workers who seemingly resist institutional ideologies, strategies, and practices. Tolerating uncertainty around risk is based on an organizational acceptance that risk can never completely be eradicated from any situation. It means providing organizational support for practising in a manner that is in opposition to a worst-case perspective. Thus, with the exception of the extreme and most obvious cases, practice involves carrying some uncertainty and allowing for fluidity and flexibility in assessment and protection planning. Here, we advocate for CPS agencies to adopt an ideological shift away from the mythical notion of non-offending mothers as ready, willing, and able to make rational choices to reduce risk and ensure immediate protection, to one that understands non-offending mothers as social actors whose protective decisions are contingent on time and circumstance rather than evidence of flawed or risky choices.

References

Alaggia, Ramona. 2002. "Cultural and Religious Influences in Maternal Response to Intrafamilial Child Sexual Abuse: Charting New Territory for Research and Treatment." *Journal of Sexual Abuse* 10, 2.

Ayre, Patrick. 2001. "Child Protection and the Media: Lessons from the Last Three Decades." *British Journal of Social Work* 31, 6.

Bell, Mark. 2011. "Man Charged with Child Rape, Mother for Failure to Protect." *Daily News Journal*, May 18.

Bolen, Rebecca M., and Jan Leah Lamb. 2000. "Ambivalence of Nonoffending Guardians after Child Sexual Abuse Disclosure." *Journal of Interpersonal Violence*

19, 2.

Broadhurst, Karen, Chris Hall, Dave Wastell, Sue White, and Andy Pithouse. 2010. "Risk, Instrumentalism and the Humane Project in Social Work: Identifying the *Informal* Logics of Risk Management in Children's Statutory Services." *British Journal of Social Work* 40, 4.

Brown, Louise. 2010. "Balancing Risk and Innovation to Improve Social Work Practice." *British Journal of Social Work* 40, 4.

Dale, Peter. 2004. "'Like a Fish in a Bowl': Parents' Perceptions of Child Protection Services." *Child Abuse Review* 13, 2.

Darlington, Yvonne, Karen Healy, and Judith A. Feeney. 2010. "Challenges in Implementing Participatory Practice in Child Protection: A Contingency Approach." *Children and Youth Services Review* 32, 7.

Davies, Linda, Julia Krane, Sara Collings, and Sharon Wexler. 2007. "Developing Mothering Narratives in Child Protection Practice." *Journal of Social Work Practice* 21, 1.

Dumbrill, Gary. 2006. "Parental Experience of Child Protection Intervention: A Qualitative Study." *Child Abuse and Neglect* 30, 1.

Journal Gazette. 2009. "Mom Accused of Letting Father Beat Children." June 4. <journalgazette.net/article/20090604/LOCAL07/306049913/1043/LOCAL07>.

Kemshall, Hazel. 2006. "Crime and Risk." In Peter Taylor-Gooby and Jens Zinn (eds.), *Risk in Social Science*. Oxford: Oxford University Press.

___. 2010. "Risk Rationalities in Contemporary Social Work Policy and Practice." *British Journal of Social Work* 40, 4.

Krane, Julia. 2003. *What's Mother Got to Do with It? Protecting Children from Sexual Abuse*. Toronto: University of Toronto Press.

Lawrence, David, Roberto Martínez, and James Sewell. 2011. *The Nubia Report: The Investigative Panel's Findings and Recommendations*. Florida: Department of Children and Families.

Littlechild, Brian. 2009. "Child Protection Social Work: Risks of Fears and Fears of Risk — Impossible Tasks from Impossible Goals?" In David Denney (ed.), *Living in Dangerous Times: Fear, Insecurity, Risk and Social Policy*. West Sussex: Wiley-Blackwell.

Lord Laming. 2009. *The Protection of Children in England: A Progress Report*. London: Stationery Office.

Lupton, Deborah. 1999. *Risk*. London: Routledge.

Macdonald, Geraldine, and Kenneth Macdonald. 2010. "Safeguarding: A Case for Intelligent Risk Management." *British Journal of Social Work* 40, 4.

Maiter, Sarah, Sally Palmer, and Shehenaz Manji. 2006. "Strengthening Social Worker-Client Relationships in Child Protective Services: Addressing Power Imbalances and 'Ruptured' Relationships." *Qualitative Social Work* 5, 2.

Munro, Eileen. 2004. "A Simpler Way to Understand the Results of Risk Assessment Instruments." *Children and Youth Services Review* 26, 9.

___. 2010. *The Munro Review of Child Protection — Part One: A Systems Analysis*. London: Department of Education.

___. 2011a. *The Munro Review of Child Protection — Interim Report: A Child's Journey*. London: Department of Education.

___. 2011b. *The Munro Review of Child Protection — Final Report: A Child-centred System*. London: Department of Education.

Palmer, Sally, Sarah Maiter, and Shehenaz Manji. 2006. "Parents' Experiences with Child Protective Services." *Child and Youth Services Review* 28, 7.

Parton, Nigel. 2008. "Changes in the Form of Knowledge in Social Work: From the 'Social' to the 'Informational'?" *British Journal of Social Work* 38, 2.

Parton, Nigel, David Thorpe, and Corinne Wattam. 1997. *Child Protection: Risk and the Moral Order*. London: Macmillan Press.

Reder, Peter, and Sylvia Duncan. 2004. "Making the Most of the Victoria Climbié Inquiry Report." *Child Abuse Review* 13, 2.

Rycos, Judith S., and Ronald C. Hughes. 2003. *Issues in Risk Assessment in Child Protective Services: Policy White Paper*. Columbus, OH: North American Resource Center for Child Welfare, Center for Child Welfare Policy.

Sedlak, Andrea, Karla McPherson, and Barnali Das. 2010. *Supplementary Analyses of Race Differences in Child Maltreatment Rates in the NIS-4*. Washington, DC: U.S. Department of Health and Human Services, Administration on Children, Youth and Families.

Spratt, Trevor. 2001. "The Influence of Child Protection Practice Orientation on Child Welfare Practice." *British Journal of Social Work* 31, 6: 933–54.

Spratt, Trevor, and Jackie Callan. 2004. "Parents' Views on Social Work Interventions in Child Welfare Cases." *British Journal of Social Work* 34, 2.

Swift, Karen, and Marilyn Callahan. 2009. *At Risk: Social Justice in Child Welfare and Other Human Services*. Toronto: University of Toronto Press.

Titterton, Mike. 2005. *Risk and Risk Taking in Health and Social Welfare*. London: Jessica Kingsley Publishers.

Trocmé, Nico, Barbara Fallon, Bruce MacLaurin, Joanne Daciuk, Caroline Felstiner, Tara Black, Lil Tonmyr, Cindy Blackstock, Ken Barter, Daniel Turcotte, and Richard Cloutier. 2005. *Canadian Incidence Study of Reported Child Abuse and Neglect — 2003: Major Findings*. Ottawa: National Clearinghouse on Family Violence.

Trocmé, Nico, Barbara Fallon, Bruce MacLaurin, Vandna Sinha, Tara Black, Elizabeth Fast, Caroline Felstiner, Sonia Hélie, Daniel Turcotte, Pamela Weightman, Janet Douglas, and Jill Holroyd. 2010. *Canadian Incidence Study of Reported Child Abuse and Neglect — 2008: Major Findings*. Ottawa: National Clearinghouse on Family Violence.

Webb, Stephen A. 2006. *Social Work in a Risk Society: Social and Political Perspectives*. New York: Palgrave Macmillan.

6.   Black Feminist Thinking, Black Mothers, and Child Sexual Abuse

Claudia Bernard

Mother-blame is one of the most persistent and confounding problems in social work practice in situations of child sexual abuse. A rich feminist scholarship challenges discourses and practices that render mothers responsible for abuse of their children while remaining silent on the responsibility of offenders. This scholarship has paid little attention to the ways in which mothers' experiences of their children's disclosure and protection are differentiated as a result of their racial and class locations. In this chapter I address this omission by describing how different layers of gendered relations interplay with the nuances of race to create particular dilemmas for Black mothers as protectors of their children. The ideas discussed here are drawn in part from my research with Black British mothers of African-Caribbean origin whose children had been sexually abused (Bernard 2001). In that study I explored mothers' emotional and behavioural responses to the discovery of the sexual abuse of their children in order to better understand what factors influenced their help-seeking and protective strategies.

Black feminist thinking can help to explore how markers of racial difference alter the gendered parenting experiences of Black mothers in the aftermath of child sexual abuse and to understand the notion of failure to protect in this context. My central argument is that accusations of failure to protect arise in a social and cultural milieu where racialized constructs of Black families operate alongside gendered assumptions about motherhood that foster a mother-blaming stance. In order to engage effectively and anti-oppressively with Black mothers and their children, a complex understanding of crucial interlocking factors that may constrain or enable Black mothers' coping processes is required. Thus, I employ a concept of intersectionality to analyze factors that impact on the emotions, reactions, and behaviours of Black mothers. I develop this concept of intersectionality from the specificities of child sexual abuse in Black families, coupled with key ideas in Black feminist thinking.

Childhood Sexual Abuse and Black Families

Although childhood sexual abuse has been shown to be a widespread phenomenon that affects families across all racial and socio-economic backgrounds (Abney and Priest 1995; Cawson et al. 2000; Finkelhor and Browne 1986; Gorey and Leslie 1996; NSPCC 2011; Trocmé and Wolfe 2001), there is a paucity of research that has looked specifically at Black families (Bernard 2001). Studies of prevalence rates of maltreatment in the U.K. have utilized small samples from Black populations, limiting reliable conclusions about child sexual abuse in Black families (Burton, Kelly and Regan 1991; Cawson et al. 2000; May-Chahal 2006; May-Chahal and Cawson 2005). Knowledge about Black children and sexual abuse is sketchy, and it remains difficult to obtain reliable figures on the occurrence of sexual abuse in Black families (Jackson 1996; Kenny and McEachern 2000; Mtezuka 1996). There is some evidence to suggest that child sexual abuse in Black families may be under-reported (Radford et al. 2011; NSPCC 2011).

A growing number of first-person accounts by Black women and men recovering from childhood sexual abuse provide insights on negative con-sequences particular to victimized Black children (Alleyne 1997; Canaan 1990; Hollies 1990; Lee 1998; Palmer Adisa 1999; Stone 2005a; Wilson 1993). A central theme woven through adult survivors' testimonies is that external devaluing messages associated with their race are a key component in shaping the dynamics of their abuse and the meanings they attach to their experiences. Several commentators (Lee 1998; Stone 2005a; Wilson 1993) have argued that accounts from adult survivors are important because they facilitate a deeper understanding of some of the familial and societal factors affecting survivors: these factors may shed light on why some sexual abuse in Black families goes unreported to child protection services.

Understanding Non-Disclosure
While prevalence rates are affected by methodological issues (Zellman and Coulborn Faller 1996), it is possible that failure to report child sexual abuse influences the accurate estimate of the prevalence of child sexual abuse in Black families (Bernard 2001; Radford et al. 2011; NSPCC 2011). A number of factors have been identified as contributing to a reluctance to report abuse to CPS authorities. Stone (2005b) noted that Black children are particularly dependent on family networks for support: this situation may make disclosure especially difficult for children, who may feel that reporting abuse represents a betrayal of their families. Reporting sexual abuse to CPS authorities in Britain also generates fear of reprisals and could incur marginalization, or even exclusion, from families and communities (Bernard 2001). Moreover, it has been noted by Kenny and McEachern (2000) that sexual abuse in Black families is not openly discussed because of the stigma, but also for fear that doing so will further contribute to the pathologization of Black families (Stone 2005b). Black families and communities also fear racist treatment and coercive surveillance by statutory agencies (Gibbons, Conroy and Bell 1995; Graham 2002; Jackson 1996; Wilson 1993). Given that racism in child protection has been extensively documented (Barn 2007; Chand 2000; Thoburn, Chand,

and Procter 2005), the fear and mistrust of statutory agencies among Black people is well founded.

Reporting and seeking help related to child sexual abuse are further influenced by a multitude of factors, including dominant constructions of Black families as inherently pathological; negative stereotypes of Black parents as "deficient" in their parenting; and negative images of Black men as absent fathers (Arnold 2011; Brown et al. 2009; Gibbons, Conroy, and Bell 1995; Reynolds 2001). Moreover, the racist demonization of Black men can silence Black women, in that raising the issue of Black men's violence in public might well invite a racist interpretation, furthering the pathologizing of Black families (Arshad 1996; Hamer 2001; Mama 1995; Mtzuka 1996; Smith et al. 2005; Wilson 1993). All these factors create obstacles for Black mothers in seeking help and may explain the silence surrounding child sexual abuse in Black communities (Wilson 1993).

Feminism, Black Mothers, and Protection from Child Sexual Abuse

During the past quarter-century, feminists have made significant contributions to challenging notions of mothers' complicity in their children's experiences of sexual abuse (Bolen 2003; Breckenridge 2006; Krane 2003; McGuffey 2005). Feminist insights into mothers' varying awareness of the abuses experienced by their children and the diversity of their help-seeking responses have brought to the fore the effects of disclosure of sexual abuse on mothers' cognitive, emotional, and social relational world (McCallum 2001). Indeed, evidence confirms that sexual abuse poses major challenges for many mothers in protecting their children (Hooper 1992; Krane 2003). Learning of the abuse can elicit a powerful grief response involving shock, numbness, denial, fear, anxiety, guilt, anger, and depression (Green 1996; Hiebert-Murphy 1998; Hooper 1997; Lewin and Bergin 2001).

The protective efforts of mothers are often complicated by their own experiences of intimate partner violence, given that these two kinds of violence often occur together (Farmer and Owen 1998; Hester and Pearson 2000; Humphreys et al. 2006; Lapierre 2010a, 2010b; Radford and Hester 2006). A child's disclosure of sexual abuse often has a significant impact on the mother-child relationship and may influence the way women as caregivers are able to protect their children (Hiebert-Murphy 2002; Krane 2003; Krane and Carlton 2009; Plummer 2006; Stone 2005b; Tamraz 1996; Wilkins 2007). Feminist thinkers have proposed that one of the most effective ways to safeguard the welfare of children victimized by sexual abusers is to understand the gendered power relationships in which their mother's lives are situated, in order to develop positive supportive relationships with non-abusing mothers in the aftermath of abuse (Breckenridge 2006; Carter 1993; Damant et al. 2008; Hester and Pearson 2000; Humphreys 1994; Mullender et al. 2002;

Plummer and Eastin 2007). However, relatively little attention has been paid in this regard to Black mothers' experiences of their children's disclosures and their ensuing help-seeking behaviours. This gap is problematic in that maternal support following disclosure of abuse is found to be a mediating factor in a child's emotional recovery and in strengthening the mother-child relationship (Alaggia 2002; Coohey 2006). Also of significance are the factors child protection workers utilize to make professional judgements about Black mothers' protection of their children after disclosure of sexual abuse. Evidence suggests that race shapes parents' responses in the aftermath of child sexual abuse. For example, racial meanings overlap with gender to produce a racialized mother-blaming discourse in relation to Black mothers, and race-based assumptions devaluing Black motherhood can be at play in how professionals judge Black mothers as protectors (McGuffey 2005).

Thus, while it could be argued that all mothers are at risk for scrutiny as the protectors of their children in response to child sexual abuse, Black mothers are doubly vulnerable to negative judgments. Being women, as well as Black, creates particular challenges to their capacity to act as protectors of their children in the aftermath of sexual abuse. How to understand Black mothers is the subject matter to which I now turn, drawing on Black feminist thinking and intersectionality frameworks to understand the influence of these interlocking oppressions.

Black Feminist Thinking as an Organising Framework

Black feminism refers to a particular school of thought that engages an intersectional analysis of the effects of gender, race, and class oppressions in understanding the social location of Black women (Athey 1996; Hill Collins 1990). This philosophical and political perspective takes as its starting point the continual interplay of race and gender (see Carby 1982; Crenshaw 1994, 2000; Davis 1981; Hill Collins 1990; hooks 1989; Lorde 1984; Mama 1995). An important feature of Black feminist discourse is the notion that Black women know and understand the social world differently from other women and therefore bring a unique perspective on racial and gendered systems of oppression. As Hill Collins (1990: 22) put it, Black feminism offers a "unique angle of vision on self, community and society and the theories that interpret these experiences." This approach is based on the position that Black women's histories — contextualized and situated within the legacy of slavery, colonialism, imperialism, and migration — profoundly shape the way they experience and construct their understandings of their social world.

Thus, knowledge about women's worlds must be grounded in Black women's life experiences (hooks 1984). To elaborate, Hill Collins (1990) contends that the standpoints of oppressed groups are suppressed or discredited by those more powerful in society: she maintains that Black women's knowledge is subjugated knowledge. Such a claim suggests that powerful groups are able to shape the content of knowledge and to decide what knowledge is legitimate. Hill Collins advanced the argument that "outsider-within" status functions not only to create new angles of vision for validating the knowledge claims of subordinate groups (Hill Collins 1990: 11), but also to give Black women unique insights into the nature of society. Accordingly, the claim is made that Black feminists are ideally placed for creating an oppositional discourse (Hill Collins 1990; James 2000). Black feminists assert that universal knowledge claims made about women's experiences are called into question when one examines the role of power in the generation, acquisition, and production of knowledge. Black feminists maintain that power dynamics operating in this process serve to marginalize and exclude the voices of those who are oppressed. Black feminist thinking challenges the assumption that Western and Eurocentric forms of knowledge are the only valid, or the most valuable, ways of knowing (Barriteau 2009; Christian 1988).

A fundamental analytic tool in Black feminist thinking is that of "intersectionality." First conceptualized by Crenshaw (1994), intersectionality can aid analyses of ways in which multiple identities of gender, race, class, and sexual orientation interact to affect the relational and contextual nature of women's experiences. In other words, the concept of intersectionality is instrumental in interrogating how multiple and intersecting systems of oppression affect the experiences of marginalized groups. An intersectional theoretical framework helps to conceptualize how categories of differences intersect and interplay in a context of social relations of power; it thus advances understanding of how divergent groups of women may experience oppression differently. To recognize multiple sites of oppression means that one understands that Black and ethnic minority women will experience gender discrimination differently than White women, and will also experience racial and ethnic discrimination differently than Black and ethnic minority men (Lorde 1984).

Through the lenses of Black feminist thinking in general, and intersectionality in particular, the complex nexus of relationships that impact the mothering role in the aftermath of children's disclosures of sexual abuse can be elucidated. I now turn to the recurring theme of "conflict" that emerged in my research, paying particular attention to the interplay of race and gender. I illuminate how a web of relationships played an important role in creating a set of dynamics that impacted how mothers prioritized their children's care and protection needs in the aftermath of abuse. Briefly, my research interviews with Black British mothers, of African-Caribbean origin, focusing on their responses to the discovery of the sexual abuse of their children, revealed that conflict arose in five interconnected strands: (1) conflict in the mother-child relationship; (2) familial conflict; (3) conflictual feelings towards their husband/partner; (4) conflict with self; and (5) conflict about using child protection services. Understanding these areas of conflict will, I suggest, engender a more complex understanding of mothers' efforts to protect as it applies to the everyday lives of Black mothers facing child protection investigations and interventions. This complex understanding is essential to ensure competent and socially just interventions.

Conflict in Mother-Child Relationships

An intersectionality lens provides an important frame of analysis to illuminate the specific nuances in the mother-child relationship in the aftermath of the abuse. In particular, ambivalent feelings and difficulties in keeping their children's needs in focus were crucial factors identified by mothers as having an effect on the relationship with their children. All the mothers expressed a range of feelings following their children's disclosures — primarily sadness, anger, self-blame, disbelief, guilt, and despair. For some mothers who had themselves been victims of childhood sexual abuse, strong feelings were aroused about their own trauma. Some experienced depression, and thus felt hindered in their ability to be emotionally receptive to the distress and behavioural disturbances presented by their children as a consequence of the sexual abuse. For some, the disclosure triggered feelings of ambivalence, which made it especially challenging for them to engage in the difficult conversations that they needed to have with their children. Others struggled to keep their children's emotional needs in focus at all times, trying to actively listen to their children recounting their experiences; nonetheless, they acknowledged that the quality of the mother-child relationship had been seriously damaged. Coming to terms with the fact that their children had felt unable to disclose the abuse to them was particularly difficult. This reality dispelled the notion that they had a close relationship with their children and negatively affected their ability to be responsive to their children's emotional needs.

Dominant ideologies of mothering romanticize the notion that an attentive mother always puts her children's emotional needs before her own. Awareness of the specificities of Black mothers' lives may help to shed light on Black mothers' coping responses. Responses that may be perceived as denial, maternal deficit, or failure to protect can actually be stages in the process that mothers go through to reconcile the discord between their own feelings and the need to act in the best interest of their children. It is important to consider, especially where the perpetrator is the child's father or stepfather, that Black women's parenting can be undermined not only by the perpetrator's grooming of the child (Jacobs 1994; Slater 1995), but also by multiple axes of oppression inherent in cultural norms stressing family loyalty (Bernard 2001; Stone 2005b). Since racism is a reality of life in Black communities, women's dependence on family networks is often complex and contradictory. There is often pressure on Black women to remain quiet about gender-based violence in their communities, for to go outside the family will be perceived as betrayal, and Black women will be labelled as race traitors (Cole and Guy-Sheftall 2003). This silence can result in CPS judgements about mothers' failure to protect. A deficit-oriented view of Black mothers can obscure the significant factors that frame their relationships with their children, and that may ultimately leave mothers vulnerable to accusations of complicity. Utilizing an intersectional lens to disentangle some of the specificities of Black women's mothering roles in the aftermath of child sexual abuse thus enables us to better understand the various influences on mothers' responsiveness.

Familial Conflicts
Family support is important for Black mothers as the family can serve essential functions in buffering the negative effects of racism that is a constant reality for them.

But there are many family factors that create conflictual relations for mothers and make it difficult for them to draw on this support. A number of the mothers reported experiencing mother-blaming through their kinship networks; some cited pressure from family members not to report suspected abuse to child protection services. Not surprisingly, mothers who reported that other family members judged their parenting suffered isolation and faced major challenges in seeking support outside of their families. In the absence of emotionally supportive familial relationships, some mothers questioned their sense of belonging, as well as the meanings they attached to their familial relationships. It was suggested by Jacobs (2004) that there are powerful sanctions on Black women to not "air their dirty laundry" in public. Rigid adherence to cultural attitudes about gendered expectations may also play a decisive role in silencing mothers; for instance, the notion that women should remain loyal to men and should protect the family from outside surveillance in a racist society provided a strong deterrent to reporting the abuse (McGuffey 2005).

Intersectionality highlights the complex networks of relationships within which women's kinship ties are embedded, and helps to illuminate the subtleties impinging on mothers' circumstances. Some feminist thinkers argue that Black women are in a contradictory position because the family is a site of resistance in struggles against the state and police racism (Mama 1993; Reynolds 2005), yet, paradoxically, the family is also a site of oppression and that can pose significant dilemmas and difficulties for Black women in the aftermath of intrafamilial sexual abuse (Wilson 1993; Wyatt 1997). The following example from a mother whose twelve-year-old daughter was abused by her husband, the child's father, illustrates this point:

I feel very alone. To everyone in the family he was seen as "Mr.

Respectable," loyal, a good provider and a good father. I was the one left carrying all the guilt, as if I was to blame. I feel they think it's my fault that my daughter was abused — it must be to do with something I am not doing right as a mother. Though my family are not coming right out and saying anything to my face, I feel they are judging me in a negative way.

Conflict with Husbands/Partners

The mothers who were married, cohabiting, or in intimate relationships with the perpetrators of the abuse experienced the greatest degree of ambivalence. They experienced conflictual feelings of powerlessness and ambivalent feelings of loyalty — all of which influenced their capacity to act. Some commentators suggest that Black women's defensiveness when presented with any criticism of Black men results in what might be considered a shared sense of collective assault by the forces of societal racism (Crenshaw 2000) and the corollary need to present a united front. Because dominant discourses negatively portray Black men as deviant, violent, or absent fathers (Reynolds 2001), the alliance with Black men may make it difficult for some Black mothers to make public their personal troubles and the familial problems resulting from child sexual abuse.

Moreover, the complexity of feelings towards their intimate partners may distort mothers' judgements, thus hindering their capacity to focus extensively on their children's needs. The silence surrounding child sexual abuse in Black families is linked to the pervasiveness of Black women's alliances with Black men and related feelings of loyalty, shame, and fear of facing accusations of being a "race traitor" (see Wilson 1993). For Wilson, different dimensions of oppression operated to contribute to keeping secret about child sexual abuse in Black families. She also asks, to whose detriment are we denying that sexual abuse occurs in Black families? Indeed, as Villarosa (1994: 520) pointed out, "silence only fuels the problem and leaves survivors feeling lost, confused, guilty and painfully alone" which presents difficulties for mothers in naming and talking about their children's experiences of sexual abuse.

Conflict with Self

Internal barriers created by shame and stigma emerged as significant issues for the mothers. It is as if the deep shame and stigma associated with child sexual abuse attacked their self-esteem and confidence, causing some mothers to feel bereft of a space in which to voice their true feelings; consequently, they retreated into silence, self-blame, and anger toward themselves. As already discussed, the emotional responses of some mothers hindered their ability to give voice to their children's abuse. Other research has also noted that shame and stigma associated with child sexual abuse can silence the voice of victims and impinge on non-abusing mothers' personal agency (Cowburn and Dominelli 1998; Fontes and Plummer 2010). Internalized racism (that is, where mothers have internalized devaluing messages and stereotypes about their racial identity) can play a role in the ways some mothers framed conceptions of themselves. Cultural scripts about the "strong Black woman" had an impact on how some mothers thought of themselves (Bernard 2001); for example, they saw their depression following disclosure of their children's abuse as a sign of weakness and felt they should have been able to cope better. The concept of "double consciousness" (Du Bois 1989) — seeing yourself through the eyes of others — provides a starting point from which to explore the relevance of the effects of racism on the mothers' sense of self, psychological functioning, and individual agency in the face of a disclosure of child sexual abuse. The following account from a mother whose ten-year-old daughter was abused by her partner (not the child's father) illustrates the nuances of the effects of racism:

> At the time I felt there was a pressure — not only from White society, but within your own society, like a lot of covering up. The pressure was there to cover up. Some of that pressure was coming from family members. When I talked to my sister about what had happened, I had really been desperate to talk to someone, to get some support about how best to deal with the problem. She was very much of the view that I should not go to the police or social services because of their racist treatment of Black families. I feel very on my own dealing with this stuff.

Conflict About Using Child Protection Services
Mothers' mistrust of statutory agencies was an influencing factor in their willingness to seek and access help. In cases of extrafamilial sexual abuse, mothers were more likely to report the matter to child protection agencies, but this was not so in intrafamilial circumstances, which generated intense ambivalence in relation to being involved with the child protection system. Fear of having their children removed from their care, professionals' lack of sensitivity to their circumstances and embedded views of Black families as dysfunctional were some of the reasons the mothers felt that child protection services would be unsupportive. Research has consistently highlighted these barriers for Black families in using child protection services (Abney and Priest 1995; Barn 2001; Barn, Ladino and Rogers 2006; Chand and Thoburn 2006; McGuffey 2005).

Building Respectful Relationships with Black Mothers

The Black feminist framework offers insights into the complex and multi-faceted nature of Black women's emotional and behavioural responses in the aftermath of their children's disclosures of child sexual abuse. It suggests that the everyday experiences of Black mothers are shaped by a racism that is a key component in the social devaluation of Black families; further, Black feminist thinking has used an intersectionality analysis to understand how markers of racial difference alter mothers' gendered experiences of parenting in the aftermath of child sexual abuse. This approach enables an examination of the different layers of mothers' experiences and illuminates nuances that might be wrongly interpreted as failure to protect. It provides a means for understanding that Black mothers experience deep conflictual loyalties, because their experiences take place in a context of race and gender oppression, making their situations multi-faceted, ambiguous, and laden with tensions.

If we understand the help-seeking attitudes, behaviours, and coping strategies of non-abusing Black mothers, there are implications for how we can think about practice interventions to work sensitively and effectively with this group of mothers. As noted previously, there is evidence to suggest that the support of non-abusing mothers plays a significant role in children's recovery (Conte and Berliner 1988; Farmer and Owen 1998; Gomes-Schwartz, Horowitz and Cardarelli 1990; Krane 2003; Strega et al. 2008). Skilled interventions that are cognizant of the relational and contextual nature of Black mothers' parenting are more likely to successfully engage mothers in elucidating what their circumstances are for providing safe care for their children. Meaningful and effective intervention with Black mothers requires child protection workers to possess good analytical skills, as well as good interpersonal communication skills and the persistence to work with the complexities of mothers' divided loyalties. This vantage point allows space to challenge conceptions of the Black mother as failing to protect her child from sexual abuse.

Building a positive respectful relationship with Black mothers is critical if practitioners are to enable them to discuss highly personal aspects of their lives. For a trusting relationship to develop, child protection workers need to start from a strengths-based approach rather than a deficit model of parenting, in order to better understand the protective stances adopted by Black mothers. In particular, a strengths-based approach to the assessment of mothers' parenting would require looking at the resources that the family draws on to protect itself from stressors during a crisis (Genero 1998). Moreover, a strengths-based approach has a much better potential to recognize that, given day-to-day experiences of racism, Black mothers have to be very resourceful in the parenting strategies they develop to build resilience in their children (Bernard 2002; Reynolds 2005). If practice interventions are to effectively engage mothers, then a strengths-based approach is better able to value their skills, abilities, and strengths for enhancing the support they can give to their children.

CPS workers need to engage in practice that is critically reflexive in order to be clear about how their own feelings and values might influence the criteria they are using to assess mothers' circumstances and to gauge good-enough mothering (Ruch 2005, 2007; Ward 2010). It is therefore important that practitioners use their supervision forums to help them think through the implications of their presuppositions and values on their professional judgments about the parenting of Black mothers. Establishing a positive respectful relationship is the only basis on which practitioners can successfully engage with mothers to make sound judgements about their interpersonal functioning and their abilities to provide emotionally responsive care to their children (Davies et al. 2007).

Finally, in situations of intrafamilial child sexual abuse where CPS workers encounter avoidant coping strategies such as silence or denial, questions may be raised about balancing children's needs with those of their mothers. The challenge for practitioners is to help mothers address uncomfortable questions about their relationships with their male partners, without being punitive or blaming. Persistence and the capacity to tolerate uncertainties and ambiguities, without losing sight of children's needs, are imperative. Indeed, the capacity of CPS workers to be empathic and create an empowering environment, one that fosters, a safe, respectful, and supportive relationship, is critical to make nuanced assessments of mothers' abilities to create safe environments for their children. A primary goal for practice interventions is to support mothers in strengthening their alliances with their children in order to assist children's recovery. Intervention strategies that demonstrate sensitivity to the complexities confronting Black mothers are the foundation of supportive child protection engagement.

Although Black feminist thinking offers an alternative lens through which to explore Black mothers' experiences of disclosure and protection, it is important to refrain from essentializing and universalizing Black women's experiences. Indeed, there are significant variations in experience based on other axes of division, i.e., class, sexual orientation, religion, education, culture, and ethnicity, which separate Black mothers from one another (hooks 1989; Lorde 1984; Smith 1983). Moreover, particular care is needed when assessing mothers' protective actions and capacities, because the needs, wishes and safety of children in vulnerable situations are of paramount importance when identifying risks and protective factors. Risks to children are better assessed if we open up for scrutiny the complex matrix of oppressions that intersect for non-abusing mothers and seek to understand the dilemmas and difficulties they face, while at the same time being aware of how silences and avoidances can leave children vulnerable. To make sense of situations where Black mothers' responses raise concern for CPS authorities, workers need to be mindful of the interpersonal familial dynamics that help or hinder their will-ingness to reach out for support. Most importantly, we have to acknowledge that the hidden nature of child sexual abuse means that we will encounter families that will be difficult to engage with. We must also be mindful of the uncomfortable truth that not all mothers provide adequate care for their children in the aftermath of abuse. Notwithstanding, CPS workers have to find ways to engage these mothers in an empathic way. In order to engage effectively in an anti-oppressive manner, practitioners must have the ability to demonstrate empathy and respect, and to be non-judgmental (Wilson et al. 2011). Essentially, social workers must convey empathic listening skills in order to develop a nuanced understanding of mothers' perspectives, without resorting to mother-blaming.

Taking into account issues at the intersection of gender and race, in the context of sexual abuse in Black families, needs to be a basic part of anti-oppressive practice with mothers. In order to establish anti-oppressive practices and make well-informed professional judgements in sexual abuse situations involving non-abusing Black mothers, practitioners need to be able to draw on knowledge that is grounded in an understanding of the broader contextual factors that impact on the mothers' daily lives. In this sense, it can be argued that making Black mothers' and children's experiences visible, with all their inherent complexities, is critically important to illuminate how mothers develop effective coping strategies. By broadening our conceptual lens, we can shed light on how Black mothers navigate the contradictory expectations that arise as a result of the disclosure of the sexual abuse of their children.

An important goal is to challenge the dominant hegemony of Eurocentric theorizing of Black families as deficient and to move away from a gender-blind approach to race. In tis regard, Black feminist thinking can provide an explanatory framework for interrogating the variety of factors that configure mothers' relational experiences and for critiquing the construction of the collusive Black mother. Above all, a Black feminist approach to the racial-izing of gender in the context of sexual abuse extends the feminist discourse of mothers by facilitating critical reflection on the specific nuances affecting Black women's mothering in the aftermath of child sexual abuse. Essentially, a Black feminist approach broadens knowledge of the effects of child sexual abuse in Black families by unravelling how multiple oppressions cohere to pose challenges. A critical Black feminist framework thus adds a new perspective from which to understand the tensions Black mothers experience and how they differ from those of other groups of non-abusing mothers.

References

Abney, Veronica B., and Ronnie. Priest. 1995. "African Americans and Child Sexual Abuse." In Lisa A. Fontes (ed.), *Sexual Abuse in Nine North American Cultures.* Thousand Oaks, CA: Sage.

Alaggia, Ramona. 2002. "Cultural and Religious Influences in Maternal Response to Intrafamilial Child Sexual Abuse: Charting New Territory for Research and Treatment" *Journal of Child Sexual Abuse* 10, 2.

Alleyne, Vanessa. 1997. *There Were Times I Thought I Was Crazy: A Black Woman's Story of Incest.* Toronto: Sister Vision.

Arnold, Elaine. 2011 *Working with Families of African Caribbean Origin: Understanding Issues around Immigration and Attachment.* London: Jessica Kingsley Publishers.

Arshad, Rowena. 1996. "Building Fragile Bridges: Educating for Change." In Kate Cavanagh and Viviene Cree (eds.), *Working with Men: Feminism and Social Work.* London: Routledge.

Athey, Stephanie. 1996. "Black Feminism." In Ernest Cashmore (ed.), *Dictionary of Race and Ethnic Relations.* Fourth edition. London: Routledge.

Barn, Ravinder. 2001. "Caribbean Families and the Child Welfare System in Britain." In Harry Goulbourne and Mary Chamberlain (eds.), *Caribbean Families in Britain and the Trans-Atlantic World.* London: Macmillan

___. 2007 "'Race,' Ethnicity and Child Welfare: A Fine Balancing Act." *British Journal of Social Work* 37, 8.

Barn, Ravinder, Carolina Ladino, and Brooke Rogers. 2006. *Parenting in Multi-Racial Britain.* London: National Children's Bureau.

Barriteau, Violet Eudine. 2009. "The Relevance of Black Feminist Scholarship: A Caribbean Perspective." *Feminist Africa Diaspora Voices* 13.

Bernard, Claudia. 2001. *Constructing Lived Experiences: Representations of Black Mothers in Child Sexual Abuse Discourses.* Aldershot, UK: Ashgate.

___. 2002. "Giving Voice to Experiences: Parental Maltreatment of Black Children in the Context of Societal Racism." *Child & Family Social Work* 7, 4.

Bernard, Claudia, and Anna Gupta. 2008. "Black African Children and the Child Protection System." *British Journal of Social Work* 38, 3.

Bolen, Rebecca. M. 2003. "Nonoffending Mothers of Sexually Abused Children: A Case of Institutionalized Sexism?" *Violence Against Women* 9, 11.

Breckenridge, Jan. 2006. "'Speaking of Mothers…' How Does the Literature Portray Mothers Who Have a History of Child Sexual Abuse?" *Journal of Child Sexual Abuse* 15, 2.

Brown, Leslie, Marilyn Callahan, Susan Strega, Christopher Walmsley, and Lena Dominelli. 2009. "Manufacturing Ghost Fathers: The Paradox of Father Presence and Absence in Child Welfare." *Child and Family Social Work* 14, 1.

Burton, Sheila, Liz Kelly, and Linda Regan. 1991. *An Exploratory Study of the Prevalence of Sexual Abuse in a Sample of 16–21 Year Olds.* London: Polytechnic of North London, Child Abuse Studies Unit.

Canaan, Andrea. R. 1990. "I Call up Names: Facing Childhood Sexual Abuse." In Evelyn C. White (ed.), *Black Women's Health Book: Speaking for Ourselves.* Seattle. WA: Seal Press.

Carby, Hazel. 1982. "White Women Listen! Black Feminism and the Boundaries of Sisterhood." In *The Empire Strikes Back: Race and Racism in 70s Britain*. Centre for Contemporary Cultural Studies, Race and Politics Group, London: Hutchinson.

Carter, Betty. 1993. "Child Sexual Abuse: Impact on Mothers." *Affilia* 8, 1.

Cawson, Pat, Corrine Wattam, Sue Brooker. and Graham Kelly. 2000. *Child Maltreatment in the United Kingdom: A Study of the Prevalence of Abuse and Neglect.* London: NSPCC.

Chand, Ashok. 2000. "The Over-Representation of Black Children in the Child Protection System: Possible Causes, Consequences and Solutions." *Child and Family Social Work* 5, 1.

Chand, Ashok. and June Thoburn. 2006. "Research Review: Child Protection Referrals and Minority Ethnic Children and Families." *Child and Family Social Work* 11, 4.

Christian, Barbara. 1988. "The Race of Theory." *Feminist Studies* 14, 1.

Cole, Johnnetta Betsch. and Beverley Guy-Sheftall. 2003. *Gender Talk: The Struggle for Women's Equality in African American Communities*. New York: One World/ Ballantine Books.

Conte, Jon, and Lucy Berliner. 1988. "The Impact of Sexual Abuse on Children: Empirical Findings." In Lenore E. Walker (ed.), *Handbook of Sexual Abuse on Children: Assessment and Treatment Issues*. New York: Springer.

Coohey, Carol. 2006. "How Child Protective Services Investigators Decide to Substantiate Mothers for Failure to Protect in Sexual Abuse Cases." *Journal of Child Sexual Abuse* 15, 4.

Cowburn, Malcolm, and Lena Dominelli. 1998. "Moving Beyond Litigation and Positivism: Another Approach to Accusations of Sexual Abuse." *British Journal of Social Work* 28, 4.

Crenshaw, Kimberle. 1994. "Mapping the Margins: Intersectionality, Identity Politics and Violence against Women of Colour." In Martha A. Fineman and Roxanne Mykitiuk (eds.), *The Public Nature of Private Violence: The Discovery of Domestic Abuse*. New York: Routledge.

___. 2000. "Demarginalizing the Intersection of Race and Sex: A Black Feminist Critique of Anti-Discriminatory Doctrine, Feminist Theory and Anti-Racist Politics." In Joy James and T. Denean Sharpley-Whiting (eds.), *The Black Feminist Reader*. Oxford: Blackwell Publishing.

Damant, Dominique, Simon Lapierre, Anne Kouraga, Andrée Fortin, Louise Hamelin-Brabant, Chantal Lavergne, and Genevieve Lessard. 2008. "Taking Child Abuse and Mothering Into Account." *Affilia* 23, 2.

Davis, Angela. 1981. *Women, Race and Class.* New York: Random House.

Davies, Linda, Julia Krane, Sara Collings, and Sharon Wexler. 2007. "Developing Mothering Narratives in Child Protection Practice." *Journal of Social Work Practice* 21, 1.

Du Bois, William Edward Burghardt. 1989. *The Souls of Black Folk*. New York: Bantam (first published 1903 in Chicago by A.C. McClung).

Farmer, Elaine, and Morag Owen. 1998. "Gender and Child Protection Process." *British Journal of Social Work* 28, 4.

Finkelhor, David, and Angela Browne. 1986. "The Traumatic Impact of Child Sexual Abuse: A Conceptualization." *American Journal of Orthopsychiatry* 55.

Fontes, Lisa, and Carol Plummer. 2010. "Cultural Issues in Disclosures of Child Sexual Abuse." *Journal of Child Sexual Abuse* 19, 5.

Genero, Nancy. P. 1998. "Culture, Resiliency and Mutual Psychological Development." In Hamilton I. McCubbin, Elizabeth A. Thompson, Anne I. Thompson and Jo A. Futrell (eds.), *Resiliency in African-American families.* Thousand Oaks, CA: Sage.

Gibbons, Jane, Sue Conroy, and Caroline Bell. 1995. *Operating the Child Protection System: A Study of Child Protection Practices in English Local Authorities.* London: HMSO.

Gomes-Schwartz, Beverley, Jonathon M. Horowitz, and Albert P. Cardarelli. 1990. *Child Sexual Abuse: The Initial Effects.* London: Sage.

Gorey, Kevin M., and Donald R. Leslie. 1996. "The Prevalence of Child Sexual Abuse: Integrative Review Adjustment for Potential Response and Measurement Biases." *Child Abuse and Neglect* 2, 4.

Graham, Makeda. 2002. *Social Work and African-Centred Worldviews.* London: Venture Press.

Green, Judith. 1996. "Mothers in Incest Families." *Violence Against Women* 2, 3.

Hamer, Jennifer. 2001. *What it Means to Be Daddy: Fatherhood for Black Men Living Away from Their Children.* New York: Columbia University Press.

Hester, Marriane, and Chris Pearson. 2000. *From Periphery to Centre: Domestic Violence in Work with Abused Children.* London: Jessica Kingsley Publishers.

Hiebert-Murphy, Diane. 1998. "Emotional Distress Among Mothers Whose Children Have Been Sexually Abused: The Role of History of Child Sexual Abuse." *Journal of Child Abuse and Neglect* 22, 5.

___. 2002. "Partner Abuse Among Mothers Whose Children Have Been Sexually Abused: An Exploratory Study." *Journal of Child Sexual Abuse* 10.

Hill Collins, Patricia. 1990. *Black Feminist Thought.* London: Unwin Hyman.

Hollies, Linda. 1990. "A Daughter Survives Incest: A Retrospective Analysis." In Evelyn C. White (ed.), *The Black Women's Health Book: Speaking for Ourselves.* Seattle, WA: Seal Press.

hooks, bell. 1984. *Feminist Theory: From Margin to Centre.* Boston: South End Press.

___. 1989. *Talking Back: Thinking Feminist — Thinking Black.* London: Sheba.

Hooper, Carol-Ann. 1992. *Mothers Surviving Sexual Abuse.* London: Routledge.

___. 1997. "Child Sexual Abuse and the Regulation of Women: Variations on a Theme." In Laura L. O'Toole and Jessica R. Schiffman (eds.), *Gender Violence: Interdisciplinary Perspective.* Second edition New York: NYU Press.

Humphreys, Catherine. 1994. "Counteracting Mother-Blaming Among Child Sexual Abuse Service Providers: An Experiential Workshop." *Journal of Feminist Family Therapy* 6, 1.

Humphreys, Catherine, Audrey Mullender, Ravi K. Thiara, and Agnes Skamballis. 2006. "Talking to My Mum: Developing Communication Between Women and Children in the Aftermath of Domestic Violence." *Journal of Social Work* 6,1.

Jackson, Valerie. 1996. *Racism and Child Protection: The Black Experience of Child Sexual Abuse.* London: Cassell.

Jacobs, Janet Liebman. 1994. *Victimized Daughters: Incest and the Development of the Female Self.* London: Routledge.

Jacobs, Michelle S. 2004. "Piercing the Prison Uniform of Invisibility for Black Female Inmates." *Journal of Criminal Law and Criminology* 94, 3.

James, Joy. 2000. "Radicalizing Feminism." In Joy James and T. Denean Sharpley-Whiting (eds.), *The Black Feminist Reader.* Oxford: Blackwell Publishers.

Kenny, Maureen C., and Adriana G. McEachern. 2000. "Racial, Ethnic and Cultural Factors of Childhood Sexual Abuse: A Selected Review of the Literature." *Clinical Psychology Review* 20, 7.

Kim, Kihyun, Penelope K. Trickett, and Frank W. Putman. 2011. "Attachment Representations and Anxiety: Differential Relationships Among Mothers of Sexually Abused and Comparison Girls." *Journal of Interpersonal Violence* 26, 3.

Krane, Julia. 2003. *What's Mother Got to Do With it? Protecting Children from Sexual Abuse.* Toronto: University of Toronto Press.

Krane, Julia, and Rosemary Carlton. 2009. "What Is So Oppressive About Protection Practice in Cases of Child Sexual Abuse: Scratch the Surface and Find the Oppression of Mothers." In Susan Strega and Jeannine Carriere (eds.), *Walking this Path Together: Anti Racist and Anti-Oppressive Child Welfare Practice.* Halifax: Fernwood Publishing.

Lapierre, Simon. 2010a. "More Responsibilities, Less Control: Understanding the Challenges and Difficulties Involved in Mothering in the Context of Domestic Violence." *British Journal of Social Work* 40, 5.

___. 2010b. "Striving to Be Good Mothers: Abused Women's Experiences of Mothering." *Child Abuse Review* 19, 5.

Lee, Brenda. 1998. *The Abused and the Abuser.* Oakland, CA: Princess Lee Publishing Co.

Lewin, Linda, and Christi Bergin. 2001. "Attachment Behaviours, Depression, and Anxiety in Non-offending Mothers of Child Sexual Abuse Victims." *Child Maltreatment* 6, 4.

Lorde, Audrey. 1984. *Sister Outsider: Essays and Speechs.* New York: Crossing Press.

Mama, Amina. 1993. "Black Women and The Police: A Place Where the Law is Not Upheld." In Winston James and Clive Harris (eds.), *Inside Babylon: The Caribbean Diaspora in Britain.* London: Verso.

___. 1995. *Beyond the Mask: Race, Gender and Subjectivity.* London: Routledge.

May-Chahal, Corinne. 2006. "Gender and Child Maltreatment: The Evidence Base." *Social Work and Society Online International Journal* 4. <http://www.socwork.net/sws/article/view/176>.

May-Chahal, Corinne, and Pat Cawson. 2005. "Measuring Child Maltreatment in the United Kingdom: A Study of the Prevalence of Child Abuse and Neglect." *Child Abuse and Neglect* 29, 9.

McCallum, Sharon. 2001. "Non-Offending Mothers: An Exploratory Study of Mothers Whose Partners Sexually Assaulted Their Children." *Violence Against Women* 7, 3.

McGuffey C. Shawn. 2005. "Engendering Trauma: Race, Class and Gender Reaffirmation after Child Sexual Abuse." *Gender and Society* 19, 5.

Mtezuka, Melody. 1996. "Issues of Race and Culture in Child Abuse." In Barbara Fawcett, Brid Featherstone, Jeff Hearn, and Christine Toft (eds.), *Violence and Gender Relations: Theories and Interventions.* London: Sage.

Mullender, Audrey, Gill Hague, Umme Iman, Liz Kelly, Ellen Malos, and Linda Regan. 2002. *Children's Perspectives on Domestic Violence.* London: Sage.

NSPCC. 2011. *Child Cruelty in the UK 2011: An NSPCC Study into Childhood Abuse and Neglect over the Past 30 Years*. London: NSPCC.

Palmer Adisa, Opal. 1999. "Children Must Be Seen and Heard." In Joan Anim-Addo and Jacob Ross (eds.), *Voice Memory Ashes — Lest We Forget*. London: Mango.

Plummer, Carol. A. 2006. "Non-Abusive Mothers of Sexually Abused Children: The Role of Rumination in Maternal Outcomes." *Journal of Child Sexual Abuse* 15, 2.

Plummer, Carol. A., and Julie Eastin. 2007. "The Effect of Child Sexual Abuse Allegations/Investigations on the Mother/Child Relationship." *Violence Against Women* 13, 10.

Radford, Lorraine, Susana Corral, Christine Bradley, Helen Fisher, Claire Bassett, Nick Howat, and Stephan Collishaw. 2011. *Child Abuse and Neglect in the UK Today*. London: NSPCC.

Radford, Lorraine, and Marianne Hester. 2006. *Mothering Through Domestic Violence*. London: Jessica Kingsley Publishers.

Reynolds, Tracey. 2001. "Caribbean Fathers in Family Lives in Britain." In Harry Goulbourne and Mary Chamberlain (eds.), *Caribbean Families in Britain and the Trans-Atlantic World*. London: Macmillan.

____. 2005. *Caribbean Mothers: Identity and Experience in the UK*. London: Tuffnell Press.

Ruch, Gillian. 2005. "Relationship-Based and Reflective Practice in Contemporary Child Care Social Work." *Child and Family Social Work* 10, 2.

____. 2007. *Post-Qualifying Child Care Social Work: Developing Reflective Practice*. London: Sage.

Slater, Anna C. 1995. *Transforming Trauma: A Guide to Understanding and Treating Adult Survivors of Child Sexual Abuse*. Thousand Oaks, CA: Sage.

Smith, Barbara. 1983. *Home Girls: A Black Feminist Anthology*. New York: Kitchen Table Women of Colour Press.

Smith, Carolyn A., Marvin D. Krone, Rebekah Chu, and Oscar Best. 2005. "African American Fathers: Myths and Realities about Their Involvement with Their Firstborn Children." *Journal of Family Issues* 26, 7.

Stone, Robin D. 2005a. "Reconciliation and Moving On." *Journal of Feminist Family Therapy* 16, 3.

____. 2005b. *No Secrets No Lies: How Black Families Can Heal from Sexual Abuse*. New York: Broadway Books.

Strega, Susan, Claire Fleet, Leslie Brown, Lena Dominelli, Marilyn Callahan, and Christopher Walmsley. 2008. "Connecting Father Absence and Mother Blame in Child Welfare Policies and Practices." *Children and Youth Services Review* 30, 7.

Tamraz, Djenane Nakhle. 1996. "Non-Offending Mothers of Sexually Abused Children: Comparison of Opinions and Research." *Journal of Child Sexual Abuse* 5, 4.

Thoburn, June, Ashok Chand, and J. Procter. 2005. *Child Welfare Services for Minority Ethnic Families: The Research Reviewed*. London: Jessica Kingsley Publishers.

Trocmé, Nico, and David Wolfe. 2001. *Child Maltreatment in Canada: Selected Results from the Canadian Incidence Study of Reported Child Abuse and Neglect*. Ottawa: Minister of Public Works and Government Services Canada.

Villarosa, Linda. 1994. *Body and Soul: The Black Women's Guide to Physical Health and Emotional Well-Being*. New York: HarperPerennial.

Ward, Adrian. 2010. "The Use of Self in Relationship-Based Practice." In Gillian

Ruch, Danielle Turney, and Adrian Ward (eds.), *Relationship-Based Social Work: Getting to the Heart of Practice*. London: Jessica Kingsley Publishers.

Wilkins Erica. J. 2007. "Using an IFS Informed Intervention to Treat African American Families Surviving Sexual Abuse: One Family's Story." *Journal of Feminist Family Therapy* 19, 3.

Wilson, Melba. 1993. *Crossing the Boundary: Black Women Survive Incest*. London: Virago.

Wilson, Kate, Gillian Ruch, Mark Lymbery, and Andrew Cooper. 2011. *Social Work: An Introduction to Contemporary Practice*. Essex: Pearson Education Limited.

Wyatt, Gail Elizabeth. 1997. *Stolen Women: Reclaiming Our Sexuality, Taking Back Our Lives*. New York: John Wiley and Sons.

Zellman, Gail L., and Kathleen Coulborn Faller. 1996. "Reporting of Child Maltreatment." In John E. Briere, Lucy Berliner, Josephine A. Bulkley, Carole Jenny, and Theresa Reid (eds.), *The APSAC Handbook on Child Maltreatment*. London: Sage.

7. Double Jeopardy

Racialized Families and Failure to Protect

Sarah Maiter, Ramona Alaggia, and Baldev Mutta

The over-representation of racialized and ethnic minority families in child protection systems is well documented in Canada and the United States (Blackstock 2007; Blackstock et al. 2004; Dettlaff and Rycraft 2010; Lavergne et al. 2008). In their review of the literature, Dettlaff and Rycraft noted racial disproportionality in the U.S. at many levels of the child protection system, including reporting, substantiation, placement in foster care, and exits from foster care (Ards et al. 2003; Rolock and Testa 2005; George and Lee 2005; Hill 2005; in Dettlaff and Rycraft 2010). Although Canadian data are scant and less robust, similar concerns have also been noted. For example, researchers have suggested that disproportionality on child protection caseloads in Canada could be due to higher rates of reporting and substantiation (Blackstock 2007; Blackstock, Trocmé, and Bennett 2004; Lavergne et al. 2008). In a 1998 *Canadian Incidence Study (CIS)* of child maltreatment, Blackstock et al. (2004) reported that Indigenous people and visible minorities (a term used by the Canadian government to refer to racialized people in the census) had higher rates of substantiation of maltreatment — 50 percent and 41 percent respectively — when compared to non-Indigenous people. Lavergne et al. (2008) found similar trends in their analysis of data from the 2003 *CIS*. For example, they found that Asian children reported for physical abuse accounted for 14 percent of the sample, a proportion that is 1.6 times greater than their proportion in census data. Asian children also had the highest substantiation rates for physical abuse. The main risk factors identified by workers for the parents of visibility minority and Asian children (personal issues and difficult housing) were reported as being lower than in other groups. In their attempts to untangle these data, Lavergne et al. (2008) speculate whether racial bias may be a factor in identifying and reporting child maltreatment, as well as in decision making by child protection services. Findings of over-representation and disproportionality could indicate a greater prevalence of maltreatment; however, studies have found no significant differences in the incidence of child maltreatment amongst different racial and ethnic groups, leading to racial and cultural bias being identified as key contributors to disproportionality in child protection service (CPS) involvement (Dettlaff and Rycraft 2010; Maiter, Alaggia, and Trocmé 2004; Sedlak and Broadhurst 1996; Sedlak and Schultz 2005).

This chapter examines issues for minority racial and ethnic families involved with the child protection system and, specifically, the impacts of failure-to-protect policies and practices on how CPS systems engage with ethno-racial mothers. As discussed in earlier chapters, the concept of failure to protect most often arises in situations of intimate partner violence or sexual abuse of a child, and the vast majority of these incidents involve male perpetrators. Emerging research on child welfare interventions generally, and in situations of intimate partner violence specifically, for racialized families suggests that there are unique contextual considerations for these families that must be understood and that efforts should be made to reduce their harmful impact. Racialized families are disadvantaged at many levels in the child protection system: for example, reporting by professionals of suspected child maltreatment is more likely to be biased (Cross 2008; Lu et al. 2004; Rolock and Testa 2005); treatment in terms of access to services is more likely to be unequal (McRoy 2004); and assessments of maltreatment are more likely to be biased (Lavergne et al. 2008). For immigrant women, a host of other problems also prevail: fear of their immigration status being jeopardized (Alaggia and Maiter 2006); harsher treatment of offenders (Bernard 2001); and judgments about their culture and community (Maiter 2009a; Jeffery 2009). Here we will explore these issues in more detail and present recommendations for improved CPS responses to immigrant, refugee, and other racialized families. In the next section we provide information on how CPS responds to intimate partner violence, followed by a discussion of the role of stereotypes of women that contribute to their being held responsible for and blamed for the violence that they experience. We then discuss stereotypes about racialized families and the potential impact of this stereotyping on assessments and interventions with families. We suggest that male violence towards women in racialized families is presented in the media and understood generally in such problematic ways by wider society that CPS policies and practices encounter great difficulty in engaging with these families in a more neutral manner. We conclude with recommendations for change.

Exposure to Intimate Partner Violence and Child Protection

Increased recognition of the overlap between intimate partner abuse and child abuse has generated awareness of the possible negative effects on children of witnessing violence against their mothers. In many jurisdictions across North America, exposure to intimate partner violence is now considered a form of child maltreatment requiring investigation and intervention (Alaggia, Jenney, and Mazzuca et al. 2007; Nixon et al. 2007). Exposure to intimate partner violence is the most frequently substantiated form of child maltreatment, and is verified at the same rate as neglect (34 percent each) (Trocmé et al. 2008). But there is still considerable debate over the impact of children's exposure to mother abuse (Edleson 2004), as well as general lack of clarity about who is to be held responsible in this situation. For example, when Minnesota instituted and then quickly repealed exposure to intimate partner violence as a category of child maltreatment, questions were raised about the fundamental aspects of its definition (Edleson, Gassman-Pines, and Hill 2006). In their Michigan study about battered women's perceptions of their interactions with child protective services workers, Johnson and Sullivan (2008) examined the research on the effects of intimate partner violence on children. Their review led them to conclude that the effect of witnessing intimate partner violence is equivocal. While some researchers concluded that many children show psychological and behavioural problems similar to those of children who have been abused themselves, other researchers found that a significant proportion show few or none of these behaviours (Johnson and Sullivan 2008). Although these equivocations can be challenged with further studies, it is our intention in this chapter to challenge the further victimization of abused women and their children that occurs when children's exposure is tied to the assumption that women can, and should, be responsible for ending the abuse perpetrated against them. Johnson and Sullivan's (2008: 242) qualitative study with twenty women who shared a history of intimate partner violence found that most felt "misunderstood and unsupported by their CPS workers and thought that their treatment harmed them and their children." They note that the perpetrators of violence escaped sanctions, contributing to further negative consequences for mothers and children.

Highlighting patriarchal ideologies in the legal responses to violence against women and drawing on the work of Epstein (1999), Johnson and Sullivan (2008) noted that mothers are valued and judged against three common maternal stereotypes: the all-sacrificing mother, the all-knowing mother, and the nurturing mother. These maternal stereotypes are further distinguished from the father's limited stereotype as breadwinner. Universally, women are expected to overcome many obstacles outside of their control, including structural barriers such as racism, classism, and sexism. They are also expected to know everything about their children, to protect their children from all harms, and to ensure that their material and emotional needs are met. Mothers are routinely held to a higher standard of parental responsibility than are fathers, even when they are the victims of intimate partner violence (Humphreys and Absler 2011; Strega et al. 2008) There is great onus on mothers to distance themselves from a perpetrating father or father-figure in order to protect their children from further exposure. This is evidenced through Humphreys and Absler's (2011) systematic content analysis of decades of child welfare studies, from which they conclude that, since mothers historically have been viewed as more amenable to CPS intervention, they are routinely dealt with as the primary client. Although there have been brief periods where perpetrating fathers have been the focus of change, by and large, mothers have been the primary targets of intervention (Humphreys and Absler 2011).

In addition to the influence of maternal stereotypes, attribution theory provides some explanation for the persistent focus on the mother's behaviour rather than on other salient factors such as the batterer's abuse, inadequate police response, lack of shelter space, inadequate action by the courts, and patriarchal social structures (Magen 1999). Fundamental attribution error occurs when problems are attributed to an individual's personality, attitudes, or values rather than to the situational context of the person. Johnson and Sullivan (2008) note that mothers in their study reported that they were held responsible by CPS workers for the violence inflicted on them by their abusers, and were expected to control the behaviour of their abusers. When they did not manage to control abusers' actions, their perception was that CPS workers acted as if this was because they chose not to. Workers often required mothers to complete parenting agreement plans that included counselling, parenting classes, extensive drug screening, and psychological testing — referrals that suggested that they were inadequate parents — while little or nothing was required of their assailants. Many of the women reported that workers threatened and intimidated them and treated them as child abuse perpetrators. These findings are significant when we consider that the sample comprised of women who shared a history of intimate partner violence were mothers who had recent CPS involvement only because they were victims of this violence and not for any other child protection concerns. We see then that failure to protect reflects attribution error in that the concept is defined in terms of the mother's actions or inactions rather than a host of other relevant factors that contribute to the existence and persistence of violence against women.

Ethno-Racialized Stereotypes

Social service encounters and CPS interventions are further complicated for women from diverse ethno-racial families who are experiencing violence from their partners. When mothers (and fathers and families) are evaluated as the racialized "Other," both in the West and in situations where White Westerners are observing them in their home countries, they are generally judged according to the negative stereotypes of non-White, non-Western families. Racialized stereotypes have been discussed extensively with respect to media, law, and human services (see, for example, Ahmed 2000; Haque 2010; Maiter 2009a; Mohanty 1994; Razack 1998, 2004; Razack, Smith, and Thobani 2010). At their core, these stereotypes perpetuate a number of inaccurate notions to justify the general perception that all women from diverse ethno-racial backgrounds are oppressed in ways that White Western women are not. Stereotypical beliefs about these women include that their behaviours are controlled by inferior and primitive religions; they are religiously observant and subservient to their religion; they are traditionally family-oriented and submissive to their husbands and other male relatives; and they are negatively tied to cultural beliefs considered outmoded in progressive Western society. In other words, the dominant stereotype is that women from diverse ethno-racial backgrounds are so oppressed that they are unable to act with any personal agency. Similarly, stereotypes of men from diverse ethno-racial backgrounds not only contribute to ideas about women and families, but also shape CPS interventions and case resolutions. In particular, these stereotypes include assumptions that patriarchal behaviours and attitudes that justify or even prescribe the oppression of women and the routine use of violence toward women and children are common and widespread.

White Western encounters with families from diverse ethno-racial backgrounds are influenced by broader social processes such as colonization, racialization, and marginalization (Ahmed 2000). These encounters are also impacted by the proliferation of highly sensationalized news reports of violence within identified minority groups — for example, the intensely reporting of supposed "honour killings" attributed to certain groups — contributing to the perspective that violence is rampant in particular non-White, non-Western cultures and family structures. Indeed, it is often difficult to know which ethno-racial group is specifically being discussed as discussions of Muslims or Sikhs or other "Others" seem to be interchangeable. We suggest that attribution theory (Magen 1999) is useful for exploring why CPS seems to view woman abuse in diverse ethno-racial families as if it were characteristic of the ethno-racial group in question (Jiwani 2010; Razack 2004; Thobani 2010). Errors derived from racially based stereotypes of women (and men) result in blaming violence, and children's exposure to it, on the culture in general and the "helpless" mother who lives inside that culture in particular. Acknowledging that violence towards women is pervasive in all cultures is a necessary step in moving towards respectful practice with diverse ethno-racial families.

Because male violence towards women in ethno-racial families is understood in such problematic ways, CPS practitioners must actively resist being influenced by these stereotypical understandings when engaging with ethno-racial families. As Haque (2010) notes in her examination of the issue of violence and ethno-racial families, discourses about family violence in ethno-racial groups emerge from many political positions. Although specifically discussing the situation of Muslim families in Canada, Haque notes that in relation to racialized cultures, the essentialized, reductive formulation is that violence is a natural consequence of the values of a fundamentalist culture. One counter measure to this reductive formulation is to identify violence as the result of patriarchy, which is a universal phenomenon with varying influence in particular groups: to conteract the influence of patriarchal values, legal enforcement of women's rights must be put in place. But what is critically important to note is that while this perspective brings gender issues to the forefront, it renders race and racial equity issues invisible. Indeed, this perspective contributes to even further stereotyping of racialized men, as they are then positioned among all men as having advanced the least and being the most traditional and patriarchal, while broader social processes of racialization are ignored. Further, as Haque (2010) notes, access to community and counselling services are deeply racialized. In Canada, for example, "soft services" for immigrant families, such as mental health and family counselling, have been drastically cut in the last ten years and replaced by language training and other employment-oriented supports for newcomers (Haque 2010: A6). A comprehensive review of mental health services (Simich, Maiter, and Ochocka 2009: 254) drew on several sources to demonstrate that "immigrants who need help coping with mental distress associated with the transition are currently underserved by existing mental health care systems, which face increasing challenges serving culturally diverse populations."

Haque (2010: 90) recommends a contextual understanding of men's violence towards women in racialized families that considers factors such as the uneven distribution of support services for particular communities, in order to avoid a "totalizing cultural explanation of racialized gendered violence." Similarly, Razack (2004) urges that any consideration of violence include an appreciation of severe economic and social constraints within ethno-racial families and communities. Reitz and Bannerjee (cited in Haque 2010: 90) note that "racial minorities have the lowest incomes and highest rates of poverty" in Canada. Income disparity for racialized communities continues into the second generation, as does an increased perception of discrimination and sense of alienation (Nakhaie 2006). Immigrant visible minorities find that even though they are highly qualified and skilled, their credentials are not readily recognized in the Canadian labour market; consequently, many work in low-skilled, low-waged, or precarious employment, often for years. In their study of ethno-racial clients involved in the child protection system, Maiter and colleagues (2009) found that one of the significant settlement stressors was the devaluation of newcomers' qualifications, impacting their ability to earn fair wages — stressors that potentially contribute to troubled family relations and parenting.

Earlier we identified how attribution errors may negatively impact CPS practices with ethno-racial families. Negative practices may also derive from what we call "comparison error." In initial encounters with ethno-racial families and subsequent efforts to provide services to them, contrasts between "West" and "East," in which these locations are posited as in "good" versus "bad" and "moral" versus "immoral" comparisons, take place due to the tendency to view Western culture as more enlightened or superior than another culture (Razack 1998; Miller and Maiter 2008). Razack (2004: 7) illustrates the challenge:

> A message of Southern cultural inferiority and dysfunction is so widely disseminated that when we in the North see a veiled woman, we can only retrieve from our store of information that she is a victim of her patriarchal culture or religion. Few alternative images or more complex evaluations are possible.

More recently, feminist scholars of colour (Razack, Smith, and Thobani 2010) have examined in detail the complex ways in which race, gender and class operate in both the Canadian context and in Western power. They highlight historical efforts by Canadian governments to maintain Canada's "racial purity," from the time of its first prime minister, Sir John A. Macdonald, in 1885 through to a half century later to another Prime Minister, Mackenzie King, and onto the early twenty-first century of prime minister Stephen Harper's Conservative government. MacDonald and King saw "African" and "Asiatic" people as members of "unwholesome" races, whose inclusion in Canada would lead to a "mongrel" race and "debase" Anglo-Saxon civilization, while their habits and nature would make it impossible for White people of European ancestry to coexist with them. In a similar vein, Harper's government recently issued a new *Citizenship Guide*, which stated, "Canada's openness and generosity do not extend to *barbaric cultural practices*" (emphasis added, in Razack et al. 2010: ix). Razack, et al. (2010: ix) go on to note:

> The new *Citizenship Guide* defends Anglo-Saxon civilizational practices against what it calls the "barbaric cultural practices" of the Others. What is notable about this suspect gesture, nominally in support of women's rights, is that it is blind to the persistence of violence against women in Canada, including the hundreds of murdered and disappeared Aboriginal women. It suggests, instead, that such violence lies within the *barbaric cultures* of non-Western — Asian, African, and Middle Eastern — societies. It is a contemporary expression of earlier representations of the impossibility that Others cannot "wholesomely amalgamate" with the dominant Canadian culture. (emphasis in original)

These discourses are so historically entrenched in the Canadian context and then reinforced at current times that they become a part of widely accepted Canadian reality and leave little room for other evaluations of these groups. These powerful forces and discourses influence CPS approaches to ethno-racial groups and contribute to the negative bias they face when they are tangled up in CPS processes.

The Child Protection Context and the Problem with Cultural Competency

The *Canadian Incidence Studies* of child abuse and neglect conducted in 1998, 2003, and 2008 provide some insights into the profiles of families served by CPS systems, including characteristics of children and families, types of abuse reported, and emotional outcomes for children. However, except for Indigenous families, *CIS* data contain only limited information on ethno-racial diversity. Specific information on exposure to violence toward women as a category of investigation with ethno-cultural families is largely unavailable. Still, there is ample evidence from other research and from practice examples that racialized women and families struggle with the CPS system.

Canadian researchers have identified higher rates of reporting of child maltreatment and decisions to substantiate maltreatment for visible minority groups (Blackstock 2007; Blackstock et al. 2004; Lavergne et al. 2008; Trocmé et al. 2009). As discussed in detail in the first chapter of this book, racialized families and Indigenous people are over-represented in Canada in the identification and reporting of child maltreatment cases to CPS, as well as in decisions about the substantiation of maltreatment. Moreover, in reviewing data from the *CIS*-2003 study (Lavergne et al. 2008), researchers found that when groups were broken out further, Indigenous children were most over-represented, followed by Blacks and Latinos, while Caucasians, Asians and Arabs were under-represented. The researchers separated reports of abuse by type of maltreatment and found that, when only physical abuse was considered, Asian children were over-represented at 14 percent of the sample, or 1.6 times higher than their percentage in the general population. Since workers did not identify "child vulnerability factors" and "parental and housing risk factors" as areas of concern for these families, the authors conclude that the results suggest a degree of racial bias in the identification and reporting of cases to CPS and in decisions to substantiate maltreatment. The authors also speculate, however, that problems within these families relating to the above factors may have been missed, thus leading them to suggest: "It is also possible that child welfare workers have more trouble identifying problems in these [visible minority] families than in others because they lack the cultural competency required to accurately decode the socio-cultural world and the family structures and dynamics of immigrants from non-Western countries" (Lavergne et al. 2008: 74).

While it is important to acknowledge the difficulties that CPS workers may experience in identifying struggles of these families, relying on "cultural competency" to understand the issues is problematic (see Maiter 2009b; Jeffery

2009). A cultural-competency approach can lead to attempts to "understand" a culture — an impossible task that can result in reifying a culture, seeing it as unchanging and set in time. The fluid and changing nature of people and communities is lost in this approach; moreover, seeing groups as outside of the "mainstream" contributes to comparison errors. More importantly, a cultural-competency approach does not allow for an examination of the pervasiveness of "Whiteness" (Jeffery 2009) and its influence on Western perceptions of "Others" and their communities, cultures, and religions. When structural issues with which these families may be struggling are mistakenly ascribed to culture, the result is often a failure to assess their need appropriately and to provide services that address these needs. Culturalized perceptions of parents can lead to essentializing a group based on stereotypes of racialized families. Thus societal perceptions of racialized families as being more violent can contribute to increased reporting and substantiating of these families. Lavergne et al. (2008) reported that, according to *CIS-2003* data, ethno-racial families were over-represented for physical abuse while under-represented for other forms of child maltreatment. However, South Asians parents who participated in a Canadian qualitative study noted that in their view child protection services became involved with them because they were experiencing the following: family conflicts; parent-teen issues; parental mental health issues; issues such as struggles with nursing; exposure to intimate partner violence; and sexual abuse (Maiter and Stalker 2011).

Complex issues in families may be more difficult to identify because of a host of barriers, including language challenges. Parental use of physical discipline can also hide some of the structural struggles families are encountering. Researchers in the United Kingdom have identified that racialized children and families overall are more likely than other children to come to the attention of CPS in crisis situations (Thoburn, Chand and Proctor 2005). Waiting until a crisis develops before children come to CPS attention can result in additional difficulties for families. For example, parents may lose the chance to give input that might have been available to them had intervention come at an earlier stage. As well, adversarial dealings between CPS professionals and parents are more likely at later stages of CPS involvement (Qureshi, Berridge, and Wennman 2000).

Assessment Issues
The discussion of CPS investigative work by Lavergne et al. (2008), who found that the under-representation of Asian children at intake for the reporting of abuse gave way to over-representation when reported physical abuse alone is considered, suggests that racial bias influences decisions about substantiation of child maltreatment. Many other researchers support this contention (see, for example, Dettlaff, and Rycraft 2010; Maiter, Alaggia, and Trocmé

2004; Sedlak and Broadhurst 1996; Sedlak and Schultz 2005). As a result, CPS caseworkers may be missing problems being experienced by ethno-racial families, with the result that families may not be provided with supports or referred to resources that might prevent escalation of difficulties.

A qualitative study of the experiences of visible minority families, mostly immigrants who had come in contact with CPS in southern Ontario between 2003 and 2005, elicited themes regarding their settlement struggles as well as issues relating to their interactions with CPS systems (Maiter, Stalker, and Alaggia 2009). Settlement issues include a deep sense of loneliness and isolation, betrayal and hopelessness, financial problems, lack of recognition of professional credentials, and language barriers. Families themselves may contribute to inaccurate CPS assessments, being either unable to fully express the complex stressors in their lives or unwilling to share these details because they are ashamed. Other factors such as concerns about being misunderstood by caseworkers and past experiences of racism may further contribute to their sense that they are perceived as inferior, causing them to be wary of sharing information (Maiter and Stalker 2011). Finally, they may hold the common fear of all vulnerable families involved with CPS: that if they share their problems, they may be misunderstood and face the temporary or permanent removal of children from their care.

The Impact on Women: Intersection of Gender, Race, and Class

Throughout this book, contributors explore the implications of failure-to-protect statutes, policies, and practices, which have come to dominate CPS responses when men assault their intimate partners or sexually assault children. Maternal response to child sexual abuse has been a dominant research focus for the past two decades, and mother-blame discourses remain prevalent. This is evidenced by studies documenting mothers' dissatisfaction with CPS responses which were steeped in criticism and judgements that leave women feeling ever more isolated and distressed (Fong and Walsh-Bowers 1998; Plummer and Eastin 2007). The small percentages of mothers who are least supportive of their abused children have received a disproportionate amount of attention (Bolen and Lamb 2002; Heriot 1996), even though ambivalent responses that change over time are not evidence of a mother's enduring failing but normative on a dynamic continuum of responses (Alaggia 2002; Bolen and Lamb 2007).

In Ontario, failure to protect is the automatic default position of CPS workers while they investigate complex case dynamics to determine if a mother has provided anything less than unqualified and unequivocal support for her child (Alaggia et al. 2007). Mother-blame discourse seems to be deeply entrenched in cases of child exposure to intimate partner violence and is perpetuated by provisions that failure to protect is strongly suspected and has to be ruled out. In other words, a mother is "guilty until proven innocent." The introductory and other chapters in this book reference the heightened attention and vigorous enforcement now brought to both actual harm and risk of harm to children. Increasingly, in both Canada and the U.S., questions are being raised about the reach of child protection statutes and policies. Some writers suggest that perhaps these have gone too far and mothers are being re-victimized by CPS interventions (see, for example, Edleson 2004; Edleson, Gassman-Pines, and Hill 2006; Jaffe, Crooks, and Wolfe 2003; Magen, Conroy, and Del Tufo 2000; Magen 1999).

One unintended consequence of failure-to-protect policies may be that they create conditions where women are hesitant to disclose violence directed at them (Jaffe, Crooks, and Wolfe 2003; Alaggia et al. 2007; Nixon et al. 2007). At the same time, perpetrators of violence are not regularly engaged by CPS (Bourassa et al. 2008). A recent study conducted in southern and eastern Ontario (Alaggia, Gadalla, and Shlonsky 2010) found that only one-third of perpetrating partners were contacted as part of the investigation; CPS workers focused instead on mothers. Mother-blaming and perpetrator-avoidance are common investigative responses (Davies and Krane 2006; DeVoe and Smith 2003; Humphreys and Absler 2011), and mothers are often accused of failing to protect their children if they are unable, or are seen to be unwilling, to leave an abusive partner. Further, they are frequently assessed as having parenting deficiencies (Kantor and Little 2003). A mother who stays with the perpetrator when involved with child protection risks longer and more intensive intervention, or even the apprehension of her children (Alaggia et al. 2007; Sev'er 2002).

The literature is replete with research that articulates very real and valid barriers for abused women who contemplate leaving abusive relationships. Nonetheless, CPS workers expect them to leave, disregarding or downplaying insurmountable structural and intra/inter-personal barriers, and perhaps even increased risk of serious harm by perpetrators after separation (Alaggia, Regehr, and Rishchynski 2009). In a sample of immigrant and refugee women in Toronto and surrounding areas, the majority of the women participants are racialized. Many of these women are sponsored by their partners: these women cited fears of deportation and other immigration vulnerabilities if they leave. These vulnerabilities included compromising their citizenship application, especially if they reported their abuser who was also their sponsor. As well, they cited a lack of economic resources to sustain their family as a single parent and the prohibitive costs of seeking a sole immigration application for themselves and their children through a protracted process under humanitarian and compassionate grounds within the *Immigration Act*. Additionally, they reported a desire to maintain family unity and noted shame related to acknowledging abuse. Not surprisingly, language barriers were noted as a significant barrier, both with interacting outside of their cultural community and also in terms of the paperwork required to continue their immigration bid. Finally, fear that surveillance by other social services could lead to CPS interventions and child apprehension, and concern that police involvement could result in harsh treatment of their partners were repeatedly identified as factors creating reluctance to involve any authorities to halt the intimate partner violence (Alaggia et al. 2009).

Findings about whether or not exposure to intimate partner violence will result in child removal are mixed. American studies claim rates of removal as high as 80 percent when intimate partner violence is considered a moderate or high risk, and/or when other forms of maltreatment coexist (English, Edleson, and Herrick 2005; Humphreys 2000). Alternatively, findings from Canada suggest that intimate partner violence is no more likely to result in removal than other forms of maltreatment (Trocmé, Fallon, MacLaurin et al. 2005; Lavergne et al. 2008). Nonetheless, parents fear the loss of their children in any encounter with CPS, and ethno-racial, immigrant, and refugee families have particular fears, including that disclosing partner abuse will set off a chain reaction of negative events; their parenting will be scrutinized and perhaps found to be "different," which would increase the likelihood of child removal; and their immigration status, or the precarious status of refugees whose files are under review, will be negatively influenced (Alaggia et al. 2007, 2009). In addition, undocumented immigrants do not want to draw attention to themselves under any circumstances (Alaggia et al. 2009).

Reports of partner abuse are often made by concerned community members or neighbours, or by school personnel who contact CPS when children exhibit troubled behaviours in class or disclose that their mothers are being abused. Although there is little data available on other racialized families in the Canadian context, research shows that Indigenous women run a higher risk of being reported to CPS for intimate partner violence (Blackstock 2007; Blackstock, Trocmé, and Bennett 2004; Lavergne, Dufour, and Trocmé et al. 2008), suggesting that ethno-racial mothers face a similar risk. Of equal concern is the possibility that intimate partner violence will remain a secret, and victims will receive no services or supports. Black's (2010) Canadian study indicates that when exposure to intimate partner violence was identified and substantiated on its own, without other co-occurring maltreatment, CPS workers tended towards shorter interventions, terminating involvement and closing 64 percent of cases after initial investigation. Once a case is closed, it is unclear what the post-investigation needs of the family may be and whether they are being met in other ways. There is a possibility that attempts will be made to hide violence in the family in order to avoid future investigations.

Differential Response Models

The differential response approach, a recent innovation in CPS, has the potential to generate better outcomes for families being investigated for exposure to intimate partner violence (Conley 2007; Waldfogel 1998). Philosophically, differential response evolved from the notion that some children and their families may benefit from voluntary community-based services, while those at high risk still require traditional child protection services (Conley 2007; Edleson 2004; Waldfogel 1998). Differential response models implemented in a number of Anglo-American jurisdictions were in part created to respond to limited resources, dramatic increases in CPS referrals, and increased public scrutiny (Friend, Schlonsky, and Lambert 2008; Trocmé, Knott, and Knoke 2003). In this approach, cases categorized as high-risk typically include sexual abuse, serious physical or emotional harm, chronic neglect, and cases where criminal charges have been laid. All other types of referral are considered less urgent and can be referred for assessment of the short- and long-term needs of the children and their families. CPS workers will then effectively link families to appropriate supportive services in t he community.

It has been suggested by Friend, Schlonsky, and Lambert (2008: 695) that a differential response in situations of intimate partner violence would start with a safety and risk assessment. Subsequently, low-risk cases would be referred to community agencies that are contracted with CPS to provide appropriate voluntary services. Representatives from violence-against-women shelters or Elders could be included to work with the community agency. Friend et al. note that these multiple perspectives may make it possible to establish good connections with the family and also have the potential to be less threatening and disempowering to women who are exposed to partner violence. For instance, within a differential response approach, more effort is likely to be exerted by CPS to connect with client strengths, and referrals for mothers and their children would promote less intrusive and more supportive interventions.

Research on service involvement and outcomes based on differential response is still in its infancy and presents a somewhat perplexing picture (Marshall et al. 2010). Implementation with ethno-racial, refugee, and immigrant families can be especially difficult for CPS, given that language and communication barriers, cultural and contextual misunderstandings, and preconceived ideas of these families can all contribute to the level of risk assigned to mothers. Services such as shelters have not necessarily been designed for transportability to all ethnic, racial, and cultural contexts. Despite well-intended referrals, racialized families may remain poorly served in the absence of community-based services that provide a good cultural "fit." Ethno-racial families require services that are free of racism; can provide for their dietary and customary needs; ensure that families feel welcomed and treated fairly without being judged; and provide interpreter and counselling services. Differential response models frequently operate with unrealistic assumptions about community capacity for providing these sorts of services.

Policy and Service Issues

We share the conviction that underlies other contributions to this book, namely, that failure-to-protect policies and practices must be abolished because they inappropriately blame women for men's violence and exculpate perpetrators and absent fathers. Families coming to the attention of CPS are identified as being isolated (Palmer, Maiter, and Manji 2006) and lacking in support networks (Manji, Maiter, and Palmer 2005). These aspects can often be heightened for racialized and immigrant families if they are newcomers to the country, are unable to secure good employment, are not able to locate helpful resources, and are struggling with language barriers. Experiences of racial discrimination further contribute to these difficulties.

CPS interventions in intimate partner violence situations require respectful collaborations with ethno-racial families and must be informed by a theoretical framework that looks beyond essentialized cultural explanations, or generalized notions of patriarchy, to truly understand the structural constraints on these families. Johnson-Odim (1991), in *Third World Women and the Politics of Feminism*, argues that "third world" women see feminism among "first world" women as being narrowly confined to a struggle against gender discrimination and its consequences. Third world women often describe their struggles as being connected to struggles with other forms of oppression, including racism and economic exploitation. This viewpoint in no way represents a lack of commitment to women's equality, but rather recognizes the intersecting oppressions in the lives of women of colour and the sense that mainstream feminism centralizes a gender-specific concern that is too narrow to include intersectionality (Mirza 2009; Razack 2004).

Finally, the need for "expanding or deepening domestic violence training" and "ensuring that CPS staff has access to domestic violence specialized expertise" has been identified, alongside the need for collaboration with skilled and experienced intimate partner violence workers (LaLiberte et al. 2010: 1645). For interventions with ethno-racial families, skills training and service provision need to reflect an understanding of the diverse contexts of these families. Developing such understanding is still in its very early stages; however, acknowledging the barriers to services that we have identified in this chapter offers a starting place for action.

Policy and Service Recommendations

One of the authors of this chapter (Mutta) has considerable direct experience of racialized families, intimate partner violence, and CPS interventions
in his role as executive director of Punjabi Community Health Services,
in Brampton, Ontario: we draw on his rich experience in making recommendations for change in CPS systems. Together with him, we suggest that
in order to be effective, CPS practices must continually be tailored to each
family. Like Johnson and Sullivan (2008), we recognize that there will be instances when removal of children from their home is warranted because of
extreme physical and/or psychological risk, but well-informed policies and
trained and empathetic workers can offer invaluable assistance to families in
intimate partner violence situations. Removal of children from their parents
also poses so many well-known risks that most alternatives must always be
considered. Most importantly, the perpetrator of abuse should be held solely
responsible for the abuse and its consequences, and CPS interventions such
as parenting plans should be targeted to the perpetrator. The case scenario
below provides a good example of missed opportunities for CPS intervention
with the perpetrator:

> CPS was called in when a racialized mother with a five-year-old son
> called the police for an incident of intimate partner violence. Dad
> was arrested and was legally ordered to leave the home. The legal
> case is now closed with no restrictions on Dad about returning home.
> CPS, however, has been visiting Mom and has informed her that, if
> Dad returns home, they will have to remove her son from her care.
> There is pressure all around from Dad and other family members
> to allow Dad to return, as he has been to anger-management and
> substance-abuse programs. CPS talks to Mom but has no contact
> with Dad.

As can be seen here, the mother in this situation is being held responsible for
the violence she has experienced and is also being asked to do the impossible:
control her partner's behaviour, including preventing him from returning to
the family home. In this situation, CPS could usefully meet directly with the
father, establish a clear plan that holds him accountable for the abuse, and
spell out the changes that are required before he returns home.

Mutta reports that Punjabi Community Health Services is routinely
involved in these situations and finds that often their role is to remind CPS
of the other major part of the CPS mandate, that is, to preserve families.
When family preservation is the goal, CPS can work collaboratively with the
perpetrator to establish the changes he must demonstrate prior to any return
to the family home. The agency also finds that intimate partner violence
situations provide great teaching opportunities about resources and services

available for individuals and families. CPS assessments must be individualized to each family so that protective factors in the family can be explored; mothers' support networks can be extended; and families can be linked to needed resources such as mental health counselling, substance abuse programs, and parenting programs. Like most mothers in intimate partner violence situations, ethno-racial mothers who do not see alternatives may think that the violence is inevitable and that there is no possibility for change. Direct intervention with perpetrators and a supportive approach to mothers can challenge such beliefs and allow for the exploration of alternatives.

These policy and practice recommendations are in accord with findings from research that explored what mothers in situations of intimate partner violence wanted from their service providers. Mothers in a study of twenty participants, half of whom were White and half African American, reported that helpful workers were those who believed them; confronted the perpetrator; offered services and referrals; engaged with and advocated for them with other systems; protected them from harassment from the assailant's family; provided information on processes and expectations; offered encouragement; placed the children with those whom they trusted if the children had to be removed; maintained contact with them after the children's removal; and testified in court on the dynamics of abuse (Johnson and Sullivan 2008: 255). These findings are congruent with those from research with CPS clients in situations not specific to intimate partner violence (Maiter and Stalker 2011; Trotter 2002). For example, parents in a study in Ontario reported that they wanted more contact with their CPS worker; instrumental and therapeutic help; better information about reasons for CPS interventions; guidance around parenting in general and parenting teens specifically; referrals to parenting and support groups; focus on the family as a whole; intensive in-home services that addressed their broader needs rather than a focus on the incident that resulted in intervention; and sensitivity to their cultural and contextual situation (Maiter and Stalker 2011: 146). These findings suggest that there are considerable possibilities for working with mothers in ways that are supportive and non-threatening and that do not hold them responsible for the violence they have experienced.

References

Ahmed, Sara. 2000. *Strange Encounters: Embodied Others in Post-Coloniality*. London: Routledge.

Alaggia, Ramona. 2002. "Balancing Acts: Reconceptualizing Support in Maternal Response to Intra-Familial Child Sexual Abuse." *Clinical Social Work Journal* 30, 1.

Alaggia, Ramona, Tahany Gadalla, and Aron Shlonsky. 2010. *Differential Response in Cases of Domestic Violence in the Child Welfare System*. Ontario Ministry of Children and Youth Services.

Alaggia, Ramona, Angelique Jenney, Josephine Mazucca, and Melissa Redmond. 2007. "In Whose Best Interest? A Canadian Case Study of the Impact of Child Welfare Policies in Cases of Domestic Violence." *Journal of Brief Therapy and Crisis Intervention* 7, 4.

Alaggia, Ramona, and Sarah Maiter. 2006. "Intimate Partner Violence and Child Abuse: Issues for Immigrant and Refugee Families." In R. Alaggia and C. Vine (eds.), *Cruel but Not Unusual: Violence in Canadian Families*. Waterloo, ON: Wilfred Laurier University Press.

Alaggia, Ramona, Cheryl Regehr, and Giselle Rishchynski. 2009. "Intimate Partner Violence and Immigration Laws in Canada: How Far Have We Come?" *International Journal of Law and Psychiatry* 32, 6.

Bernard, Claudia. 2001. *Constructing Lived Experiences: Representations of Black Mothers in Child Sexual Abuse Discourses*. Aldershot: Ashgate Publishing.

Black, Taro. 2010. "Children's Exposure to Intimate Partner Violence (IPV): Challenging Assumptions about Child Protection Practice." Unpublished doctoral dissertation, University of Toronto.

Black, Tara, Nico Trocmé, Barbara Fallon, and Bruce MacLaurin. 2008. "The Canadian Child Welfare System Response to Exposure to Domestic Violence Investigations." *Child Abuse and Neglect* 32, 3.

Blackstock, Cindy. 2007. "Residential Schools: Did They Really Close or Just Morph Into Child Welfare?" *Indigenous Law Journal* 6, 1.

Blackstock, Cindy, Nico Trocmé, and Marlyn Bennett. 2004. "Child Maltreatment Investigations Among Aboriginal and Non-Aboriginal Families in Canada." *Violence Against Women* 10, 8.

Bolen, Rebecca, and Leah J. Lamb. 2002. "Guardian Support of Sexually Abused Children: A Study of its Predictors." *Child Maltreatment* 8, 3: 265–76.

___. 2007. "Can Nonoffending Mothers of Sexually Abused Children Be Both Ambivalent and Supportive?" *Child Maltreatment* 12, 2.

Bourassa, Chantal, Chantal Lavergne, Dominique Damant, Geneviève Lessard, and Pierre Turcotte. 2008. "Child Welfare Workers' Practice in Cases Involving Domestic Violence." *Child Abuse Review* 17, 3.

Conley, Amy. 2007. "Differential Response: A Critical Examination of a Secondary Prevention Model." *Children and Youth Services Review* 29, 11.

Cross, Terry L. 2008. "Disproportionality in Child Welfare." *Child Welfare* 87, 2.

Davies, Linda, and Julia Krane. 2006. "Collaborate with Caution: Protecting Children, Helping Mothers." *Critical Social Policy* 26, 2.

Dettlaff, Alan J., and Joan R. Rycraft. 2010. "Factors Contributing to Disproportionality in the Child Welfare System: Views from the Legal Community." *Social Work* 55, 3.

DeVoe, Ellen R., and Erica L. Smith. 2003. "Don't Take My Kids: Barriers to Service Delivery for Battered Mothers and Their Young Children." *Journal of Emotional Abuse* 3, 3–4.

Edleson, Jeffrey L. 2004. "Should Childhood Exposure to Adult Domestic Violence Be Defined as Child Maltreatment under the Law?" In Peter G. Jaffe, Linda L. Baker, and Alison J. Cunningham (eds.), *Protecting Children from Domestic Violence: Strategies for Community Intervention*. New York: Guilford Press.

Edleson, Jeffrey L., Jenny Gassman-Pines, and Marissa B. Hill. 2006. "Defining Child

Exposure to Domestic Violence as Neglect: Minnesota's Difficult Experience." *Social Work* 51, 2.

English, Diana J., Jeffrey L. Edleson, and Mary E. Herrick. 2005. "Domestic Violence in One State's Child Protective Case Load: A Study of Differential Case Dispositions and Outcomes." *Children and Youth Services Review* 27, 11.

Epstein, Deborah. 1999. "Effective Intervention in Domestic Violence Cases: Rethinking the Role of Prosecutors, Judges, and the Court System." *Yale Law Journal* 11, 3–9.

Fong, Josephine, and Richard Walsh-Bowers. 1998. "Voices of the Blamed: Mothers' Responsiveness to Father-Daughter Incest." *Journal of Family Social Work* 3, 1.

Friend, Colleen, Aron Shlonsky, and Liz Lambert. 2008. "From Evolving Discourses to New Practice Approaches in Domestic Violence and Child Protective Services." *Children and Youth Services Review* 30, 6.

Haque, Eve. 2010. "Homegrown, Muslim and Other: Tolerance, Secularism and the Limits of Multiculturalism." *Social Identities* 16, 1.

Heriot, Jessica. 1996. "Maternal Protectiveness Following the Disclosure of Intrafamilial Child Sexual Abuse." *Journal of Interpersonal Violence* 11, 2.

Hill, Robert B. 2007. "An Analysis of Racial/Ethnic Disproportionality and Disparity at the National, State and County Levels." <http://www.aecf.org/KnowledgeCenter/Publications.aspx?pubguid={86210406-E174-44F4-88A6-8E7A3DC338E6}>.

Humphreys, Cathy. 2000. *Social Work, Domestic Violence and Child Protection: Challenging Practice.* Bristol: Policy Press.

Humphreys, Cathy, and Deborah Absler. 2011. "History Repeating: Child Protection Responses to Domestic Violence." *Child & Family Social Work* 16, 4.

Jaffe, Peter G., Claire Crooks, and David A. Wolfe. 2003. "Legal and Policy Response to Children Exposed to Domestic Violence: The Need to Evaluate Intended and Unintended Consequences." *Clinical Child and Family Psychology Review* 6, 3.

Jeffery, Donna. 2009. "Meeting Here and Now: Reflections on Racial and Cultural Difference in Social Work Encounters." In Susan Strega and Sohki Aski Esquao (Jeannine Carrière) (eds.), *Walking this Path Together: Anti-Racist and Anti-Oppressive Child Welfare Practice.* Halifax: Fernwood Publishing.

Jiwani, Yasmin. 2010. "Doubling Discourses and the Veiled Other: Mediations of Race and Gender in Canadian Media." In Sherene H. Razack, Malinda Smith, and Sunera Thobani (eds.), *States of Race: Critical Race Feminism for the 21st century.* Toronto: Between the Lines.

Johnson, Susan P., and Cris M. Sullivan. 2008. "How Child Protection Workers Support or Further Victimize Battered Mothers." *Affilia: Journal of Women and Social Work* 23, 3.

Johnson-Odim, Cheryl. 1991. "Common Themes, Different Contexts: Third World Women and Feminism." In Chandra Talpade Mohanty, Ann Russo, and Lourdes Torres (eds.), *Third World Women and the Politics of Feminism,* Bloomington and Indianapolis: Indiana University Press.

Kantor Glenda Kaufman, and Liza Little. 2003. "Defining the Boundaries of Child Neglect: When Does Domestic Violence Equate with Parental Failure to Protect?" *Journal of Interpersonal Violence* 18, 4.

Kohl, Patricia L., Richard P. Barth, Andrea L. Hazen, and John A. Landsverk. 2005.

"Child Welfare as a Gateway to Domestic Violence Services." *Children and Youth Services Review* 27, 11.

LaLiberte, Traci, Jessie Bills, Narae Shin, and Jeffery L. Edleson. 2010. "Child Welfare Professionals' Responses to Domestic Violence Exposure Among Children." *Children and Youth Services Review* 32, 12.

Lavergne, Chantal, Sarah Dufour, Nico Trocmé, and Marie-Claude Larrivee. 2008. "Visible Minority, Aboriginal, and Caucasian Children Investigated by Canadian Protective Services." *Child Protection* 87, 2.

Lu, Yuhwa Eva, John Landsverk, Elissa Ellis-Macleod. Rae Newton, William Ganger, and Ivory Johnson. 2004. "Race, Ethnicity, and Case Outcomes in Child Protective Services." *Children and Youth Services Review* 26, 5: 447–61.

Magen, Randy H. 1999. "In the Best Interests of Battered Women: Reconceptualizing Allegations of Failure to Protect." *Child Maltreatment* 4, 2.

Magen, Randy H., Kathryn Conroy, and Alisa Del Tufo. 2000. "Domestic Violence in Child Welfare Preventative Services: Results from an Intake Screening Questionnaire." *Children & Youth Services Review* 22, 3–4.

Maiter, Sarah. 2009a. "Using an Anti-Racist Framework for Assessment and Intervention in Clinical Practice." *Clinical Social Work* 37, 4.

____. 2009b. "Social Justice Not Assimilation or Cultural Competence." In Susan Strega and Sohki Aski Esquao (Jeannine Carrière) (eds.), *Walking this Path Together: Anti-Racist and Anti-Oppressive Child Welfare Practice.* Halifax: Fernwood Publishing.

Maiter, Sarah, Ramona Alaggia, and Nico Trocmé. 2004. "Perceptions of Child Maltreatment by Parents from the Indian Subcontinent: Challenging Myths about Culturally Based Abusive Parenting Practices." *Child Maltreatment* 9, 3.

Maiter, Sarah, and Carol Stalker. 2011. "South Asian Immigrants' Experience of Child Protection Services: Are We Recognizing Strengths and Resilience?" *Child and Family Social Work* 16, 2.

Maiter, Sarah, Carol Stalker, and Ramona Alaggia. 2009. "The Experiences of Minority Immigrant Families Receiving Child Welfare Services: Understanding How to Reduce Risk and Increase Protective Factors." *Families in Society* 90, 1.

Manji, Shehenaz, Sarah Maiter, and Sally Palmer. 2005. "Community and Informal Support for Recipients of Child Protective Services." *Child and Youth Services Review* 27, 3.

Marshall, Sheila K., Grant Charles, Kristin Kendrick, and Vilmante Pakalniskiene. 2010. "Comparing Differential Responses Within Child Protective Services: A Longitudinal Examination." *Child Welfare* 89, 3.

McRoy, Ruth. 2004. "The Color of Child Welfare." In K. Davis and T. Bent-Goodley (eds.), *The Color of Social Policy.* Alexandria, VA: Council on Social Work Education.

Miller, Wayne, and Sarah Maiter. 2008. "Fatherhood and Ethnicity: Moving Beyond Cultural Competence." *Journal of Cultural and Ethnic Diversity in Social Work* 17, 3.

Mirza, Heidi Safia. 2009. "Plotting a History: Black and Postcolonial Feminisms in 'New Times'." *Race Ethnicity and Education* 12, 1.

Mohanty, Chandra Talpade. 1994. "Under Western Eyes: Feminist Scholarship and Colonial Discourse." In Patricia Williams and Laura Chrisman (eds.), *Colonial*

Discourse and Post-Colonial Theory: A Reader. New York: Columbia University Press.

Nakhaie, M. Reza. 2006. "A Comparison of the Earnings of the Canadian Native-Born and Immigrants, 2001." *Canadian Ethnic Studies* 38, 2.

Nixon, Kendra L., Leslie Tutty, Gillian Weaver-Dunlop, and Christine Walsh. 2007. "Do Good Intention Beget Good Policy? A Review of Child Protection Policies to Address Intimate Partner Violence." *Children and Youth Services Review* 29, 12.

Palmer, Sally, Sarah Maiter, and Shehenaz Manji. 2006. "Effective Intervention in Child Protective Services: Learning from Parents." *Child and Youth Services Review* 28, 7.

Plummer, Carol, and Julie A. Eastin. 2007. "System Intervention Problems in Child Sexual Abuse Investigations: The Mothers' Perspectives." *Journal of Interpersonal Violence* 22, 6.

Qureshi, Tarek, David Berridge, and Helen Wenman. 2000. *Where to Turn? Family Support for South Asian Communities — A Case Study.* London: National Children's Bureau.

Razack, Sherene. 1998. *Looking White People in the Eye: Gender, Race and Culture in Courtrooms and Classrooms.* Toronto: University of Toronto Press.

___. 2004. "Imperilled Muslim Women, Dangerous Muslim Men and Civilised Europeans: Legal and Social Responses to Forced Marriages." *Feminist Legal Studies* 12, 2.

Razack, Sherene H., Malinda Smith, and Sunera Thobani. 2010. *States of Race: Critical Race Feminism for the 21st Century.* Toronto: Between the Lines.

Rolock, Nancy, and Mark. F. Testa. 2005. "Indicated Child Abuse and Neglect Reports: Is the Investigation Process Racially Biased?" In Dennette Derezotes, John Poertner, and Mark F. Testa (eds.), *Race Matters in Child Welfare: The Overrepresentation of African American Children in the System.* Washington, DC: CWLA Press.

Sedlak, Andrea J., and Diane D. Broadhurst. 1996. *Third National Incidence Study of Child Abuse and Neglect.* Washington, DC: U.S. Department of Health & Human Services, National Clearinghouse on Child Abuse and Neglect Information.

Sedlak, Andrea J., and Dana Schultz. 2005. "Racial Differences in Child Protective Services Investigation of Abused and Neglected Children." In Dennette Derezotes, John Poertner, and Mark F. Testa (eds.), *Race Matters in Child Welfare: The Overrepresentation of African American Children in the System.* Washington, DC: CWLA Press.

Sev'er, Aysan. 2002. "A Feminist Analysis of Flight of Abused Women, Plight of Canadian Shelters: Another Road to Homelessness." *Journal of Social Distress and Homelessness* 11, 4.

Simich, Laura, Sarah Maiter, and Joanna Ochocka. 2009. "From Social Liminality to Cultural Negotiation: Transformative Process in Immigrant Mental Wellbeing." *Anthropology and Medicine* 16, 3.

Strega, Susan, Claire Fleet, Leslie Brown, Lena Dominelli, Marilyn Callahan, and Christopher Walmsley. 2008. "Connecting Father Absence and Mother Blame in Child Welfare Policies and Practice." *Children and Youth Services Review* 30, 7: 705–16.

Thobani, Sunera. 2010. "White Innocence, Western Supremacy: The Role of

Western Feminism in the 'War on Terror'." In Sherene H. Razack, Malinda Smith, and Sunera Thobani (eds.), *States of Race: Critical Race Feminism for the 21st Century.* Between the Lines: Toronto.

Thoburn, June, Ashok Chand, and Joanne Proctor. 2005. *Child Welfare Services for Minority and Ethnic Families.* London: Jessica Kingsley Publishers.

Trocmé, Nico, Barbara Fallon, Bruce MacLaurin, Joanne Daciuk, Caroline Felstiner, Tara Black et al. 2005. *Canadian Incidence Study of Reported Child Abuse and Neglect — 2003: Major Findings.* Ottawa: Minister of Public Works and Government Services Canada.

Trocmé, Nico, Barbara Fallon, Bruce MacLaurin, Vandna Sinha, Tara Black, Elizabeth Fast, Caroline Felstiner, et al. 2008. "Characteristics of Substantiated Maltreatment (Chapter 4)." *Canadian Incidence Study of Reported Child Abuse and Neglect — 2008: Major Findings,* <phac-aspc.gc.ca/cm-vee/csca-ecve/2008/cis-eci-08-eng.php>.

Trocmé, Nico, Della Knoke, Barbara Fallon, and Bruce MacLaurin. 2009. "Differentiating Between Substantiated, Suspected, and Unsubstantiated Maltreatment in Canada." *Child Maltreatment* 15, 1: 4–16.

Trocmé, Nico, Theresa Knott. and Della Knoke. 2003. "An Overview of Differential Response Model, 2003 (1)." Toronto, ON. Center of Excellence for Child Welfare. Faculty of Social Work, University of Toronto. <cecw-cepb.ca/publications/452>.

Trotter, Chris. 2002. "Worker Skill and Client Outcome in Child Protection." *Child Abuse Review* 11, 1.

Waldfogel, Jane. 1998. "Differential Response: A New Paradigm for Child Protection." In Jane Waldfogel (ed.), *The Future of Child Protection: How to Break the Cycle of Abuse and Neglect.* Cambridge, MA: Harvard University Press.

8. Creating Islands of Safety

Contesting Failure to Protect and Mother-Blaming in Child Protection Cases of Paternal Violence against Children and Mothers

Cathy Richardson and Allan Wade

Dedication
We dedicate this chapter to the Métis and First Nation families who have inspired this work, particularly those who bravely participated in the Islands of Safety pilot project on Vancouver Island.

We have been directly and indirectly involved in child protection cases for thirty years and have witnessed first-hand both beautiful responses to Indigenous families in cases of paternal violence against women and children, and humiliating responses that replicate colonial domination and enable further violence by the offender. In response to the latter kinds of cases, we obtained funding from the B.C. Law Foundation to develop and apply an alternative model for child protection for Métis and urban Indigenous families in cases of paternal violence against children and mothers, working in partnership with Métis Community Services in Victoria. This chapter describes the main tenets and key practices of the Islands of Safety model.

We chose the name Islands of Safety for several reasons. We live and work in an extraordinary archipelago and wanted to attach the model to the land, just as many Indigenous activists attach their social justice work to the land. For instance, the Liard Aboriginal Women's Society (LAWS) named its community development and residential school response, "Let's Get Together on the Land." Second, we wanted to stress that Indigenous (and non-Indigenous) families do not inhabit a benign world. Rather than a sea of safety and equality surrounding islands of violence, the reality is that families face a sea of violence and inequality surrounding islands of safety. As other writers in this book note, this reality is also common for other racialized and marginalized families. Finally, we wanted to acknowledge the Signs of Safety model, developed by Turnell and Edwards (1999) with Indigenous families in Australia, for its rigorous approach to safety and risk assessment in child protection. Previous chapters in this book analyzed failure to protect and its application in CPS systems. In this chapter, we demonstrate a way of working that contests many of the unhelpful practices common to failure-to-protect approaches.

We use the terms violence and equality in a broad sense. Colonial and intimate partner violence both entail physical domination and attacks on the dignity of victims. Paternal violence, an identified feature of all the cases we worked with in applying the Islands of Safety model, refers to violence, including threats and intimidation, physical violence and humiliation, unpredictability, surveillance and interrogation, financial coercion, and sexualized violence, by a father or father-figure against his partner, attacks on the mother-child bond, and violence directly against children. We purposely include harm to a spouse or intimate partner as a form of paternal violence. Some cases involved all these forms of violence, while others involved only partner assault. Throughout this chapter, we use the terms "violence" and "paternal violence" interchangeably to refer to the forms of violence mentioned above.

Origins of the Work

This chapter is based primarily on an ongoing collaborative project involving the development of response-based practice, resistance knowledges, and dignity-oriented therapies (Richardson 2008b; Richardson and Reynolds 2012; Wade 1995, 1997), all of which are counselling approaches that are used to assist in the recovery of those who have experienced violence. It is also based on our research in the areas of violence, resistance, language, and the well-being of Indigenous families in the context of colonialism (Richardson 2004, 2006, 2008a, 2008b; Richardson and Wade 2008; Wade 2000). We also draw on findings from an external evaluation of the Islands of Safety model that explored aspects of the practice in the context of offering services to a Vancouver Island community (Emerson and Magnusson 2009).

Child protection work is an organized social response to violence and other forms of adversity where children are harmed or at risk of violence and other forms of mistreatment. Encounters between CPS and families are charged moments in which the power of the state is enacted with some of the most vulnerable members of society, including Indigenous peoples, who already face the burdens created by dire living conditions, government policies rooted in colonialism, and high levels of violence in their communities. Numerous reports reveal chronic problems in how CPS work is conceptualized and practised, in general, and with Indigenous peoples specifically (Thibodeau and Peigan 2007; Richardson and Wade 2008; Richardson 2008a; Sinclair 2007). When CPS interventions are poorly handled, they humiliate already violated family members, create less safety rather than more, and further alienate family members from one another, from the community, and from participation in civil society. The Islands of Safety model is an orchestrated social response to this reality, a method built on Indigenous cultural teachings and a response-based approach to direct service in cases of violence.

Social Responses

The term "social response" refers to the actions of family, friends, and authorities, such as CPS and police, toward the victim and offender, whenever violence is identified. By violence, we are referring primarily to physical and sexualized violence against people of all ages. However, discussion of trends around disclosure and contacting CPS authorities relate to those with access to these opportunities, such as adults or youth. Issues around disclosure for young people, and children's responses and resistance to violence, relate to issues of context, developmental levels and levels of connection, and/or isolation in terms of community and support people (Richardson and Wade in press).

Research shows that the quality of social responses may be the single best predictor of the level of victim distress (see, for example, Andrews, and Brewin 1990; Andrews et al. 2003; Moorcroft 2011). People who have experienced violence and receive positive social responses tend to recover more fully, to report violence, and to cooperate with authorities. Conversely, victims who receive negative social responses, such as being blamed or judged, not being believed, or experiencing delayed responses in the criminal justice system, tend to experience more intense and lasting distress. These victims are more likely to receive a mental illness diagnosis and less likely to work cooperatively with authorities. The quality of social responses is also a primary consideration for those who perpetrate violence. Men who commit intimate partner assault, for example, and who receive swift and certain social responses from the criminal justice system are more likely to complete treatment programs and less likely to reoffend (Gondolf 2009, 2004; Gondolf and White 2000).

Members of already marginalized and oppressed groups (including people with disabilities; people who identify as gay, queer, lesbian, bisexual, transsexual or transgendered; people who belong to racial and ethnic minorities) are more likely to receive negative social responses than are members of majority populations (Blackstock 2007; Blackstock et al. 2004; Dettlaff and Rycraft 2010; Lavergne et al. 2008). In Canada, two identifiable groups who are likely to receive negative social responses from authorities are Indigenous people and women violated by a male partner. Numerous investigations document extensive violence against Indigenous women, many of whom are mothers; these investigations demonstrate that the response of authorities has been highly inadequate. For example, many deaths and disappearances of Indigenous women were not investigated, partially because reports of missing Indigenous women were not taken seriously, or were dismissed because the women were considered to be surviving sex workers. These oversights led to the "Sisters in Spirit" campaign to acknowledge the lives of these women (Aboriginal Women's Action Network 2001; Amnesty International Canada 2004; Amnesty International 2009; Moorcroft 2011). Other researchers document that Indigenous mothers are more likely to be targeted by CPS

(Blackstock 2007; Blackstock, Trocmé, and Bennett 2004; Richardson and Nelson 2007). Moreover, because Indigenous children are apprehended at a much higher rate than the general population, in Canada as well as other Anglo-American jurisdictions such as the U.S. (Roberts 2002; Sedlak and Schultz 2005) and Australia (Tilbury 2009), they are more likely to experience the negative consequences associated with being "in care" (Blackstock 2007; Blackstock, Trocmé, and Bennett 2004; Richardson and Nelson 2007).

Negative social responses can also involve mistreatment and/or neglect in professional or medical situations. A low-income mother may wait for long hours with children in a clinic, without having access to a regular doctor, which could add to her distress. Lengthy delays in a court process intended to address violence are likely to amplify a mother's concerns for safety and stability, while a dangerous perpetrator is on the street. These types of social responses could be linked to sexism, homophobia, racism, able-ism, or classism. Some negative social responses are linked to structural or systemic issues, such as lack of funding for community clinics, child care, and safe houses. But this does not explain why some non-marginalized victims also receive negative social responses, or why professionals who espouse good client care also provide negative social responses in certain cases. Sometimes women who are abused by an intimate partner are exposed to a form of stigmatization or negative attitudes by others who think they should "just leave." But as James Scott (1990) points out, in *Domination and the Arts of Resistance*, what appears to be happening on the outside is often very different from the inner reality of violence and oppression. It is often impossible for others to know what is really going on in these types of situations. Indigenous mothers have experienced contempt and racism in negative dealings with police (Moorcroft 2011), in courts (Coates 2000; Coates and Wade 2007), and in mainstream services. For example, in "Taking Resistance Seriously" (Richardson and Wade 2008), the authors present a case study of "Lily," an Indigenous woman who was inappropriately arrested and charged immediately after she had been assaulted. Taken to jail, she was subjected to racist slurs by police, received no medical treatment, and was denied any information about her young daughter, who had been placed in a foster home. As we discuss elsewhere (Richardson and Wade 2008), since Indigenous people are exposed to interpersonal and structural racism on a daily basis, these responses from authority figures simply add to the negative social responses they experience daily.

Another indicator of negative social responses to people who have been harmed is the hesitancy to use the descriptive term "victim." Although the word "victim" means only that a person has been wrongly harmed, it is now used as an insult, as if it reflects the person's whole identity. Indigenous women are prime targets for this contempt because, as a group, they are more likely to experience multiple forms of violence (Monture-Agnes 1995);

less likely than other women to be actively protected by the state and larger society (Amnesty International 2004); already widely regarded in racist and classist terms as submissive and state-dependant; more likely to have been in state care as children (Blackstock 2007) and, therefore, seen as disordered; and less able to effectively challenge authorities due to inadequate legal and political representation. These realities underline the need for culturally based analysis and responses to violence, such as the Islands of Safety approach.

Islands of Safety

Islands of Safety is a pilot project involving a model and process for safety planning with Indigenous families. It was developed and piloted in 2007 and 2008, with Métis and urban Indigenous families, by Cathy Richardson in collaboration with Allan Wade from the Centre for Response-Based Practice. It was created as an alternative dispute resolution process by which CPS concerns could be addressed outside of the court system.

Islands of Safety is oriented toward human rights and informed by a gendered and culturally based analysis of violence (Burstow 1992; Kelly 1998). It integrates elements of response-based practice with attention to social justice issues, such as a family's access to services, rights, and culture in the context of colonialism (Richardson and Wade 2008); it also includes elements of the rigorous safety planning approach used in Signs of Safety (Turnell and Edwards 1999). The way of working is Indigenous, in that it includes all family members who want to participate and who can demonstrate a commitment to safety, and it encourages Indigenous healing practices that create safety. It is contextual and holistic in that it creates a space to address the context of colonial domination in Canada, past and present. This includes genocidal and ethnocidal activities, such as the violence committed against children and families by governments and churches responsible for the residential school system; the displacement of Indigenous peoples from their lands; and punitive child protection interventions (Blackstock 2007; Richardson and Nelson 2007). Islands of Safety challenges racist and classist practices rooted in the colonial view that Indigenous people must be managed and educated by state professionals (Todd and Wade 2003). This model could be adapted for use in other cultural groups, particularly communities that are collective in orientation, that are culturally oriented, and that are healing from various forms of state violence, as well as violence against the women in the family. The work aims to restore dignity to those who have suffered affronts, both past and present.

As a way of working, it is seeped in Indigenous culture and worldview. The role of the facilitators is to serve as a bridge between Indigenous cultural practices and the bureaucratic culture and language of CPS. Indigenous families are sometimes unfamiliar with bureaucratic and legal terms, court timelines, and government processes. The families involved in Islands of Safety prefer to work in a more holistic manner, with time taken to tell the accounts of their lives, including their family's internment in residential schools and previous encounters with CPS or other professional services. Family members often talk about their commitments to holding on to their children, as well as to helping the men in their lives who use violence. Cultural ceremonies are sometimes included in the meetings, such as the use of prayers, smudge, the inclusion of Elders, and cultural teachings.

The objectives of Islands of Safety include:

- to address violence in the family from a holistic perspective, restoring dignity and harmony whenever possible;
- to create a safety plan that will satisfy CPS needs and return children to their mother;
- to acknowledge and uphold the mother-child bond (which is often severed both through paternal violence against children and mothers, and through child protection decisions influenced by failure-to-protect approaches); and
- to include healing practices that acknowledge the historical colonial practices, including kidnapping, residential school internment, the destruction of culture and language, and past violence in the child welfare system.

The model is loosely organized around the symbolism of four blankets of different sizes, layered one upon the other, with the smallest blanket on top to highlight the place of children in family and community life. Blankets are used to represent the roles and responsibilities of family members; values and roles; and the interconnections between community members and all forms of life. The outer and largest blanket represents men, whose traditional role includes the responsibility to protect and provide for their family and for the larger community. The third and next largest blanket represents women, whose traditional role is to maintain the life of the community through their social, political, and cultural work, and by bringing community members together. The second blanket represents the Elders, the aunties and uncles, and grandparents, whose traditional role is to provide guidance to adults and oversee the care and education of children. The top blanket, the innermost and smallest, represents children, who are at the centre of life. The four blankets together represent "right relations" or "the proper order of life," according to Indigenous teachings, and are based on a larger blanket representing community and environment.

Structure Surrounding the Process

Although Islands of Safety can be practised by CPS teams with training and under supervision, it was conceived as a service external to CPS. There are a number of steps involved in the process:

1. A referral is received from CPS or an Indigenous community agency or an individual.
2. Islands of Safety meets with the CPS worker to receive more information about the situation, such as the worker's view of the family; evidence the worker saw that Islands of Safety might be a good fit for the family, with signs of safety and risk identified by the worker; challenges the worker faced; and what the worker hoped to achieve with the family.
3. The CPS worker gives the family the Islands of Safety contact information.
4. A meeting is held with the parents, with an emphasis on the father's participation.
5. The mother is established as a point of accountability, because any safety plan must attend to her safety, as well as the safety of children.
6. A series of meetings with the parents and the CPS workers takes place, both separately and together, to prepare for a larger conference and to ensure clarity and "buy-in" to the process.
7. Working with a larger group chosen primarily by the father, a one-day safety planning meeting is held, to develop and document a safety plan with goals, timelines, and criteria for evaluation.

The majority of referrals to the Islands of Safety program involved a male perpetrator and a mother who was trying to support him to change, while simultaneously trying to parent her children apart from him. Less frequent were referrals involving both the mother and the father enacting some kind of violence, often referred to as "fighting" by the CPS worker. We found that it was important to engage with the father or father-figure as soon as possible in the process, given that men often avoid the CPS worker and sometimes lose contact with their families (Strega et al. 2009). CPS workers may contribute to this avoidance because of concerns about the father's aggression, or because they believe he will not change and should not see the children. Workers may see the mother as responsible and "failing to protect" her children for a variety of reasons. Mother-blaming attributions commonly applied to mothers by CPS workers include: "she chose poorly in entering into a relationship with a violent man"; "she did not leave the relationship when he became violent"; or "she lacked appropriate boundaries" and therefore became involved with a violent man (Johnson and Sullivan 2008; Richardson and Wade 2008).

Because so much CPS practice involves failure-to-protect biases and assumptions about parents, it is necessary for Islands of Safety facilitators to contest these formulations throughout the process, offering more informed, contextual, and cultural information about the mother and her existing efforts to protect her child. Because even violent fathers make efforts, at times, to attend to the safety of their partners and their children, it was important to also bring these to the attention of CPS workers. Islands of Safety work requires eliciting accurate descriptions and analyses of both safety and risk, as well as accurately documenting the many ways that mothers resist violence.

Beginning the Conversation

In the first contact we ask to meet with the father and the mother in order to introduce ourselves, explain the Islands of Safety approach, and answer questions. We emphasize that participation is voluntary: they can withdraw at any time, as can we. We stress that the process will involve some difficult conversations. In order to understand the situation, we will have to talk frankly and in detail about the violence itself and how family members responded, both at the time and since. We explain that we will need the father to provide a release of confidentiality, so that we can obtain any third-party information, such as police reports, about the violence. If the mother and the father agree to move forward, we then discuss who will meet first. In all cases, we have at least one private meeting with the mother. This ensures she has an opportunity to discuss information that she feels cannot be presented safely in the presence of her partner.

When we sit down together for the first full meeting, we may begin with a prayer and by burning some Indigenous cleansing medicines, such as sage or sweet grass. We spread the blankets out, along with some cultural items, such as children's moccasins, an eagle feather, medicines, children's toys, or a birch bark basket on a table.[1] These become the basis for conversations about communal and family life, often sparked by our questions: What do men do in your family? How do they relate to children? What do women do? Where do the Elders fit in? How about children? We develop a comprehensive map of the family and the ancestors, asking about which family members are involved in the present circumstances. This creates space for family members to talk about where they come from and to identify present and past family members, their collective history, different roles in the family, how the family usually works, what they like to do together, their relationship to culture and language, and their challenges and aspirations. We learn about the quality of relationships, express appreciation for the privilege of sitting together, and share some information about ourselves, who we are, where we come from, and how we came into the work.

Response-Based Practice

We are then in a position to ask family members how they became involved with CPS authorities. There is always a history to the current crisis, often a series of interventions over several years, even generations, and prior involvement with a series of professionals, from police to psychiatrists. We try to get a sense of how family members are experiencing the present intervention, how they relate to the CPS worker, and how they see violence or what the CPS worker identities as "protection concerns," in relation to legislation and policy. This begins a more focused interview on the violence itself, which we facilitate in accordance with the principles of response-based practice.

Response-based practice evolved from direct work with victims and perpetrators of violence (Response-Based practice 2011; Todd and Wade 2003; Wade 1995, 2000, 2007). Like others before us (Burstow 1992; Kelly 1988; Scott 1990), we saw that victims of violence invariably resist the violence, either covertly or overtly, depending on the combination of dangers and opportunities in their unique situations. This simple but important observation forced us to review our entire approach to working with violence. Professional training in the field of family violence focuses on identifying and treating the effects or impacts of violence. But resistance is a response to violence and cannot be understood or discussed in the language of effects and impacts. We began to see that such language portrays victims as passive recipients of violence and conceals their resistance. For us, response-based practice became a process of elucidating and honouring the victim's resistance to violence, not a process of treating its so-called effects. Consider the following example:

> A woman and man return home to their children after a dinner out, and send the babysitter home. The man then begins to berate and threaten the woman, who responds by trying to keep quiet so as not to awaken and scare the children. However, the man becomes more aggressive and then physically violent. The oldest child comes downstairs and is terrified by the scene. The man swears and spits on the woman and kicks her in the ribs before he kicks the door open and leaves.

Would it make sense that the woman would feel terrified for herself and her children? Would it make sense that she would lie awake, night after night, wondering what will happen next? Will the police come? Will CPS take her children? Would it make sense that the woman would "cocoon" herself, because she is too tired and sad to interact with friends and family? Would it make sense that the woman would stop doing the things that gave her pleasure, such as going to the gym after work, seeing friends for coffee, watching the kids at dance class? Would it make sense that the woman would feel intense despair and even consider killing herself? When she was a little girl, she saw her father beat her mother, and she promised herself her children would never see such terror. Now they have and she feels like hell.

Would it make sense that, because she is focused on safety, on what might happen next, on getting through the day, on making her children feel safe, the woman would have trouble remembering the hundreds of details a parent needs to remember every day?

Would it make sense that the woman might eat high-carbohydrate foods to comfort herself, or refuse to eat at all because she is sick to death of violence and fear? Suppose the woman goes to the local mental health centre, where the policy is that a psychiatric diagnosis is necessary before services are provided. Given that much of what is described above are symptoms of clinical depression, she would almost certainly be seen as clinically depressed. Treatment would be aimed at her depression, because "it" would be seen as illness or disorder, or perhaps as a reactive syndrome. In effect, the treatment would be aimed at eliminating what we, as response-based practitioners, see as this woman's most immediate and poignant forms of protest, in the name of therapy. This is precisely like engaging all the starving people in the world in a psycho-educational program to eliminate their appetite. It makes no more sense.

From a response-based perspective, we can describe how the woman resisted the violence as it occurred and after, in part through her physical, emotional, intellectual, and spiritual responses. To characterize those responses as symptoms of illness is to transform understandable and healthy resistance into a disorder. With this shift in our approach, we begin to see more clearly that perpetrators take deliberate steps to suppress the resistance of their victims. Men who use violence also use many strategies to isolate women (e.g., surveillance, threats, accusations, physical control, control of money, isolation from friends and family) and to prevent them from disclosing the violence (e.g., threats, secrecy, deception, violence, child abuse). A woman who has been threatened with more violence may be reluctant to contact the authorities, particularly if the perpetrator has also made threats relating to the children's safety and future custody. A woman who faces real danger and does not have a network that she can count on for positive responses is the least able to overtly resist violence. Yet the helping professions tend to denote intimate partner assault as an effect of forces, such as anger, tension, alcohol, and/or masculinity, that compel the man to use violence; they do not see that he may have made a decision to do so. The formulation of a perpetrator as "out of control" or "just losing it" conceals the deliberate nature of the violence and obscures the man's responsibility. Examples of this type of discourse, including the use of hydraulic metaphors, can be found in the cycle theories of violence that shape most services for victims — and perpetrators — of intimate partner violence (Richardson and Wade 2008).

Our observations raised important questions. If victims always resist violence, why are they portrayed as passive or dysfunctional people who fail to protect their children? If perpetrators take deliberate steps to suppress that resistance, why are they portrayed as hapless individuals who are driven to violence by forces they do not understand and cannot control? These questions forced us to examine how language is used to misrepresent violence. For instance, although violence is unilateral in that it consists of harmful actions by one person against another, it is often described as mutual or joint, as though the victim shares responsibility. Linda Coates' (2000) research on language used in courts in cases of violence shows that a unilateral assault or attack is often later mutualized as "a conflict" or "a fight." For example, if a perpetrator shoves his tongue down a person's throat, it is often referred to as "kissing" in court.

In criminal justice and human services work, including CPS, language is often used to conceal violence, obscure perpetrator responsibility, conceal victim responses and resistance, and blame and pathologize victims (Coates and Wade 2003, 2007). In stark contrast, our intention in response-based practice is to expose violence, clarify perpetrator responsibility, elucidate and honour victim responses and resistance, and contest the blaming and pathologizing of victims. These practices rely on evidence, on events in context, and on gathering clear accounts of who is doing what to whom and how the other is responding to these actions.

Obtaining Clear Descriptions of Violent Actions in Context
We argue that it is crucial, in CPS cases of paternal violence, to obtain clear and accurate descriptions of actions in immediate settings and larger social and historical context, with a minimum of psychological jargon. We use language that reveals the deliberate and unilateral nature of violence and the victim's responses and resistance to that violence. If we learn that Bob hit Sue, for example, we want to learn how he hit Sue, who else was around, and what else was happening. We will ask Bob what he did and how he did it, but we avoid language that portrays Bob as out of control, and instead highlight actual actions that show Bob was actually in control of his behaviour. Paradoxically, these descriptions often reveal that Bob already possesses forms of awareness and self-control that have not been previously acknowledged (Lehmann and Simmons 2009). For example, we can pose a more psychological question pertaining to perpetrators, "What is wrong with someone that they would commit violence?" or we could offer different formulations, such as: What conditions are in place that would permit someone to commit violence and get away with it? Under what conditions would a person choose not to enact violence? These reformulations get to the heart of the social and contextual pre-conditions for violence in society.

Focus on Victim and Offender Responses to the Violence
As we develop a clear description of Bob's actions in context, we begin to focus on how Sue responded at the time and how at least some of her responses can be understood as forms of resistance. We will ask Sue to describe what she did and felt, outwardly and inwardly, and try to understand the situation from her point of view. Asked about interactional details, she might report how she tried to move her body to protect herself from blows or to move closer to the door. She might clarify how she deliberately avoided screaming so as to not wake the children, or how she secretly dialed 911 on her cell phone and then hid the phone from the perpetrator's view. As we get a picture of Sue's responses, we begin to ask more focused questions. How did you manage to stay so calm and remember to protect your children? So, when you closed the bedroom door did you say anything to your children? Is this the first time you have had to stand up for yourself in this way? In what other ways were you taking care of yourself and your children? In accordance with the philosophy of response-based practice, these questions acknowledge Sue's resistance and put her more directly in touch with her own capacities. They also contest the notion that Sue was passive, or lacked boundaries, or chose an abusive husband, or failed to protect her children (Richardson and Wade 2008). The view that victims are socialized into submission and lack boundaries is common in the anti-violence field, including in the cycle theory of violence first circulated by Lenore Walker. Walker described some forms of women's resistance, but then adopted the theory of learned helplessness to explain their alleged passivity.

> If she has been through several cycles already, the knowledge that she has traded her physical and psychological safety for this temporary dream state adds to her self-hatred and embarrassment. She is selling herself for brief periods of phase-three behaviour. She becomes an accomplice to her own battering (69). [Battered women's] behaviour is determined by their negative cognitive set, or their perceptions of what they could or could not do, not by what actually existed. (1979: 48)

Here, women's presumed submissiveness is presented as the catalyst of the abuse. Women are portrayed as active only to the extent that they invite violence (i.e., they "build the gateway" and "grant abusers") while violence by men is portrayed as an effect of forces ("tensions") they cannot control (Ciraco 2001).

We also focus on Bob's responses to his own actions and to Sue's responses, both at the time of an attack and afterwards. When you saw that Sue was afraid of you, what did you do? Once you sat back and thought this over, what did you think? What are your concerns about this? Since taking stock of the fact that you were violent to Sue, and that you terrified your children, what have you done to ensure it will not happen again? What is important to you at this time? In what ways have you been working to help your children overcome their fear and feel safe at home? In this way we begin to build a description of how Bob makes sense of his own actions and how he orients to his own responsibility for violence and for positive change. These questions point to Bob's responsibility for non-violent and respectful behaviour by asking him to talk about his own concerns and what actions he has taken or will take to increase the safety of his partner and children. Also, Bob may take the opportunity to express how violence is wrong but how he learned about it from the adults in his life (for example, as a child imprisoned in a residential school) and how he received no help from the adults that he told. This provides a context of his early learning about violence. This process may be important for his dignity, which may make him more interested in participating in ongoing conversations about safety for his children and his partner. The Islands of Safety model acknowledges colonialism as a precondition for violence in Canada; it is acknowledged as a form of violence that created the conditions for future violence to be perpetuated, often with impunity. Exploring these contextual factors and the realities of life for Indigenous families sets this method apart from many Euro-Canadian services.

Identify Social Responses

As we noted earlier, the quality of social responses is profoundly important in cases of intimate partner violence. We ask the victim and offender, both Bob and Sue, to talk about what kinds of social responses they have received from family and friends, and from criminal justice and human services professionals. We might ask Sue: When your mom and dad found out that Bob had assaulted you and that the police were involved, what did they say? What did they do? What do your friends think? How did it go with the police? What happened when the CPS worker came over? How did that conversation go for you? From Sue's responses, we begin to build a picture of the system of social responses available to her. Often, victims of violence report negative and quite demoralizing responses from others (Andrews and Brewin 1990; Andrews et al. 2003; Moorcroft 2011; Richardson and Wade 2008).

We have found that asking perpetrators about social responses can be an effective way to create safety and facilitate the conversation. Men who have been abusive to their female partners also report negative and humiliating social responses from professionals; they say they are treated as nasty, one-dimensional, and non-redeemable. We listen carefully as men like Bob describe negative social responses. We not only want to show that we understand their desire for dignity, but we also find that in describing their experiences men often reveal their own belief in the importance of fairness and a sense that everyone deserves to be treated with respect. This information supports findings that there is a context to every form of negative behaviour, even violence. Staff at the Calgary Women's Shelter, who also provide services for men with accountability to women, have made a practice of exploring the particular context of violence (Todd et al. 2009). Many Indigenous men who perpetrate violence have themselves been exposed to various forms of violence, often in residential school and foster care settings (Richardson and Nelson 2007); they need to discuss this aspect of their history as well as to receive opportunities for their own healing and recovery. Understanding that Indigenous men and women have both been stereotyped and have both experienced unhelpful interactions, we also ask questions about what kinds of social responses have been helpful. Who do you think has made a real effort to understand your concerns? What did they say or do that was helpful? Who else has been helpful? How?

Focus on Responses to Social Responses

Finally, we ask victims and perpetrators to talk about their responses to both positive and negative social responses. For example: So, Bob, once you saw that the social worker was not interested in how you see things, how did you respond? What did you do? Had I been a fly on the wall, how would I have known you were feeling silenced? How did you then manage that relationship? We might ask Sue: When the police officer asked you why you picked abusive men, and suggested you were a bad mother, what did you do? What was that like for you? How did you manage to hang on to the fact that you did your very best to protect your children? In what other ways have you protected yourself when you have been blamed for Bob's behaviour? In replying to these questions, victims and offenders begin to detail the many overt and covert ways they have for trying to maintain their autonomy, manage the power of "the system," and retain their dignity. These conversations also create space for family members to talk about residential school, foster care, and how they have responded to other forms of adversity they may have faced in the context of Canadian colonialism. By acknowledging these experiences, we affirm the dignity of all family members.

Honouring Resistance and Building Safety

To provide a culturally appropriate way of understanding Indigenous responses to adverse events, we rely on a tool called the Medicine Wheel of Responses (Richardson 2008b).

This visual tool acknowledges how individuals resist all forms of violence and reassert their dignity — physically, intellectually, emotionally, and spiritually. Stories of surviving the Canadian prison camps, euphemistically called residential schools, and stories of those who did not survive, demonstrate

Medicine Wheel of Responses

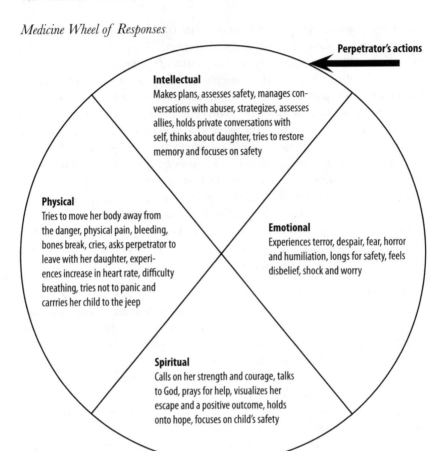

how many small acts of living can honour a dignified life, even in the face of murder and violence. Similarly, we contend that women routinely respond to, and resist, violence by their male partners, both as it occurs and often long after. As we have demonstrated elsewhere (Wade 1995; Coates and Wade 2007; Richardson 2008a, 2008b; Richardson and Wade 2008), wherever there is violence, people resist that violence in some way. An important feature of the Islands of Safety process is its capacity to generate accurate descriptions of the interaction between acts of violence and responses in situations involving parents and children. The process is guided by a commitment to safety for victims and justice that is not biased toward perpetrators of violence.

Walking the Middle Ground

Indigenous people must negotiate the spaces "between" various cultural worlds. One of the most important services we provide through Islands of Safety is to interpret the often complex language of CPS and legal professionals for Indigenous families, while simultaneously translating Indigenous cultural worldviews and values for professionals and caseworkers in state systems. This translation can be accomplished when a facilitator is culturally grounded in working with Indigenous communities and aware of the particular context, values, and cultural factors related to communication in a particular Indigenous community. Similarly, familiarity with professional systems and discourses, such as the legal, child-welfare, and psychological theories related to violence and abuse, is crucial to be able to convey this information to Indigenous families. One key purpose of this knowledge is to make sure that Indigenous parents are not subjected to the "shifting bar" that they report experiencing, thinking they have addressed a CPS worker's concerns only to find the worker presents a new list of concerns. Indigenous knowledge is an important resource that can be used to develop safety in child protection cases, promote peaceful coexistence in communities, and honour human dignity in general. Culturally based insights and wisdom are revealed in beautiful and tragic forms through individual and collective resistance to violence and oppression of all kinds, from wife-assault to administrative domination. We witness this through retrospective accounts of Indigenous children in residential school and their actions to protect one another from the violence and mistreatment of abusers. This is an aspect of response-based inquiry and community healing in which the Islands of Safety approach takes an important place.

Additional dignifying practices include gestures, such as asking permission before asking intrusive questions; acknowledging that we are probing into very sensitive and personal areas and showing an apologetic demeanor while doing so; ensuring cultural safety by offering tea and food; creating an Indigenous environment in decor; acknowledging the family's past history of interaction with professionals; and exploring what worked and what did not work well for them. We offer as much choice as possible in all aspects of structuring the meetings, although the primary participants with the mother at the centre are involved in contacting us to arrange meeting times. One of the Islands of Safety agreements is that we do not "track them down" for meetings. Primary participants take the lead in making major decisions, such as deciding who should be present at the larger safety conference. Considerations such as the availability of office space and the CPS worker's schedule dictate some of the structure, so exploration and negotiation are always a part of the process.

Our experience is that the Islands of Safety approach has been effective in our work with children, particularly in relation to Indigenous cultural precepts such as the beliefs that children are a gift from the Creator, and that children should be surrounded with loving relatives and a sense of belonging. Violence frequently disrupts a child's connection with members of family and community. Violence also forces children to respond and resist, but many forms of children's resistance continue to be ignored or seen as pathology. With rare exceptions, it is entirely inappropriate and often harmful to expose Indigenous children who have experienced violence to traditional psychiatric and psychological diagnostic practices. In Islands of Safety, we aim to enhance the full spectrum of social responses, from friends to professionals to policy makers, in part by revealing the emergent capacities of family members as they confront and resist violence, and by moving through the social response system to a place that recovers the joys of family life. We aspire to assist children and families to regain a sense of the sacred connections to their relatives, to the community, and to their land and culture. Once a family reconnects with the dignity that has been affronted, many more opportunities for reconnection tend to present themselves.

Although we developed Islands of Safety for use with Indigenous families in Canada, we believe it can be usefully applied with families from diverse ethno-racial cultures, drawing on what is most sacred for individuals within their own communities. We believe that cultural groups who have been displaced from a homeland and who look to their family traditions and spiritualty as a source of inspiration are likely to be most open to the Islands of Safety process.

Note

1. Many of these objects are from my own family; some made by my mother (Richardson); using these objects keeps the sacredness of the work alive and relevant from my own cultural perspective.

References

Aboriginal Women's Action Network. 2001. *"Research Report on the Implications of Restorative Justice for Women and Children in Isolated Communities in BC with Documented Histories of Violence."* Ottawa: Law Commission of Canada.

Amnesty International Canada. 2004. "Stolen Sisters: A Human Rights Response to Discrimination and Violence against Indigenous Women in Canada." <http://www.amnesty.org/en/library/info/AMR20/003/2004>.

___. 2009. "No More Stolen Sisters: The Need for a Comprehensive Response to Discrimination and Violence against Indigenous Women in Canada." <http://www.amnesty.org/en/library/info/AMR20/012/2009/en>.

Anderson, Kim. 2007. *A Recognition of Being: Reconstructing Native Womanhood.* Toronto: Sumach Press.

Andrews, Bernice, and Chris Brewin. 1990. "Attributions of Blame for Marital

Violence: A Study of Antecedents and Consequences." *Journal of Marriage and the Family* 52.

Andrews, Bernice, Chris Brewin, and Suzanna Rose. 2003. "Gender, Social Support and PTSD in Victims of Violent Crime." *Journal of Traumatic Stress* 6, 4.

Blackstock, Cindy. 2007. "Residential Schools: Did They Really Close or Just Morph into Child Welfare?" *Indigenous Law Journal*, 6, 1.

Blackstock, Cindy, Nico Trocmé, and Marlyn Bennett. 2004. "Child Maltreatment Investigations among Aboriginal and Non-Aboriginal Families in Canada." *Violence against Women* 10, 8.

Brown, Laura. 1991. "Telling a Life: Self-Authorization as a Form of Resistance." In C. Gilligan, A.G. Rogers, and D.L. Tolman (eds.), *Reframing Resistance: Women, Girls, and Psychotherapy*. New York: Haworth Press

Burstow, Bonnie. 1992. *Radical Feminist Therapy*. Newbury Park: Sage.

Ciraco, V.N. 2001. "Fighting Domestic Violence with Mandatory Arrest, Are We Winning? An Analysis In New Jersey." *Women's Rights Law Reporter* 22, 2 (Spring).

Coates, Linda. 2000. "Twice a Volunteer: Mutualizing Violence." Paper presented at the Women's Resistance Group, Duncan, BC.

Coates, Linda, and Allan Wade. 2007. "Language and Violence: Analysis of the Four Discursive Operations." *Journal of Family Violence* 22, 7.

_____. 2003. "Telling It Like It Isn't: How Psychological Constructs Obscure Responsibility for Sexual Assault." *Discourse and Society* 15, 5.

Dettlaff, Alan J., and Joan R. Rycraft. 2010. "Factors Contributing to Disproportionality in the Child Welfare System: Views from the Legal Community." *Social Work* 55, 3.

Department of Justice Canada. 2009. "Spousal Abuse: A Fact Sheet from the Department of Justice Canada." <http://www.justice.gc.ca/eng/sch-rch/sch-rch.asp?ResultStart=61&SearchTerms=self-defence&SearchIn=general>.

Ehrlich, Susan. 2001 *Representing Rape: Language and Sexual Consent*. London: Routledge.

Eliot, George. 2010. *Daniel Deronda*. Project Gutenberg release date February 5, 2010. Original work published 1876. <http://www.gutenberg.org/ebooks/7469>.

Emerson, Darcie, and Douglas Magnusson. 2009. "An Evaluation of Islands of Safety for Victims and Perpetrators of Violence in Families." University of Victoria, B.C.

Gondolf, Edward. 2004. "Evaluating Batterer Treatment Programs: A Difficult Task Showing Some Effects and Implications." *Aggression and Violent Behaviour* 9: 605–31.

_____. 2009. "The Survival of Batterer Treatment Programs: Responding to Evidence-Based Practice and Improving Program Operation." A position paper presented at the policy symposium "Batterer Intervention: Doing the Work and Measuring the Progress of the National Institute of Justice and Family Violence Prevention Fund." Bethesda, Maryland (Dec. 3–4).

Gondolf, Edwards, and Robert White. 2000. "Consumer Recommendations for Batterer Programs. *Violence Against Women* 196.

Goffman, Irving. 1961. *Asylums*. New York NY: Doubleday.

Johnson, Susan P., and Chris Sullivan. 2008. "How Child Protection Workers

Support or Further Victimize Battered Mothers." *Affilia: Journal of Women and Social Work* 23, 3.

Kelly, Liz. 1998. *Surviving Sexual Violence*. Minneapolis, MN: University of Minnesota Press.

Lamb, Sharon. 1991. "Acts Without Agents: An Analysis of Linguistic Avoidance in Journal Articles on Men Who Batter Women." *American Journal of Orthopsychiatry* 61, 2.

Lamb, Sharon, and Susan Keon. 1995. "Blaming the Perpetrator: Language That Distorts Reality in Newspaper Articles on Men Battering Women." *Psychology of Women Quarterly* 19, 2.

Lavergne, Chantal, Sarah Dufour, Nico Trocmé, and Marie-Claude Larrivee. 2008. "Visible Minority, Aboriginal, and Caucasian Children Investigated by Canadian Protective Services." *Child Protection* 87, 2.

Lehmann, Peter, and Catherine Simmons. 2009. *Strengths-Based Batterer Intervention: A New Paradigm in Ending Family Violence*. New York: Springer Publishing.

Monture-Agnus, Patricia. 1995. *Thunder In My Soul: A Mohawk Woman Speaks*. Winnipeg: Fernwood.

Moorcroft, Lois. 2011. "If My Life Depended on It: Yukon Women and the RCMP." Whitehorse, YT: Victoria Faulkner Women's Centre. <http://www.policereview2010.gov.yk.ca/pdf/If_My_Life_Depended_On_It_Yukon_women_and_the_RCMP_Jan.pdf>.

Response-Based Practice. 2011. "Greetings." <http://responsebasedpractice.com/>.

Reynolds, Vikki. 2010. "Doing Justice: A Witnessing Stance Alongside Survivors of Torture and Political Violence." In J. Raskin, S. Bridges, and R. Niemeyer (eds.), *Studies in Meaning 4, Constructivist Perspectives on Practice, Theory and Social Justice*. New York: Pace University Press.

Richardson, Catherine. 2006. "Métis Identity Creation and Tactical Responses Oppression and Racism." *Variegations* 2: 56–71.

___. 2008a. "Métis Experiences of Social Work Practice." In S. Strega and J. Carriere (eds.), *Walking This Path Together: Anti-Racist and Anti-Oppressive Child Welfare Practice*. Winnipeg, MB: Fernwood.

___. 2008b. "A Word Is Worth a Thousand Pictures: Working With Aboriginal Women Who Have Experienced Violence." In Lynda R. Ross (ed.), *Feminist Counselling: Theories, Issues and Practice*. Toronto: Women's Press.

___. 2009. "Islands of Safety and the Social Geography of Human Dignity: A Child and Mother Safety Planning Initiative for Cases of Paternal Violence in Child Welfare." *Federation of Community Social Services of B.C., Research to Practice Network*.

Richardson, Catherine, and Bill Nelson. 2007. "A Change of Residence: Government Schools and Foster Homes as Sites of Forced Aboriginal Assimilation." *First Peoples Child and Family Review* 3, 2: 75–84.

Richardson, Catherine, and Vikki Reynolds. 2012. "Here We Are, Amazingly Alive in the Work." *International Journal of Child, Youth and Family Studies* 3, 1: 1–19.

Richardson, Catherine, and Allan Wade. 2008. "Taking Resistance Seriously: A Response-Based Approach to Social Work in Cases of Violence Against Indigenous Women." In Susan Strega and Jeannine Carriere (eds.), *Walking This Path Together: Anti-Racist and Anti-Oppressive Child Welfare Practice*. Winnipeg MB: Fernwood.

____. 2010. "Islands of Safety: Restoring Dignity in Violence Prevention Work with Indigenous Families." *First Peoples Child and Family Review* 5, 1.

____. In press. *Points of Light: Children's and Mothers' Resistance to Violence.* Whitehorse, YT: Kaushee's Place Women's Transition Home.

Roberts, Dorothy. 2002. *Shattered Bonds: The Color of Child Welfare.* New York: Basic Books.

Scott, James. 1990. *Domination and the Arts of Resistance: Hidden Transcripts.* New Haven: Yale University Press.

Sedlak, Andrea, and Dana Schultz. 2005. "Racial Differences in Child Protective Services Investigation of Abused and Neglected Children." In Dennette Derezotes, Mark Testa, and John Poertner (eds.), *Race Matters in Child Welfare: The Overrepresentation of African American Children in the System.* Washington, DC: CWLA Press.

Sinclair, Raven. 2007. Identity Lost and Found: Lessons from the Sixties Scoop. *First Peoples Child and Family Review* 3, 1: 65–81.

Snow, Alison. 2001. "Cost of Batterer Treatment Programs: How Much and Who Pays?" *Journal of Interpersonal Violence* 15, 6.

Strega, Susan, Leslie Brown, Marilyn Callahan, Lena Dominelli, and Christopher Walmsley. 2009. "Working with Me, Working at Me: Fathers' Narratives of Child Welfare." *Journal of Progressive Human Services* 20, 1.

Thibodeau, Steven, and Faye Peigan. 2007. "Loss of Trust among First Nations People: Implications for Implementing Child Protection Treatment Interventions." *First People Child and Family Review* 3, 4: 50–58.

Tilbury, Clare. 2009. "The Over-Representation of Indigenous Children in the Australian Child Welfare System." *International Journal of Social Welfare* 18.

Todd, Nick, and Allan Wade. 2003. "Coming to Terms with Violence and Resistance. From a Language of Effects to a Language of Responses." In T. Strong and D. Pare (eds.), *Furthering Talk: Advances in the Discursive Therapies.* New York: Kluwer.

Todd, Nick, Gillian Weaver-Dunlop, and Cynthia Ogden. 2009. *The Subject of Violence: A Response-Based Approach to Working with Men Who Have Abused Others.* Calgary, AB: Calgary Women's Shelter.

Turnell, Andrew, and Stephen Edwards. 1999. *Signs of Safety. A Solution and Safety Oriented Approach to Child Protection Casework.* New York: WW Norton.

Wade, Allan. 1995. "Resistance Knowledges: Therapy with Aboriginal Persons Who Have Experienced Violence." In P.H. Stephenson, S.J. Elliott, L.T. Foster, and J. Harris (eds.), *A Persistent Spirit: Towards Understanding Aboriginal Health in British Columbia.* Vancouver: University of British Columbia.

____. 1997. "Small Acts of Living: Everyday Resistance to Violence and Other Forms of Oppression." *Journal of Contemporary Family Therapy* 19: 23–39.

____. 2000. "Resistance to Interpersonal Violence: Implications for the Practice of Therapy." Unpublished doctoral dissertation, University of Victoria, British Columbia.

____. 2007. "Despair, Resistance, Hope: Response-Based Therapy with Victims of Violence." In C. Flaskas, I. McCarthy and J. Sheehan (eds.), *Hope and Despair in Narrative and Family Therapy: Adversity, Forgiveness and Reconciliation.* Hove: Brunner-Routledge.

Walker, Lenore. 1979. *The Battered Woman.* New York: Van Nostrand Reinhold.

9. Child Protection Policy and Indigenous Intimate Partner Violence

Whose Failure to Protect?

Kendra Nixon and Kyllie Cripps

Although the ultimate goal of social policy is to improve the welfare of citizens, some policies that are introduced with the best intentions can have the opposite effect (Midgley 2000). Social policies can unintentionally further oppress and marginalize the very people they are designed to help. They can also have a gendered effect, meaning that women and men are impacted differently. Indigenous and other marginalized people are impacted in unique and profound ways when social policies disrupt and disconnect them from their cultural and kinship practices and responsibilities, or exacerbate their historical trauma, often associated with interventions related to dispossession, dislocation, and child removal. Racism either intentionally or unintentionally can also feature in this experience. Unfortunately, few social policies are adequately researched to determine their impacts and possible unintended consequences (Wharf and McKenzie 1998). In this chapter, we undertake such an examination with respect to child protection policies that are intended to address violence in the family.

Over the past decade, child welfare authorities in jurisdictions around the globe have made significant changes to child protection services (CPS) policies that attempt to protect children exposed to intimate partner violence. In a relatively small number of jurisdictions, statutory definitions of child maltreatment have been amended to include children's exposure to intimate partner violence as a form of child maltreatment (Nixon et al. 2007). This chapter specifically examines CPS policy in this area, focusing on Canada and Australia, with particular attention to potential impacts on Indigenous women, children, families, and communities. We argue that CPS policies regarding intimate partner violence may have especially devastating impacts for Indigenous women, given their unique experience with both the child protection system and intimate partner violence.

CPS policies aimed at protecting children may indeed have the opposite effect — that children will remain in abusive environments because their mothers are deterred from seeking services for fear that they and their children will be reported to CPS. As we discuss below, CPS intervention can often be unsupportive and even detrimental to children, with lasting consequences on their social and emotional well-being. The current CPS system attempts to keep children safe by focusing attention on abused mothers as non-protective caregivers and by defining the problem of intimate partner violence as indicative of individual or family dysfunction. Rarely is attention given to wider, systemic factors, such as patriarchy, colonization, racism, poverty, and women's social and economic inequality, that form the context in which men perpetrate violence against female intimate partners. Throughout this chapter, we argue that, given the current CPS context it is not the individual abused mother who is failing to protect her children from her own victimization, but rather it is the direct perpetrators of the violence, the CPS workers who hold mothers accountable for the violence perpetrated against them, and the policy makers who define the problem of intimate partner violence as essentially "failure to protect." It is our position that CPS policy makers must examine intimate partner violence (and other potential forms of child maltreatment) from a gendered perspective, as well as from a culturally appropriate perspective that takes into account the needs of Indigenous women, families, and communities.

Overview of Children's Exposure to Intimate Partner Violence

Wife abuse has been a concern in child protection work since the beginning of the child welfare profession. A key work on the history of family violence in the United States reveals that wife-beating was "common in [child welfare] case records" from 1870 through 1960 (Gordon 1988: 7). Despite the prevalence of woman abuse and the possible harm associated with children's exposure to such intimate partner violence, until quite recently child protection systems have not considered violence against mothers as an obvious concern unless children were directly harmed during a violent incident. In fact, the child protection system's mandate to uphold the best interests of the child has often precluded the interests and safety needs of battered women. Yet today, the issue has become a significant social concern, as indicated by the explosion of research on the immediate and long-term impact of children's exposure to violence in the home (Øverlien 2009).

The past two decades have seen a significant increase in research contending that witnessing violence may be damaging to a child's emotional and physical well-being (English et al. 2009; Evans, Davies, and DiLillo 2008; Holden and Ritchie 1991; McCloskey et al. 1995; Wolfe et al. 2003). Although significant limitations have been noted regarding this research, and children vary considerably in their responses, as discussed in Chapter 3, several meta-analytic studies conducted of this research (DiLillo 2008; Evans, Davies, and DiLillo 2008; Kitzmann, Gaylord, Holt, and Kenny 2003; Wolfe et al. 2003) conclude that there is a general consensus that exposure to violence in the home has a significant and measurable negative effect on children's functioning, relative to children from non-violent homes. Nevertheless, the complex and varied experiences and responses among children exposed to intimate partner violence, as well as the methodological limitations of research, indicate that the risks to children should be assessed and interpreted cautiously. Moreover, because of the difficulty of pinpointing the detrimental impact of intimate partner violence on children, policies that automatically assume that children are negatively impacted must be questioned.

Over the last decade or so, researchers have studied the impact of abuse on parenting, concluding that being abused has a direct and negative impact on behaviour as a parent, thus putting children at greater risk of physical and emotional harm (Holden et al. 1998; Levendosky et al. 2000). However, the conclusion that women's experiences of intimate partner violence have negative consequences for their mothering has been questioned: a growing number of studies provide evidence to refute these claims, concluding instead that these women often manage to be competent, nurturing parents (Casanueva et al. 2008; Letourneau, Fedick, and Willms 2007; Sullivan et al. 2000).

Despite the limitations of the current state of knowledge, child protection professionals and children's advocates typically view exposure to intimate partner violence as a serious form of child maltreatment (Nixon et al. 2007; Weithorn 2001). Widespread acceptance of the negative impacts of children's exposure to intimate partner violence has resulted in significant changes in child protection policy — not only in legislation, but also in standards, protocols, and organizational policies (Nixon et al. 2007).

Child Protection Policy and Intimate Partner Violence

In 2009, an estimated 6 percent of Canadians reported experiencing spousal violence within the last five years. Of these, over half (52 percent) of victims with children reported that their children had heard or seen assaults on them (Statistics Canada 2011). A national study on child maltreatment found that exposure to violence in the home was the second most common form of substantiated child maltreatment in Canada (excluding Quebec). An estimated 50,000 cases in which child exposure to violence was the only or primary maltreatment were substantiated by CPS in 2003 (Trocmé et al. 2005). The Australian Bureau of Statistics *Personal Safety Survey 2005* found that 0.9 percent (68,100) of men and 2.1 percent (160,100) of women aged fifteen years or older experienced current partner violence. Of these, 49 percent (111,700) reported that they had children in their care at some time during the relationship, and an estimated 27 percent (60,700) said that these children had witnessed the violence. The survey also asked respondents about violence from a past partner. Fifteen percent of women aged fifteen years and older reported being a victim of such abuse, with approximately 40 percent reporting that their children had witnessed the violence (Australian Bureau of Statistics 2006). More recently, children's exposure to intimate partner violence in Indigenous families in Victoria, Australia, was identified as the single biggest risk factor for child abuse notifications, being present in 64 percent of cases (Victorian Government Department of Justice 2008).

Briefly, CPS legislation provides the legislative grounds for intervention that legally defines which children are in need of protection; it is these grounds that determine the basis for protective intervention. Most jurisdictions include such harm as physical abuse, sexual abuse, emotional/psychological abuse, and neglect. In a new development, some CPS authorities have amended their legislation to include children's exposure to intimate partner violence as a form of child maltreatment, although this remains the exception. In the U.S., only Montana and West Virginia explicitly include child exposure to such violence as a form of child maltreatment within their statutory definitions of child abuse and neglect. In Australia, child exposure to intimate partner violence is explicitly defined in child maltreatment legislation only in New South Wales, the Northern Territory, the Australian Capital Territory, and Tasmania. However, all districts incorporate considerations with respect to child exposure to intimate partner violence in their child maltreatment policy and practice guidelines (see, for example: Department of Human Services - Victoria 2007; Families SA 2008).

In Canada, the Northwest Territories and seven provinces — Alberta, Saskatchewan, Quebec, New Brunswick, Nova Scotia, Prince Edward Island, and Newfoundland — have expanded the statutory definition of child abuse to include children who are exposed to intimate partner violence. It is important to note that many jurisdictions, in Canada and elsewhere, still intervene without having taken this step, usually by incorporating children's exposure to intimate partner violence in existing provisions for neglect or emotional abuse (Nixon et al. 2007; Weithorn 2001). In Ontario, for example, child exposure is not explicitly defined as a form of child maltreatment in the *Child and Family Services Act* (1990) but is incorporated under the provision for emotional harm. Similarly, exposure to family violence is recorded in Australia as a sub-category of emotional abuse (Department of Human Services — Victoria 2007). Child protection authorities have also attempted to address the impacts of violence in the home through the development of regulations and standards or interagency protocols, either in addition to, or instead of, amending their legal definitions of child abuse and neglect (Nixon et al. 2007; Weithorn 2001). Regardless of the type or level of policy change, CPS authorities are increasingly intervening in situations of children's exposure to intimate partner violence.

These recent changes not only allow workers to intervene when violence is reported, but also allow them to remove children from the home. This has sparked a contentious debate, with critics asserting that this new policy direction further victimizes abused women, ignores male perpetrators, and ultimately fails to protect children (Jaffe, Crooks, and Wolfe 2003; Nixon 2009b; Strega 2006). This is similar to the situation of child sexual abuse, as discussed by Carlton and Krane in Chapter 2, where non-abusing mothers are often deemed responsible. Indigenous women, children, and families may be even more detrimentally impacted, given the high incidence of family violence in these communities, the public nature of that violence, and the attention that it brings from police and child protective services (Robertson 1999, SCRGSP 2011). While official figures are not known as to how many Indigenous children are being removed as a consequence of policies relating to intimate partner violence exposure, what is known is that Indigenous children and their families are already significantly over-represented in out-of-home care by ten times the rate of non-Indigenous children (AIHW 2012). For Indigenous families, this policy may be a stark reminder of the historical policies and practices of child removal, which was a fundamental part of the colonial regime in both Australia and Canada. On the other hand, proponents assert that legislating child protection intervention in cases of exposure may sensitize front-line professionals and alert CPS to higher-risk families, leading to better assessment and intervention for children and families (Jaffe et al. 2003; Weithorn 2001). It is also argued that clearly defining exposure as maltreatment in legislation may enhance coordination and cooperation, promoting greater consistency in the handling of intimate partner violence cases amongst the various agencies involved (Weithorn 2001). Further, some believe that defining exposure as a form of child abuse may compel parents to stop the violence or to seek help in protecting their children (Jaffe et al. 2003; Weithorn 2001). Finally and perhaps most importantly, legally defining child exposure to intimate partner violence as child maltreatment is believed to send a clear message that violence in the home will not be condoned or tolerated in our society (Jaffe et al. 2003).

Nonetheless, many researchers and women's advocates have demonstrated that recent policy changes have resulted in unintended negative consequences, including blaming women for the violence that is perpetrated against them. It is argued that when intimate partner violence cases are brought to the attention of CPS workers, their efforts to keep children safe are presented as demands and instructions to mothers, further victimizing abused women (Humphreys 1999; Magen 1999; Miccio 1995; Nixon 2002, 2009a). A concentrated and narrow focus on child safety also ignores the actual perpetrators of the violence (Edleson 1998; Nixon 2002; 2009a; Strega et al. 2008). Miccio (1995) notes that the focus on mothers frames the problem of intimate partner violence in terms of what the abused woman failed to do, rather than looking at the perpetrator's violent actions within the family.

Although the concept of failure to protect originates in the American child welfare system, it is also routinely applied to women in Canada,

Australia, New Zealand, and the U.K. Child protection authorities often view women as "quasi-perpetrators," who are culpable for exposing their children to their own victimization; hence, the authorities may respond punitively to them, including removing their children from their care (Humphreys and Absler 2011; Nixon 2009b). For example, in Nixon's (2009b) study of thirteen abused mothers involved with CPS, the women were routinely mandated to undergo parenting assessments, drug assessments, and drug-testing, and to attend intimate partner violence groups. Many of the women also had their children removed, even in the absence of additional maltreatment concerns. Nixon (2009b) found that the mothers whose children were apprehended by CPS experienced overwhelming panic, grief, and loss (Nixon, Radtke, and Tutty in press), which culminated in serious health problems (e.g., headaches, depression, increased substance use, and suicidal thoughts). Other studies of abused mothers have reported similar reactions when children were removed from their care (Johnson 2006; Kellington n.d.).

There is justifiable and serious concern that defining exposure as a form of child maltreatment may lead to a reluctance on the part of abused women to disclose abuse to helping professionals, most notably the police and shelter workers, if they believe that they will be reported to CPS and that their children could be apprehended (Devoe and Smith 2003; National Council of Juvenile and Family Court Judges Family Violence Department 1999; Nixon 2009b). Indeed, abused women's fears of possible child apprehension appear to be valid; several studies have indicated that abused mothers are at greater risk of having their children apprehended than are non-abused mothers (Gordon, Hallahan, and Henry 2002; Hartley 2004; Law Reform Commission of Nova Scotia 1995; Robertson 1999; Stark and Flitcraft 1988; Wild and Anderson 2007).

It is not only abused women who may be prevented from getting help, but also their children. Again, women may be unwilling to access services for their children if they believe that there is a risk of CPS notification. When mothers and their children become involved with CPS because of suspected intimate partner violence (or other forms of suspected child maltreatment), the intervention can often be unsupportive and even detrimental to children, with lasting consequences on their social and emotional well-being (Nixon 2009b; Parkinson and Humphreys 1998; The "Failure to Protect" Working Group 2000). Further, the additional stress of CPS involvement can further compromise an abused woman's parenting ability, reducing her capacity to meet her children's emotional needs (Parkinson and Humphreys 1998). In cases of intimate partner violence, CPS workers routinely insist that women separate from their abusive partners, which often forces mothers and their children to leave their home, possessions, and neighbourhood. Not surprisingly, this is very stressful for mothers and children.

Moreover, separation often creates financial hardship for both mothers and their children (Parkinson and Humphreys 1998). Additionally, in one of the chapter author's experience (Cripps) in Australia, the parent who is the victim of intimate partner violence is often ordered to attend counselling and parenting and anger management programs. The costs associated with such services are to be borne by the parent. Some mothers simply cannot afford to participate in these mandated services, but failing to do so can result in delayed reunification, adversely affecting mothers and their children. Similar financial burden has also been noted in some Canadian jurisdictions. Nixon (2009b) found that while mothers did not have to pay for mandated programs, they often had to pay the transportation costs to attend programs, substantially adding to their financial stress and insecurity.

Indigenous Women and Child Protection Policy

The attention to children's exposure to intimate partner violence by CPS policy makers is relatively new; consequently, the specific impact of these policy changes on Indigenous women, and other groups who are already disproportionately involved with child protection authorities, has yet to be studied in any detail. Despite this significant gap, it is reasonable to predict that the shifts in policy direction and legislation in recent years will have especially devastating impacts for Indigenous women, given their unique experience with both the child protection system and intimate partner violence.

CPS involvement has had a disastrous impact on Indigenous families and communities. In Australia, it has been estimated that child welfare intervention affected between one in three and one in ten Indigenous families at different times during the period 1910–1970; it has been acknowledged that no Indigenous family escaped the effects of the forcible removal of their children (Human Rights and Equal Opportunity Commission 1997). In both Australia and Canada, government policies of assimilation targeted Indigenous children for removal from their families and communities. Government officials theorized that, by forcibly removing Indigenous children and indoctrinating them into the culture and values of the dominant society, over time they would effectively "merge" with the non-Indigenous population. Once taken, many of the children had limited opportunities to visit or reconnect with their families in the period immediately after their removal or in the years that followed. In Australia, Indigenous people commonly refer to these children as the "Stolen Generation" (Human Rights and Equal Opportunity Commission 1997). It should be noted that, due to the trauma of removal, as well as the physical, emotional, and sexual abuse and exploitation that they endured, children who were forcibly taken from their families were essentially denied their childhood. The effects of such removals were not limited to the children. For the family and kin left behind, their grief and trauma continued to be felt every day, compounded by the continued experience of profound disadvantage, including exclusion and control, racism, and poverty (Human Rights and Equal Opportunity Commission 1997; Petchkovsky et al. 2004; Silburn et al. 2006).

The effects of child removal are felt intergenerationally. Many people who are removed from their families as children will grow up without the necessary skills and supports to parent successfully: they miss out on the opportunity to draw on traditional child-care practices and kinship supports that would have been available to them had they grown up in their natural families and communities. These Indigenous-specific skills are not taught in parenting programs mandated by CPS and are difficult to obtain for this Stolen Generation, who are now parents, particularly if reunification with their natural families and/or communities has not been possible or has been limited in some way. For example, parents may have passed away before an adult child returns, or an Aboriginal community may not accept the individual as being who they say they are. Consequently, successive generations of family members fall under the surveillance of CPS, with increased risks of children being taken away or being exposed to destructive models of parental behaviour (Haebich 2000; Human Rights and Equal Opportunity Commission 1997; Johansen 2000; MacQueen 2000; Read 1999). Despite the elimination of policies that officially sanctioned the removal of Indigenous children from their families, Indigenous children continue to be over-represented in CPS interventions. In 2010–2011, Indigenous children in Australia were seven-and-a-half times more likely to be the subject of a child protection substantiation of abuse as non-Indigenous children; in June 2011 there were 12,358 Aboriginal and Torres Strait Islander children in out-of-home care — ten times the rate for non-Indigenous children (Australian Institute of Health and Welfare 2012). In Canada, in 2000–2002, between 30 and 40 percent of children and youth placed in out-of-home care were Indigenous, yet Indigenous children made up less than 5 percent of the total child population (Gough et al. 2005). Furthermore, CPS investigations are more likely to be substantiated for Indigenous families in Canada, and case files are more likely to be kept open for ongoing services (Blackstock et al. 2004).

With respect to experiencing intimate partner violence, Indigenous women are arguably more vulnerable to violence and more likely to be victims of it than any other group of society (Al-Yaman et al. 2006; Brownridge 2008; Cripps et al. 2009; Statistics Canada 2006). A Canadian study found that the rate of intimate partner violence against Indigenous women was more than three times higher than the rate for non-Indigenous women (Statistics Canada 2006). The same study noted that the severity and impacts of intimate partner violence are also greater: Indigenous women were significantly more likely to experience the most severe and potentially life-threatening forms of violence, including being beaten or choked, having had a gun or knife used against them, or being sexually assaulted. In Australia, the injuries for Indigenous women are equally significant. In the two-year period from July 1999 to June 2001, in a study of injury-related hospital separations in four of eight Australian states (Northern Territory, Western Australia, South Australia, and Queensland), Berry et al. (2009) found that Indigenous females had a forty-seven-fold greater hospitalization rate for intimate partner violence than that of non-Indigenous women. Head injuries caused by bodily force were the most common injury recorded. More recently, hospital separation data from five Australian jurisdictions, as well as from public hospitals in the Northern Territory, indicate that Indigenous women were hospitalized for partner-assault-related injuries thirty times more often than non-Indigenous females (SCRGSP 2011: Table 4A 11.8). This is not new information. Numerous Indigenous family violence inquiries have reported the seriousness of injuries inflicted upon Indigenous women and children for more than a decade (see, for example, Aboriginal Child Sexual Assault Taskforce 2006; Atkinson 1990; Robertson 1999; Wild and Anderson 2007).

The higher rates of violence experienced by Indigenous women are linked to the presence of multiple and interrelated risk factors. These include factors specific to belonging to an Indigenous minority: colonization policies and practices; dispossession and cultural dislocation; the damage to family and community structures caused by this history; and the added layer of forcible removal of children from many families. Other risk factors reflect broader social determinants, including unemployment, poverty, welfare dependency, disability, past history of abuse, substance addictions, and social marginalization (Al-Yaman et al. 2006; Cripps 2007, 2008). Cripps et al. (2009) also found potentially higher risks for women who are between the ages of fifteen and forty-four, who live by themselves, and who were removed from their families as children.

Indigenous women are also more likely than non-Indigenous women to come into contact with the police because of intimate partner violence due to the context in which the violence takes place. While it does often occur in the home. the violence can also take place in a public context, for example, in the front yard or on the street, thus drawing the attention of other relatives, community members, or neighbours, who inevitably call the police to assist, particularly when Indigenous women are sustaining quite serious injuries as a consequence of this violence. Circumstances like these, in which the police are called to intervene, are likely to increase due to the resent changes in legislation; for example, in Australia, the Northern Territory passed amendments in 2009 to the *Domestic and Family Violence Act* that mandate all adults to report intimate partner and family violence to police if they think someone has or is likely to suffer serious physical harm from this violence. Adults who fail to report domestic violence risk being charged with an offence under the *Act* and being fined a maximum of $22,000. Further, given the severe nature of the injuries that many Indigenous women sustain, it is probable that they will more often come to the attention of health care professionals, who in turn may report them to CPS. As a consequences of mandatory reporting or as a result of referrals from other agencies involved in attending to the violence and its aftermath, notably the police or health services, Indigenous women are now more likely to come to the attention of social agencies due to the (Aboriginal Child Sexual Assault Taskforce 2006; Gordon et al. 2002; Memmott et al. 2001; Mow 1992; Robertson 1999; Victorian Indigenous Family Violence Taskforce 2003; Wild and Anderson 2007). Given that police and social agencies are increasingly reporting children's exposure to intimate partner violence to child protection authorities (Humphreys 2008), Indigenous mothers are almost certainly at greater risk of CPS involvement in cases of intimate partner violence than non-Indigenous mothers; this involvement includes the possibility of having their children apprehended from their care. However, the lack of empirical research in this area precludes any definitive conclusions. In fact, a recent study actually revealed a lower risk of CPS involvement for Indigenous women. Trocmé et al. (2006) found that exposure to intimate partner violence was the primary substantiated form of abuse in 20 percent of Indigenous child maltreatment investigations, whereas in non-Indigenous child maltreatment investigations, exposure was the primary substantiated form in 30 percent of investigations.

However, statistics do not reveal the complexities of the experiences of Indigenous women who come to the attention of CPS as the result of intimate partner violence. They do not capture the nuances of kinship or community relationships and obligations, nor can they adequately capture the consequences of historical traumas upon women and their families or the daily experiences of racism that are often a feature of living as a racialized minority in a White society. But what statistics do tell us quite clearly is that Indigenous mothers who come to the attention of CPS authorities are typically younger, have higher rates of poverty and lower income levels, and lower educational attainment levels than their non-Indigenous counterparts. Furthermore, risk factors such as drug and alcohol abuse, mental health problems, past histories of abuse with prior partners or as children, and a criminal history are often more prevalent than for non-Indigenous women (Ivec et al. 2009; Queensland Government 2009; Statistics Canada 2009). A study by Cripps et al. (2009) found that Indigenous mothers who have been removed from their natural families as children have increased odds of being victims of violence, especially in remote settings where the odds of occurrences of violence were three times greater than in less remote communities. These historical and contextual factors mean that Indigenous women are more vulnerable to extended monitoring and surveillance by CPS, a situation frequently exacerbated by their difficulties accessing the supports that they require to meet CPS requirements.

As mentioned earlier, fear of CPS involvement may prevent women from disclosing abuse or from seeking services that could assist them and their children. This may be especially true for Indigenous women. Indeed, a Canadian study by Proulx (2006) reported that Indigenous mothers who were abused by their intimate partners were reluctant to seek help from professionals because of their overwhelming fear of losing their children to CPS. Being fearful of disclosing violence to social agencies, notably police and emergency shelters, negatively impacts women's access to the protection and support that they and their children deserve, putting them at greater risk of future violence. This reality must be taken into account by those responsible for developing and implementing child protection policies and practices as they explore ways to address children's exposure to intimate partner violence, including the particular situation of Indigenous women and their families. In Australia, steps towards this goal are taking place through the National Framework for Protecting Australia's Children, supported by the Council of Australian Governments. This framework promotes a public health approach to protecting children, focusing on strengthening families by providing supports and services to prevent harm. It also provides a staged approach to regulatory intervention determined by risk assessment when and if required (Council of Australian Governments 2009). In practice, the latter can involve practices such as family group conferencing in which all parties (i.e., CPS, parents, extended family members, community elders, support services, and foster families) meet together to discuss the care arrangements for a particular child. In this setting a multitude of information can be shared, issues can be discussed, and strategies for supporting the family are considered. Such conferences, when conducted well, can mobilize individual, family, and community strengths to support the mother and her children, in order to meet their immediate, medium, and longer term needs, thus potentially avoiding future interventions from CPS (Bamblett et al. 2010). From a cultural standpoint the engagement of appropriate family and community partners in this process is in keeping with traditional Indigenous parenting processes of "growing up" Indigenous children together as a collective, with Elders in particular playing an active role in passing on cultural knowledge (Bourke 1993).

Future Directions for CPS Policy Makers

As we have shown, new directions in CPS policy and practices over the past decade, including statutory amendments that explicitly include children's exposure to intimate partner violence as a form of child maltreatment, may have devastating impacts on Indigenous families, especially mothers.

It is essential to ask whether or not CPS authorities are in fact positioned to truly assist Indigenous children and women. The current context of child protection work must take into account such key factors as child welfare's colonialist and mother-blaming history (Gordon 1988; Human Rights and Equal Opportunity Commission 1997; Libesman 2004; Swift 1995), the well-documented CPS predilection to focus on individual and family dysfunction explanations rather than contextual factors (Callahan 1993, Ivec et al. 2012), and the chronic under-resourcing of CPS and ancillary services (Blackstock et al. 2005, Walmsley 2005).

Child protection authorities in Anglo-American jurisdictions are presently confronted with serious system design problems. Their present capacity is limited by a threshold system focused on individual family deficiencies and a preoccupation with risk. In this environment, resources of the financial and human kind are always going to be under stress, less available to people outside of the dominant population group. Rapid staff turnover due to heavy caseloads, low morale, public and media focus on blaming individual workers when "things go wrong," and the crisis-driven nature of CPS work create an environment that provides little opportunity for training, critical reflection, and improvements to practice (Davidson-Arad and Benbenishty 2010). In this climate it is impossible for CPS authorities to properly and adequately intervene in intimate partner violence cases, regardless of what direction may be provided by policy. More specifically, sufficient resources have not accompanied the increased number of child maltreatment investigations generated by legislative or policy changes designating exposure to intimate partner violence as maltreatment (Trocmé and Siddiqi 2002). We contend that this shortfall in resources is also evident in the failure to provide culturally appropriate services for Indigenous women and children. Further, recent CPS policy changes aimed at protecting children from exposure to violence in the home have not adequately addressed the complexities specific to Indigenous and other marginalized families struggling with intimate partner violence.

Consideration should be given in this context to two useful policy shifts. First, the safety of women and their children could be better ensured through the introduction and implementation of policies facilitating the removal of the violent partner from the home. Additionally, there must be guidelines directing CPS workers to make every effort to keep the child with the non-offending parent (usually the mother). If someone needs to be removed from the home to ensure the family's safety, it should be the actual perpetrator of the violence. Intervention by CPS workers in cases of intimate partner violence must not hold mothers accountable for the violence and abuse that is perpetrated against them. Instead, perpetrators should be held accountable and responsible for their abusive behaviour and the consequences on their families. Second, the introduction and funding of culturally appropriate services, offered in a timely manner, that not only hold men accountable for their violence but also teach them how to be non-violent, nurturing fathers, should be a priority. These changes are especially important for Indigenous families because interventions that demand the breaking up of families to secure safety are culturally unacceptable to Indigenous communities. Finding alternative methods for engaging with all parties safely is a priority for Indigenous families and communities. In Australia and in Canada there are several examples of initiatives engaging with Indigenous men in the ways described above (Ball 2010; Cripps and Davis 2012; Inteyerrkwe Statement 2008); however, further evaluations are needed to determine best practices with domestically violent fathers.

While the impact of including child exposure to intimate partner violence within CPS policies is not yet completely clear, the problematic outcomes that have come to light to date underline the need for careful development of guidelines for implementation of new policies and the implications these hold for current CPS system design. On a practical level, an assessment of the availability of resources and the potential impact of these policies on the safety of women and children, especially Indigenous women and children, must also be made. We recommend that Indigenous community stakeholders be included in the process at both policy development and review stages. This engagement would provide the opportunity to evaluate how historical and contemporary experiences manifest in the disproportionate involvement of Indigenous families with CPS authorities. It would also open up a space for innovation and best practice if the parties are committed to negotiating a way forward that responds to the specific circumstances of Indigenous families and respects Indigenous cultural and familial strengths. A necessary element to this process is regular review and evaluation so that this process that always starts with good will is maintained via the opportunity to share and resolve problems, as well as success stories. In Australia, following the National Apology to the Stolen Generations in 2008, the Australian government committed to a campaign of "Closing the Gap" of disadvantage, health inequalities, and lower life expectancy for Indigenous Australians. Part of this process involves a biannual report detailing the statistics on all social determinants that impact the life circumstances of Indigenous peoples, so that progress can be measured on major indicators. These reports make government accountable for achieving a standard and necessitate the active involvement of Indigenous people, families, communities, and services in the process. This is also occurring in respect of the new "Framework for Protecting Australia's Children." What is important in these initiatives is that government and their agencies recognize that Indigenous peoples have the right and the interest to make decisions about their futures and that it is the government's responsibility to ensure that the space is created for the voices of Indigenous people to be heard.

Alaska provides a compelling example of implementing initiatives designed to prevent children being inappropriately removed from the care of the non-offending caregiver, usually the mother. While Alaska does not include exposure to intimate partner violence as a designated category of child maltreatment, state legislation explicitly disfavours removing a child from the custody of the victim of abuse and makes protection of the victim, as well as the child, a departmental mandate (Alaska Statutes 2006). Further, it makes clear that if anyone should be removed from the home, it should be the offender and not the child (Alaska Statutes 2006; Weithorn 2001). Alaska's legislation and policy demonstrate the importance of offering support and protection to mothers as an integral part of the traditional CPS mandate to protect the well-being of the child.

Along with the police and courts, which must improve efforts to hold perpetrators responsible for the abuse that is committed against female intimate partners, CPS can also take an active role in preventing violence against mothers. Doing so requires that the problem of children's exposure to intimate partner violence be considered within the larger, gendered framework of violence against women. A gendered approach locates the causes of violence against women within wider, patriarchal social structures that legitimize men's use of force and dominance in the family (Bograd 1990). Such contextual evaluation is rarely called for in CPS policies and rarely evident in CPS practices. Instead, CPS tends to construct problem behaviours as stemming from individual and family dysfunction, including prevailing perceptions about inadequate parenting and protective ability on the part of abused women. This preoccupation with abused women's supposed parenting deficits is evident in the routine mandated use of parenting assessments and parenting programs by CPS workers (Johnson 2006; Nixon 2009b). We do not suggest that individual or familiar factors ought to be entirely disregarded. However, these factors should not be the primary basis for policy making when intimate partner violence intersects with the care and protection of children. More contextualized CPS approaches that acknowledge and address women's social and economic inequality have the potential to be more supportive to mothers and more protective of children.

In the current CPS practice environment, it is commonplace for reactive, intrusive, and punitive measures to be directed solely at mothers. This is seen in the routine use of supervision orders and mandatory parenting classes, and the too frequent removal of children from the home (Johnson 2006; Nixon 2009b). Practice efforts emphasize controlling women's behaviour in specific ways rather than providing support and assistance for the existing protective efforts of mothers. The end result is that policies designed to protect children ultimately fail to protect them and may even increase danger to children and to their mothers. By problematizing the behaviour of mothers rather than the behaviours of perpetrators, policy makers divert attention away from the political, social, and economic forces that contribute to male violence, including patriarchy, misogyny, and women's social and economic inequity. Consequently, policy preferences focus on making abused women "better" mothers and not on significant contributing factors, such as the lack of safe and affordable housing. Scholars and women's advocates have demonstrated that women's economic inequality and financial dependence on their male partners are major barriers to escaping (and remaining free) from abusive intimate relationships (Kurz 1998; Raphael 2001). Therefore, in addition to mandating support services such as counselling for abused women and their children, CPS policies must mandate the provision of resources, so that abused mothers can address their needs for housing, legal services, child care, financial assistance, and other pragmatic concerns. As mentioned earlier, Alaska may provide a useful template for policy changes as its current child maltreatment policy requires that the state make internal changes, including mandatory training for CPS workers; the development of protocols guiding case assessment and intervention; and the building of collaborative relationships with community agencies that work with intimate partner violence (Alaska Statutes 2006; Weithorn 2001).

The most urgent task is for policy makers to develop policies that support CPS workers' efforts to engage the actual perpetrators of the violence and focus on their behaviour. Policies that mandate direct engagement with domestically violent men will more effectively address the safety needs of abused women and their children. When policies fail to address the actions of the actual perpetrator of violence and the perpetrator's responsibilities for reducing risk and increasing safety, a climate is created in which it is easy for CPS workers to hold non-offending mothers accountable and inappropriately remove children from their care. As we noted earlier, in the Indigenous context, women generally believe that men must be part of the solution and not be excluded from policies, practices, or programs. Some Anglo-American jurisdictions have instituted intervention programs that both hold men accountable for their violence and teach them to be better fathers. For example, Time Out Services in Victoria (Australia) is a facility where violent men can go to stay after being removed from the home; here they receive counselling and support from Indigenous staff, including male Elders. The Time Out program also provides support for their partners and children; if all parties desire, the program offers support to bring them safely together in a counselling context.

The development of new legislation or policies would be best served through an inclusive approach to policy development that makes adequate provision for meaningful input from a broad representation of stakeholders, including Indigenous families and communities. Any invitation to comment on existing or draft legislation or policy must include a concrete commitment to incorporating the feedback provided. We encourage CPS authorities to embrace a partnership model that includes all relevant stakeholders working together. The *Victorian Indigenous Family Violence Task Force Report* (2003) describes a model of community engagement that includes establishing local and regional Indigenous family violence action groups and an overarching statewide Indigenous Family Violence Partnership Forum. The action groups include Elders, women, men, young people, and community leaders, as well as local Indigenous and non-Indigenous service providers. Their task is to work collaboratively to assess the needs of the local community and plan appropriate services to achieve better outcomes for those affected by violence. They then feed their knowledge and experiences up to a statewide partnership forum that meets regularly, again with the aim of improving the collective interagency responses to families. The model in is not without its flaws, as it requires an early recognition of the power inequities that might inhibit full participation from all stakeholders. Processes can be built into the model to empower and support all members to have a voice, as well as for declaring and managing potential conflicts. The model can also be grounded in the existing evidence base of what works and does not work in responding to intimate partner violence in Indigenous contexts. A basic principle is ensuring that there are services available for all those affected by the violence, whether they are victims, witnesses, or perpetrators. A second important principle is that interventions are targeted at multiple levels, not only at the crisis end, but also, most importantly, at the day-to-day level, providing support for struggling families. Prevention efforts provide education to the community about how to build safe nurturing environments for children that are free from violence. (For a more detailed description of this initiative, see Cripps 2007; Cripps and Davis 2012; and Wild and Anderson 2007.)

Little evidence exists, to date, to support the efficacy or usefulness of including child exposure to intimate partner violence as a category within child maltreatment statutes. As this chapter and others in the book demonstrate, CPS policies that aim to protect children exposed to intimate partner violence in the home often have the opposite and unintentional effect; that is, they increase danger for both abused mothers and their children. Some years ago Canadians scholars Jaffe, Crooks, and Wolfe (2003) recommended a moratorium on legislation to address children exposed to intimate partner violence until evaluations and reviews of both the intended and unintended impacts could be conducted. Further research is urgently needed to support the development of alternative policy approaches that incorporate gendered and decolonizing methodologies in their analysis of the impact of child protection policies and practice, with particular focus on the experiences of Indigenous mothers and their children. This would then need to be implemented immediately in order to ensure that the disproportionate disadvantage levelled at Indigenous women is addressed and creation of a second "stolen generation" may be averted Lastly, CPS and other systems, including the police and courts, must take the issue of violence against female intimate partners seriously and must operate in ways that hold the actual perpetrators of abuse accountable, not the non-offending mothers.

References

Aboriginal Child Sexual Assault Taskforce. 2006. *Breaking the Silence: Creating the Future. Addressing Child Sexual Assault in Aboriginal Communities in NSW.* Sydney: Attorney General's Department.

Alaska Statutes. 2006. Title 47, Chapter 17, §47.17.035.

Al-Yaman, Fadwa, Mieke Van Doeland, and Michelle Wallis. 2006. *Family Violence Among Aboriginal and Torres Strait Islander Peoples.* Canberra: Australian Institute of Health and Welfare.

Atkinson, Judy. 1990. *Beyond Violence: Finding the Dream.* Barton: National Domestic Violence Education Program, Office of Status of Women, Department of Prime Minister and Cabinet.

Australian Bureau of Statistics. 1997. "1996 Women's Safety Survey." Belconnen: Commonwealth of Australia.

___. 2006. "Personal Safety, Australia, 2005 (Reissue)." <abs.gov.au/ausstats/abs@.nsf/mf/4906.0/>.

Australian Institute of Health and Welfare. 2008. "Aboriginal and Torres Strait Islander Health Performance Framework 2008 Report: Detailed Analyses." AIHW Cat. No. IHW 22. Canberra, Australia: Author.

___. 2012. "Child Protection Australia 2010–11." Child Welfare Series no. 53. Cat. No. CWS 41. Canberra, Australia: Author.

Ball, Jessica. 2010. "Indigenous Fathers' Involvement in Reconstituting 'Circles of Care'." *American Journal of Community Psychology* 45.

Bamblett, Muriel, Howard Bath, and Rob Roseby. 2010. *Growing Them Strong, Together: Report of the Board of Inquiry into the Child Protection System in the Northern Territory.* Darwin: Northern Territory Government, Department of the Chief Minister.

Berry, Jesia, James Harrison, and Philip Ryan. 2009. "Hospital Admissions of Indigenous and Non-Indigenous Australians due to Interpersonal Violence, July 1999 to June 2004." *Australian and New Zealand Journal of Public Health* 33, 3.

Blackstock, Cindy, Tara Prakash, John Loxley, and Fred Wien. 2005. "Wen:de: We are Coming to the Light of Day." Ottawa: First Nations Child and Family Caring Society.

Blackstock, Cindy, Nico Trocmé, and Marlyn Bennett. 2004. "Child Maltreatment Investigations Among Aboriginal and Non-Aboriginal Families in Canada." *Violence against Women* 10, 8.

Bograd, Michele. 1990. "Feminist Perspectives on Wife Abuse: An Introduction." In Kersti Yllö and Michele Bograd (eds.), *Feminist Perspectives on Wife Abuse.*

Newbury Park: Sage.

Bourke, Eleanor. 1993. "The First Australians: Kinship, Family and Identity." *Family Matters* 35.

Brownridge, Douglas A. 2008. "Understanding the Elevated Risk of Partner Violence Against Aboriginal Women: A Comparison of Two Nationally Representative Surveys of Canada." *Journal of Family Violence* 23, 5.

Callahan, Marilyn. 1993. "The Administrative and Practice Context: Perspectives from the Front Line." In Brian Wharf (ed.), *Rethinking Child Welfare in Canada*. Toronto: Oxford University Press.

Casanueva, Cecilia, Sandra L. Martin, Desmond K. Runyan, Richard P. Barth, and Robert H. Bradley. 2008. "Quality of Maternal Parenting Among Intimate Partner Violence Victims Involved With the Child Welfare System." *Journal of Family Violence* 23, 6.

Child and Family Services Act, R.S.O. 1990, c.11.

Council of Australian Governments. 2009. Protecting Children Is Everyone's Business: National Framework for Protecting Australia's Children 2009-2020. Canberra: FaHCSIA.

Cripps, Kyllie. 2007. "Indigenous Family Violence: From Emergency Measures to Committed Long Term Action." *Australian Indigenous Law Review* 11, 2.

____. 2008. "Indigenous Family Violence: A Statistical Challenge." *INJURY: International Journal of the Care of the Injured* 39, 5.

Cripps, Kyllie, Catherine Bennett, Lyle Gurrin, and David Studdert. 2009. "Victims of Violence Among Indigenous Mothers Living with Dependent Children." *Medical Journal of Australia* 191, 9.

Cripps, Kyllie, and Megan Davis. 2012. "Communities Working to Reduce Indigenous Family Violence." *Indigenous Justice Clearinghouse Brief* 12.

Davidson-Arad, Bilha, and Rami Benbenishty. 2010. "Contribution of Child Protection Workers' Attitudes to Their Risk Assessments and Intervention Recommendations: A Study in Israel." *Health and Social Care in the Community* 18, 1.

Department of Human Services — Victoria. 2007. "Protecting Victoria's Children — Child Protection Practice Manual. Abuse and Harm — Legal and Practice Definitions." <dhs.vic.gov.au/office-for-children/cpmanual/Output%20files/Practice%20context/Output%20files/Execute/1008_abuse_and_harm_legal_and_practice.pdf>.

Devoe, Ellen, and Erica Smith. 2003. "Don't Take My Kids: Barriers to Service Delivery for Battered Mothers and Their Young Children." *Journal of Emotional Abuse* 3, 3/4.

DiLillo, David E. 2008. "Exposure to Domestic Violence: A Meta-Analysis of Child and Adolescent Outcomes." *Aggression and Violent Behavior* 13, 2.

Domestic and Family Violence Act. 2007. (NT).

Edleson, Jeffrey. L. 1998. "Responsible Mothers and Invisible Mothers: Child Protection in the Case of Adult Domestic Violence." *Journal of Interpersonal Violence* 13, 2.

English, Diana J., Christopher Graham, Rae R. Newton, Terri L. Lewis, Richard Thompson, Jonathan B. Kotch, and Cindy Weisbart. 2009. "At-Risk and Maltreated Children Exposed to Intimate Partner Aggression/Violence:

What the Conflict Looks Like and Its Relationship to Child Outcomes." *Child Maltreatment* 14, 2.

Evans, Sara E., Corrie A. Davies, and David K. DiLillo. 2008. "Exposure to Domestic Violence: A Meta-Analysis of Child and Adolescent Outcomes." *Aggression and Violent Behavior* 13, 2.

"Failure to Protect" Working Group. 2000. "Charging Battered Mothers with 'Failure to Protect': Still Blaming the Victim." *Fordham Urban Law Journal* XXVII.

Families SA. 2008. *Child Protection Manual of Practice*. Adelaide: South Australian Government, Family and Youth Services.

Gordon, Linda. 1988. *Heroes of Their Own Lives: The Politics and History of Family Violence*. New York: Penguin Books.

Gordon, Sue, Kay Hallahan, and Darrell Henry. 2002. "Putting the Picture Together: Inquiry into Response by Government Agencies to Complaints of Family Violence and Child Abuse in Aboriginal Communities." Perth: State Law Publisher. <http://www.strongfamilies.wa.gov.au/UserDir/Documents/Public/Putting%20the%20Picture%20Together.pdf>

Gough, Pamela, Nico Trocmé, Ivan Brown, Della Knoke, and Cindy Blackstock. 2005. "Pathways to the Overrepresentation of Aboriginal Children in Care." CECW Information Sheet #23E. <cecw-cepb.ca/publications/424>.

Haebich, Anna. 2000. "Broken Circles. Fragmenting Indigenous Families 1800–2000." Fremantle: Fremantle Arts Centre Press.

Hartley, Carolyn. 2004. "Severe Domestic Violence and Child Maltreatment: Considering Child Physical Abuse, Neglect, and Failure to Protect." *Children and Youth Services Review* 26.

Holden, George W., and Kathy L. Ritchie. 1991. "Linking Extreme Marital Discord, Child Rearing, and Child Behavior Problems: Evidence from Battered Women." *Child Development* 62, 2.

Holden, George. W., Joshua D. Stein, Kathy L. Ritchie, Susan D. Harris, and Ernest N. Jouriles. 1998. "Parenting Behaviours and Beliefs of Battered Women." In George W. Holden, Robert A. Geffner, and Ernest N. Jouriles (eds.), *Children Exposed to Marital Violence: Theory, Research, and Applied Issues*. Washington: American Psychological Association.

Human Rights and Equal Opportunity Commission. 1997. "Bringing Them Home: National Inquiry into the Separation of Aboriginal and Torres Strait Islander Children from Their Families." Canberra: Commonwealth of Australia.

Humphreys, Catherine. 1999. "Avoidance and Confrontation: Social Work Practice in Relation to Domestic Violence and Child Abuse." *Child and Family Social Work* 4, 1.

___. 2008. "Problems in the System of Mandatory Reporting of Children Living with Domestic Violence." *Journal of Family Studies* 14, 2.

Humphreys, Cathy, and Deborah Absler. 2011. "History Repeating: Child Protection Responses to Domestic Violence." *Child and Family Social Work* 16, 2.

"Inteyerrkwe Statement" 2008. <caac.org.au/malehealthinfo/malehealthsummit-2008sorry.pdf>.

Ivec, Mary, Valerie Braithwaite, and Nathan Harris. 2009. "'Resetting the Relationship' in Indigenous Child Protection: Public Hope and Private Reality." Regulatory Institutions Network Occasional Paper 14. Canberra: Australian

National University.

Ivec, Mary, Valerie Braithwaite, and Nathan Harris. 2012. "'Resetting the Relationship' in Indigenous Child Protection: Public Hope and Private Reality." *Law and Policy* 34, 1.

Jaffe, Peter G., Claire V. Crooks, and David A. Wolfe. 2003. "Legal and Policy Responses to Children Exposed to Domestic Violence: The Need to Evaluate Intended and Unintended Consequences." *Clinical Child and Family Psychology Review* 6, 3.

Johansen, Bruce E. 2000. "Education — The Nightmare and the Dream: A Shared National Tragedy, A Shared National Disgrace." *Native Americas* 17, 4.

Johnson, Susan P. 2006. "Child Welfare and Domestic Abuse: The Intersection of Safety and Accountability." Doctoral dissertation. Retrieved from ProQuest. (Publication No. 3216138).

Kellington, Stephanie. n.d. "Missing Voices: Mothers at Risk for or Experiencing Apprehension in the Child Welfare System in BC." Vancouver: National Action Committee on the Status of Women.

Kitzmann, Katherine M., Noni K. Gaylord, Aimee R. Holt, and Erin D. Kenny. 2003. "Child Witnesses to Domestic Violence: A Meta-Analytic Review." *Journal of Consulting and Clinical Psychology* 71, 2.

Kurz, Demie. 1998. "Old Problems and New Directions in the Study of Violence Against Women." In Raquel K. Bergen (ed.), *Issues in Intimate Partner Violence*. Thousand Oaks, CA: Sage.

Law Reform Commission of Nova Scotia. 1995. "From Rhetoric to Reality: Ending Domestic Violence in Nova Scotia: Final Report." Halifax: Author.

Letourneau, Nicole. L., C.B. Fedick, and J.D. Willms. 2007. "Mothering and Domestic Violence: A Longitudinal Analysis." *Journal of Family Violence* 22, 8.

Levendosky, Alytia A., Shannon M. Lynch, and Sandra A. Graham-Berman. 2000. "Mothers' Perceptions of the Impact of Woman Abuse on Their Parenting." *Violence Against Women* 6.

Libesman, Terri. 2004. "Child Welfare Approaches for Indigenous Communities: International Perspectivies." *National Child Protection Clearinghouse, Child Abuse Prevention Issues* 20.

MacQueen, A. 2000. "Four Generations of Abuse: Canada's Unfinished Business of Compensation." *Native Americas* 17, 4.

Magen, Randy. H. 1999. "In the Best Interests of Battered Women: Reconceptualizing Allegations of Failure to Protect." *Child Maltreatment* 4, 2.

McCloskey, Laura A., Aurelio J. Figueredo, and Mary P. Koss. 1995. "The Effects of Systemic Family Violence on Children's Mental Health." *Child Development* 66.

Memmott, Paul, Rachel Stacy, Catherine Chambers, and Catherine Keys. 2001. "Violence in Indigenous Communities: Full Report." Barton: Commonwealth of Australia.

Miccio, Kristian. 1995. "Deconstructing the Myth of the Passive Battered Mother and the 'Protected Child' in Child Neglect Proceedings." *Albany Law Review* 58.

Midgley, James. 2000. "The Definition of Social Policy." In James Midgley, Martin B. Tracy, and Michelle Livermore (eds.), *The Handbook of Social Policy*. Thousand Oaks: Sage.

Mow, Karen E. 1992. "Tjunparni: Family Violence in Indigenous Australia: A

Report and Literature Review for the Aboriginal and Torres Strait Islander Commission." Canberra: Aboriginal and Torres Strait Islander Commission.

National Council of Juvenile and Family Court Judges Family Violence Department. 1999. "Effective Intervention in Domestic Violence and Child Maltreatment Cases: Guidelines for Policy and Practice." Reno: Author.

Nixon, Kendra L. 2002. "Leave Him or Lose Them: The Child Protection Response to Woman Abuse." In Leslie M. Tutty and Carolyn Goard (eds.), *Reclaiming Self: Issues and Resources for Women Abused by Intimate Part*ners. Halifax, NS: Fernwood Publishing and RESOLVE.

____. 2009a. "Intimate Partner Woman Abuse in Alberta's Child Protection Policy and the Impact on Abused Mothers and Their Children." *Currents: New Scholarship in the Human Services* 8, 1.

____. 2009b. "The Construction of Intimate Partner Woman Abuse in Alberta's Child Protection Policy and the Impact on Abused Mothers and Their Children." Unpublished doctoral dissertation, University of Calgary.

Nixon, Kendra, H. Lorraine Radtke, and Leslie M. Tutty. In press. *"Every Day It Takes a Piece of You Away*: The Experiences of Grief and Loss Among Abused Mothers Involved with Child Protective Services." *Journal of Public Child Welfare*.

Nixon, Kendra L., Leslie M. Tutty, Gillian Weaver-Dunlop, and Christine A. Walsh. 2007. "Do Good Intentions Beget Good Policy? A Review of Child Protection Policies to Address Intimate Partner Violence." *Children and Youth Services Review* 29.

Øverlien, Carolina. 2009. "Children Exposed to Domestic Violence: Conclusions from the Literature and Challenges Ahead." *Journal of Social Work* 10, 1.

Parkinson, Patrick, and Catherine Humphreys. 1998. "Children Who Witness Domestic Violence: The Implications for Child Protection." *Child and Family Law Quarterly* 10, 2.

Petchkovsky, Leon, Craig San Roque, Rachel Napaljarri Jurra, and Sally Butler. 2004. "Indigenous Maps of Subjectivity and Attacks on Linking: Forced Separation and Its Psychiatric Sequelae in Australia's Stolen Generation." *Australian e-Journal for the Advancement of Mental Health* 3, 3.

Proulx, Jocelyn, Cheryl Fraehlich, and Cheryl Laurie. 2006. "Women's Access to Services for Abuse: Barriers Related to Culture, Religion, and Immigration Issues." Paper presented at the RESOLVE Research Day, Saskatoon, SK.

Queensland Government. 2009. *Characteristics of Parents Involved in the Queensland Child Protection System. Report 6: Summary of Key Findings*. Brisbane: Queensland Government, Department of Communities.

Raphael, Jody. 2001. "Domestic Violence as a Welfare-to-Work Barrier: Research and Theoretical Issues." In Claire. M. Renzetti, Jeffrey L. Edleson, and Raquel K. Bergen (eds), *Sourcebook on Violence Against Women*. Thousand Oaks, CA: Sage.

Read, Peter. 1999. *A Rape of the Soul So Profound: The Return of the Stolen Generations*. St Leonards: Allen and Unwin.

Robertson, Boni. 1999. "The Aboriginal and Torres Strait Islander Women's Taskforce on Violence Report." Brisbane: Queensland Government.

SCRGSP (Steering Committee for the Review of Government Service Provision). 2011. *Overcoming Indigenous Disadvantage: Key Indicators 2011*. Productivity Commission, Canberra.

Silburn, Sven, Stephen Zubrick, David Lawrence, Francis Mitrou, John DeMaio, Eve Blair, Adele Cox, Robin Dalby, Judith Griffin, Glenn Pearson, and Colleen Hayward. 2006. "The Intergenerational Effects of Forced Separation on the Social and Emotional Wellbeing of Aboriginal Children and Young People." *Family Matters* 75, 10.

Stark, Evan, and Flitcraft, Anne H. 1988. "Women and Children At Risk: A Feminist Perspective on Child Abuse." *International Journal of Health Services* 18, 1.

Statistics Canada. 2006. "Measuring Violence Against Women: Statistical Trends 2006: Violence Against Aboriginal Women." <statcan.gc.ca/pub/85-570-x/2006001/findings-resultats/4054081-eng.htm>.

___. 2009. "Women in Canada: A Gender-based Statistical Report." <statcan.gc.ca/pub/89-503-x/89-503-x2005001-eng.htm>.

___. 2011. "Family Violence in Canada: A Statistical Profile." <statcan.gc.ca/pub/85-224-x/85-224-x2010000-eng.htm>.

Strega, Susan. 2006. "Failure to Protect? Child Welfare Interventions When Men Beat Mothers." In Ramona Alaggia and Cathy Vine (eds.), *Cruel But Not Unusual: Violence in Canadian Families*. Ottawa: Wilfrid Laurier University Press.

Strega, Susan, Claire Fleet, Leslie Brown, Lena Dominelli, Marilyn Callahan, and Christopher Walmsley. 2008. "Connecting Father Absence and Mother Blame in Child Welfare Policies and Practice." *Children and Youth Services Review* 30, 7.

Sullivan, Cris M., Huong Nguyen, Nicole Allen, Deborah Bybee, and Jennifer Juras. 2000. "Beyond Searching for Deficits: Evidence that Physically and Emotionally Abused Women Are Nurturing Parents." *Journal of Emotional Abuse*, 2, 1.

Swift, Karen J. 1995. *Manufacturing "Bad Mothers": A Critical Perspective on Child Neglect.* Toronto: University of Toronto Press.

Trocmé, Nico, Barbara Fallon, Bruce MacLaurin, Joanne Daciuk, Caroline Felstiner, Tara Black, Lil Tonmyr, Cindy Blackstock, Ken Barter, Daniel Turcotte, and Richard Cloutier. 2005. "Canadian Incidence Study of Reported Child Abuse and Neglect — 2003: Major Findings." Ottawa: Minister of Public Works and Government Services Canada.

Trocmé, Nico, Bruce MacLaurin, Barbara Fallon, Della Knoke, Lisa Pitman, and Megan McCormack. 2006. "Mesnmimk Wasatek: Catching a Drop of Light. Understanding the Overrepresentation of First Nations Children in Canada's Child Welfare System: An Analysis of the Canadian Incidence Study of Reported Child Abuse and Neglect (CIS-2003)." Ottawa: First Nations Child and Family Caring Society of Canada.

Trocmé, Nico, and Jasmine Siddiqi. 2002. "Child Maltreatment Investigations in Canada: Judicial Implications." Paper presented at the National Judicial Institute's Child Protection and the Law Seminar, Ottawa.

Victorian Government, Department of Justice. 2008. "Measuring Family Violence in Victoria — Victorian Family Violence Database (Volume 3): Seven Year Trend Analysis 1999–2006." Melbourne: Author.

Victorian Indigenous Family Violence Task Force. 2003. "Victorian Indigenous Family Violence Task Force Final Report." Melbourne: Department of Victorian Communities.

Walmsley, Christopher. 2005. *Protecting Aboriginal Children*. Vancouver: UBC Press.

Weithorn, Lois A. 2001. "Protecting Children from Exposure to Domestic Violence:

The Use and Abuse of Child Maltreatment Statutes." *Hastings Law Journal* 53.

Wharf, Brian, and Brad McKenzie. 1998. *Connecting Policy to Practice in the Human Services*. Toronto: Oxford University Press.

Wild, Rex, and Patricia Anderson. 2007. "Ampe Akelyernemane Meke Mekarle: 'Little Children are Sacred,' Report of the Northern Territory Government Inquiry into the Protection of Aboriginal Children from Sexual Abuse." Darwin: Department of the Chief Minister.

Wolfe, David. A., Claire V. Crooks, Vivien Lee, Alexandra McIntyre-Smith, and Peter G. Jaffe. 2003. "The Effects of Children's Exposure to Domestic Violence: A Meta-analysis and Critique." *Clinical Child and Family Psychology Review* 6, 3.